CONSCIOUSNESS AND ITS OBJECTS

CONSCIOUSNESS AND ITS OBJECTS

Colin McGinn

CLARENDON PRESS · OXFORD

OXFORD
UNIVERSITY PRESS

Great Clarendon Street, Oxford OX2 6DP

Oxford University Press is a department of the University of Oxford.
It furthers the University's objective of excellence in research, scholarship,
and education by publishing worldwide in

Oxford New York

Auckland Bangkok Buenos Aires Cape Town Chennai
Dar es Salaam Delhi Hong Kong Istanbul Karachi Kolkata
Kuala Lumpur Madrid Melbourne Mexico City Mumbai Nairobi
São Paulo Shanghai Taipei Tokyo Toronto

Oxford is a registered trade mark of Oxford University Press
in the UK and in certain other countries

Published in the United States
by Oxford University Press Inc., New York

British Library Cataloguing in Publication Data

Data available

Library of Congress Cataloging in Publication Data

Data available

ISBN 0-19-926760-X

1 3 5 7 9 10 8 6 4 2

Typeset by Kolam Information Services Pvt. Ltd, Pondicherry, India
Printed in Great Britain on acid-free paper by
Biddles Ltd., King's Lynn, Norfolk

ACKNOWLEDGEMENTS

The following articles have been reproduced with the permission of the publisher.

'What Is It not Like to Be a Brain?', in Van Loocke (ed.), *The Physical Nature of Consciousness* (Benjamins, 2001), 257–68.

'Consciousness and Space', *Journal of Consciousness Studies* 2 (1995): 220–30.

'How Not to Solve the Mind-Body Problem', in C. Gillett and B. Loewer (eds.), *Physicalism and Its Discontents* (Cambridge University Press, 2001).

'Solving the Philosophical Mind-Body Problem', *Festschrift for Dieter Henrich* (Gieseking, 2000).

'The Problem of Philosophy', *Philosophical Studies* 76 (1994): 133–56.

'Consciousness and Cosmology', in M. Davies and G. W. Humphreys (eds.), *Consciousness* (Blackwell, 1993).

CONTENTS

INTRODUCTION

I intend this book as a sequel to my 1991 book, *The Problem of Consciousness*. Since writing that book I have produced a number of papers extending and clarifying my earlier position; it seemed a good idea to bring them together. In addition, there are papers on neighbouring topics that act as an antidote to the theoretical pessimism of my writings on the mind-body problem. All the papers deal with consciousness in one way or another. I have not seen reason to modify or retract any of my earlier views, which I know will disappoint some of my readers. The chief change during the last decade or so has been the inclusion of my position, under the label 'mysterianism', in the canon of possible positions concerning the mind-body problem. Initially, my view was, I think, regarded as an eccentricity, a marginal and eminently neglectable theoretical option. While I have not made many converts in the succeeding years, mysterianism has, nevertheless, become a standard alternative in these debates—it is regarded as a contender. I confess that when the view first occurred to me I expected it to be eagerly embraced by many who have found themselves irremediably perplexed by consciousness—since it had, for me, such a liberating and illuminating power. I suppose I shouldn't be surprised that this was not the general reaction, for reasons both worthy and suspect. Worthy, because it could hardly be said that I *demonstrated* the correctness of mysterianism; but suspect, because surely a large part of the resistance stems from a powerful desire to preserve the omnicompetence of the human intellect (it is not as if you are supposed to *like* the view). I remain convinced, however, that mysterianism makes the best overall sense of our predicament with the mind-body problem, as many of the papers here aim to show. It is, indeed, a complex position, with many facets and inspirations, not reducible to a single argument or thesis, and is best taken in the round; which is one reason why I thought it fit to bring the various papers together. No one should become a mysterian over night, after a single exposure to the view; it is something that creeps up on you until, one crepuscular dawn, you find yourself thinking 'Yes, it really *has* to be so, doesn't it—nothing else works, and it certainly makes sense of it all.' Maybe, in fact, it is the kind of view that one has to arrive at oneself, rather than as a result of the discursive coercion of others. So I am really only planting seeds.

As I reflect on these papers, I detect an implicit principle, or policy, that has guided me, which might be called 'methodological radicalism'. My approach has been to venture ideas and theories that say something surprising, heterodox, perhaps disconcerting. A spirit of adventurism pervades these pages. This is not because I value provocation for its own sake; it is because I believe that what the philosophy of mind primarily needs at this point is new ideas, and some shaking up. As a methodological precept, then, my aim is not to curb excess but to encourage it—responsible excess, of course. In my view, the philosophy of mind in particular, and to a lesser extent philosophy generally, has followed a policy of methodological conservatism, in the sense that it has tried to account for the mind in the most restricted and 'kosher' terms possible. The attempt to shoehorn the mind into a box shaped like the body is only the most conspicuous example of this tendency—behaviourism, functionalism, and central-state materialism. There has been a pervasive effort to counter the supposed excesses of Cartesian dualism—to maintain as much distance as possible from this view. We all desperately want to avoid the supernatural ghost lurking unintelligibly inside the clanking machine. I see this as the analogue of the desire, within the philosophy of language, to avoid the supposed excesses of Meinong, with his menagerie of non-existent but robust and populous objects (and one of the papers in this volume, 'The Objects of Intentionality', is far more deferential to Meinong than most philosophers these days deem respectable). Ontological modesty is the prevailing mantra, for fear of meta-physical monsters. If that means denying the appearances, then so be it.

I think these fears are misplaced. Occam's razor quickly turns into Procrustes' bed. Modesty becomes a retreat from ambition. Parsimony transmutes into miserliness. In a word: the philosopher loses a sense of *reality*—of what he or she is actually confronted with. What we must do is face the mental facts and develop adequate descriptive and explanatory theories—or admit that we can't. Trimming the data to mask the inadequacy of our under-standing is not a reputable option. Meinongian munificence is preferable to Occamite blinkeredness. For too long the philosophy of mind (and psychology) has been hampered by the likes of empiricism, positivism, and behaviourism; we need to look beyond ideologies and confront the mind in all its splendour and intractability. We need to kick our theorizing into a higher gear, because the mind will not submit to purblind attempts to cut it down to size. That, at any rate, is my conviction. Another rule of thumb: whenever a view is held by one's contemporaries to be absolute anathema that is the time to look at it seriously. Of course, this is offered only as a methodological suggestion—it is not that the maximally provocative view is bound to be *true*. But sometimes radicalism is what the field calls for, in philosophy as in science, and in my view that is the situation we face now. We have had long enough of trying to get by with the minimum (a pro-gramme much favoured by Quine, in particular); we should be aiming rather for theoretical ascendancy, the shock of the new, a shaft of sharp insight. Much of this will no doubt take us on frustrating trips down dark alleys, or submerge us in deep waters of obscurity, but—as Popper never tired of insisting—error is sometimes more fruitful than truth (if the truth is too unambitious and restrained). Hence, my methodological radicalism.

I regard the papers collected here, then, as essentially exploratory, not as lapidary dogma. I positively look forward to seeing some of them falsified, and I certainly expect vigorous criticism of some of my bolder breaks with tradition. The mood of the papers here is 'What if?' and 'Let's suppose' and 'It just may be'. In some of them (especially 'Inverted First-Person Authority') I have myself wavered considerably before coming down on one side of the issue; I have even resorted to bringing in aliens to express views that seem to me worth exploring ('Consciousness and Cosmology'). There are many loose ends here and much more to be said, but my aim has largely been to start hares rather than to deliver them stuffed and odourless to your front door. That said, there are also many points on which I am entirely convinced and as dogmatic as might be wished. Open-mindedness is indeed an important intellectual virtue, but there is also a lot to be said for the burnished shield of firm conviction.

Let me also enter a plea for *lightness* in philosophy. I don't mean lack of seriousness; I mean a willingness to let ideas play among themselves, so to speak. That is, there should be a place for the unimpeded flow of ideas, not weighed down by the heaviness of doctrine and 'professionalism'. Thought must be allowed to dance to its own music, to follow its own inclinations. There should, sometimes at least, be that slight smile of pleasure as one perceives ideas taking on their own life and leading one down a path that may have seemed forbidding or blocked. Philosophy should not lose its affinity to play, its capacity to amuse and delight. And tone of philosophical voice matters.

I

What Constitutes the Mind-Body Problem?

How do we know there is a mind-body problem? In what does our awareness of this problem consist? That is: granted that there is a problem, how should we characterize our knowledge that it exists? Obviously, we must know something about consciousness and something about the brain from which it follows that there is a problem about relating the two in a theoretically satisfactory way. But *what* do we know and what kind of knowledge do we have of it? In particular, what kind of knowledge of consciousness do we have from which its problematic relation to the brain follows?

Presumably, we have some kind of knowledge of the *essence* of consciousness that produces the conviction that there is a philosophical problem here: this knowledge of essence tells us that consciousness is somehow special, not transparently related to known facts about the brain, deeply puzzling. And there is a strong impression that our knowledge of the problem somehow outruns our ability to formulate it explicitly: we sense more than we can say. We may not be able to articulate precisely what it is about consciousness—about its nature—that defies explanation, but we feel strongly that there is a deep problem here. We want to ask, in a tone of incredulity, 'How could *this* (consciousness) just be *that* (the brain)?' Yet if we are asked to characterize just what property of consciousness poses the problem we run into doubt and controversy; and then it can seem that we are falling for a mystery that isn't really there. Opponents with their proposed solution in hand then take themselves to be entitled to dismiss our inchoate perplexities.

My first task in this paper is to make sense of this situation; not to persuade those who are convinced there is no problem, but to expose the cognitive predicament we are in when we think there is. To this end I am going to make heavy use of Russell's old distinction between knowledge by acquaintance and knowledge by description, which I think has not been fully appreciated: it is more radical than commonly assumed. Roughly, then, my suggestion will be that we know the essence of consciousness by acquaintance and not by description, and this is enough to produce our (justified) sense of the problem. Here is how Russell formulates the distinction:

Knowledge of things, when it is of the kind we call knowledge by *acquaintance*, is essentially simpler than any knowledge of truths, and logically independent of knowledge of truths, though it would be rash to assume that human beings ever, in fact, have acquaintance with things without at the same time knowing some truth about them . . . We shall say that we have *acquaintance* with anything of which we are directly aware, without the intermediary of any process of inference or any knowledge of truths. Thus in the presence of my table I am acquainted with the sense-data that make up the appearance of my table—its colour, shape, hardness, smoothness, etc.; all these are things of which I am immediately conscious when I am seeing and touching my table. The particular shade of color that I am seeing may have many things said about it—I may say that it is brown, that it is rather dark, and so on. But such statements, though they make me know truths *about* the colour, do not make me know the colour itself any better than I did before: *so far as concerns knowledge of the color itself, as opposed to knowledge of truths about it, I know the colour perfectly and completely when I see it, and no further knowledge of it itself is even theoretically possible* [my italics]. Thus the sense-data which make up the appearance of my table are things with which I have acquaintance, things immediately known to me just as they are.[1]

Later Russell notes that we also have acquaintance with states of consciousness, such as seeing the sun or sensations of pain: 'This kind of acquaintance, which may be called self-consciousness, is the source of all our knowledge of mental things.'[2] Such self-consciousness distinguishes us from animals, he says, because although animals are acquainted with sense-data, they are never acquainted *with* this acquaintance. Thus we know our minds in a way that animals do not. We know our own minds by being acquainted with them.

Several points need to be noted here. The first is that knowledge by acquaintance and knowledge by description are mutually independent, conceptually speaking. We are all familiar with the idea that knowledge by description does not entail knowledge by acquaintance, since we may have no direct awareness of something whose existence we know only by inference, but Russell is equally adamant that the converse entailment also fails to hold. The mental act in which we are acquainted with a colour, say, gives us knowledge of the colour—of its nature, its essence—that is quite independent of any truths we know about it: that is, the acquaintance-based knowledge does not inherently involve any propositional knowledge (knowledge of truths, in Russell's terminology). In the case of animals, we may suppose that this logical independence is actually realized: they have knowledge by acquaintance of colours but (in some cases, at least) no propositional knowledge about colours—they do not know *that* there is a red patch in front of them, say (they don't even have the concept of red).[3] Thus knowledge by acquaintance is not in any way reducible

---

[1] Bertrand Russell, *The Problems of Philosophy* (Oxford University Press, 1967; originally published 1912), 25.

[2] Ibid 27.

[3] This is on the assumption that all propositional knowledge is conceptual. But there is room for the view that animals may have non-conceptual propositional

to propositional knowledge—to knowledge of truths. We are simply directly aware of something and this gives us a type of knowledge of the thing of which we are aware: we know *what it is* that we are aware of. And notice that the acquaintance relation itself is not to be identified with the knowledge it generates: acquaintance *gives* us a type of knowledge; this knowledge is not *reducible* to the acquaintance relation that founds it. In virtue of knowledge by acquaintance, then, we may know the nature of something without being able to *describe* it.

Second, this type of knowledge has a certain kind of solidity or completeness to it, because it gives me insight into the essence of that with which I am acquainted. It is not to be supposed defective compared to knowledge by description (propositional knowledge). It is not some sort of half-hearted attempt at real propositional knowledge, but a specific type of knowledge in its own right. Just because I cannot express in propositions what I know in this way is no reason to downgrade such knowledge, or regard it as suspect. Indeed, according to Russell, knowledge by acquaintance is the basis of all knowledge, so that knowledge by description presupposes it. No propositional knowledge would be possible unless we knew some things in the non-propositional way.

Third, we have such knowledge of our own conscious states, as well as of their intentional objects: we know their nature in this direct non-propositional way (as well as propositionally). This means that this type of knowledge, too, is logically independent of descriptive knowledge: we may in fact have such descriptive knowledge, but our knowledge by acquaintance of our own conscious states does not reduce to it. Thus we know *what consciousness is* by means of knowledge by acquaintance. Paraphrasing Russell, then, when I am directly aware of my own consciousness 'I know it perfectly and completely.'

knowledge. For the purposes of this paper I am equating Russellian knowledge of truths with conceptual knowledge, but in fact I think that non-conceptual propositional knowledge is a genuine possibility. (I intend to write about this elsewhere.)

Now I shall say that some of our concepts are *acquaintance-based*, meaning that our grasp of them depends upon our being acquainted with what they denote.[4] The concept of an electron is not like that, but the concept of pain is. I suggest that the general concept of consciousness is acquaintance-based: we are acquainted with consciousness and our concept of consciousness depends upon this acquaintance. To have the concept of consciousness is to know what consciousness is (in one sense), and this knowledge is produced by our acquaintance with consciousness; more succinctly, we know what consciousness is by acquaintance. If this is right, then we can say two things: first, that this knowledge is enough to ground our sense that there is a mind-body problem; and second, that it explains why we feel that our sense of the problem outstrips our ability to articulate it. On the first point, mere acquaintance with consciousness could suffice to give us the knowledge that there is indeed a problem about linking the mind and the brain: for, if we know the essence of consciousness by means of acquaintance, then we can just see that consciousness is not reducible to neural or functional processes (say)—just as acquaintance with the colour red could ground our knowledge that redness is not the same as greenness, say. Secondly, granted that knowledge by acquaintance does not entail knowledge by description, it could be that we have a type of knowledge here that we cannot formulate propositionally: we know the nature of consciousness by acquaintance but we cannot express that nature in the form of truths about consciousness. Here we are a bit like animals and their objects of acquaintance. Thus we resort, helplessly, to metaphors to express what we antecedently know by acquaintance: that consciousness is like a mirror, a stream, a light, a receptacle, or a theatre. When you know something that you

[4] I am thinking here of bats and blind people—cases in which, through lack of the relevant kinds of experience, the associated concepts cannot be possessed. That is: we can't know what it is like to be a bat, and congenitally blind people can't know what it is like to see colours.

cannot express, you are apt to wax poetic.[5] We know quite well what consciousness is *not*, but we cannot *say* what it is about it that prevents it being those things. It is the possibility of such inarticulate (but real) knowledge that explains our cognitive predicament in formulating the mind-body problem. In other terminology, we have *implicit* knowledge of the problem, not *explicit* knowledge. (Note that I am not trying to *prove* that there is an unsolved problem here, or that 'physicalism' is false; my aim is merely to make epistemological sense of our predicament in appreciating and trying to formulate the mind-body problem.)

It may help if I contrast what I am suggesting with some other ways of explaining our knowledge that there is a mind-body problem. Thus it is standardly said that consciousness has certain properties (meets certain descriptions) from which it follows that it is problematically related to the brain: it is subjective; it has intentionality; it is essentially reflective; it is known infallibly. I think these observations, however correct and illuminating, strike us as expressing consequential not intrinsic aspects of what is distinctive of consciousness. Thus it is a consequence of consciousness being what it is that a specific form of it can be grasped only from the point of view of one who shares that form: this is an epistemic feature of consciousness—how it can be known—rather than an intrinsic ontological feature.[6] Similarly for infallible

---

[5] It is hard not to be reminded here of Wittgenstein's distinction between saying and showing in the *Tractatus*. Presumably what can only be shown is an instance of knowledge, but it cannot be an instance of propositional knowledge—or else it could be said. There is thus quite a close analogy between Russell's notion of propositionally inexpressible knowledge-by-acquaintance and Wittgenstein's notion of what can only be shown; and similarly for knowledge of truths and what can be said. I have not seen this analogy remarked upon but it is striking once you notice it. Was Wittgenstein developing an idea whose roots lie in Russell's distinction (though of course transforming it and putting it to a different use)?

[6] I am referring here to Thomas Nagel's formulation of the notion of subjectivity: see *The View From Nowhere* (Oxford University Press, 1986).

access: this too is an extrinsic epistemic feature of consciousness—how it relates to our cognitive faculties. Intentionality also appears to miss the mark: it is arguably neither necessary nor sufficient for being a conscious state, and again seems not to lie at the heart of what consciousness *is*. And the same can be said about the reflectiveness of consciousness. None of these quite captures our intuitive introspection-based sense of what makes a conscious state what it is. We have an ability to sort things into the conscious and the non-conscious, based upon our knowledge by acquaintance of what consciousness is, and these attempts to capture that knowledge fall short of its real content. We know just by means of self-consciousness what the essence of consciousness is, and this is not caught by these kinds of attempt at specifying this essence. Our acquaintance-based concept of consciousness is not capturable in these attempts at knowledge by description. This is why we can sense a problem about consciousness just by introspecting it, without yet having articulated any of the properties listed: hence our natural, if excessively blunt, question: 'How can *this* be *that*?' The bare demonstratives say it all.

I am saying, then, that the knowledge we have of consciousness, from which it follows that there is a mind-body problem, is of this acquaintance-based kind; it is not the kind that consists in specifying in propositional form exactly what it is about consciousness that makes it problematically related to the brain. Of course, we keep trying to express it that way and never quite succeed; my point is that this should now seem quite intelligible, resulting from the distinction between Russell's two types of knowledge. If someone were to claim that red is reducible to green, we would be within our rights to reply that we know this has to be false simply by acquaintance with the two colours; we wouldn't need to be able to specify something about red that *shows* that it is not green. I think we are in essentially this position with respect to the question of whether consciousness is reducible to neural firings; at any rate,

I hope to have given reasons to open up that option in a principled way.[7]

I now want to go further and argue that there are structural reasons why the mind-body problem cannot be solved: the problem that we sense in the way I have suggested is not one that we can solve with our current cognitive faculties.[8] To know whether a given problem is soluble, we clearly need to know what conditions of adequacy a solution should meet. I propose that any solution to the mind-body problem has to exhibit consciousness as *conservatively emergent* on brain processes: that is, we must be able to explain how consciousness emerges from the brain in such a way that the emergence is not *radical* or *brute*. Analytic functionalism fulfils this condition: if it were true, it would show that the mind is conservatively emergent on the body and brain, since it *analyses* conscious states as a certain type of physical state—causal roles, physically described, can clearly be realized by brain states. Conservative emergence is what we find in the standard cases of reduction: transparent bottom-up necessity from the reducing facts to the reduced facts.[9] I won't repeat what others have argued here—I will simply accept their conclusion,

[7] This explains why *argument* seems so futile in these debates: the knowledge we have of the nature of consciousness extends further than we can discursively articulate, and hence is not available for use as an argumentative premiss. One is quickly reduced to exclaiming 'But can't you *see*?!'

[8] This continues earlier work of mine: see *The Problem of Consciousness* (Basil Blackwell, 1991), *Problems in Philosophy: The Limits of Inquiry* (Basil Blackwell, 1993), and *The Mysterious Flame* (Basic Books, 1999). Let me also take this opportunity to make reference to Frank Jackson's 'Epiphenomenal Qualia', *Philosophical Quarterly* 32: 127–36, which in addition to the well-known 'knowledge argument' contains a brief but eloquent statement of what we might call the 'ignorance argument', i.e. the thesis that human knowledge may not be cut out to solve the mind-body problem. This statement of something very like my cognitive closure thesis did not come to my attention until after I had written my first papers propounding it, but there is an eerie similarity to some of my own formulations (obviously Jackson could not have been influenced by my work, given the timing). I note, however, that this theme seems to have retreated in his later work, and is never fully worked out.

[9] This has been particularly well argued by Joseph Levine in 'On Leaving Out What It's Like', in *The Nature of Consciousness*, (eds.) Ned Block, Owen Flanagan, and Guven Guzuldere (MIT Press, 1997), and elsewhere.

namely that reduction is possible only in the presence of a priori entailments from one set of facts to the other.[10] Any identities stated in the reduction must be backed by such a priori entailments; they cannot be merely stipulated or posited. What I want to point out are the *consequences* of accepting that the reduction must meet the requirement of conservative emergence via a priori entailments; so from now on I shall take this condition of adequacy as given.

The solution must accordingly completely close the explanatory gap. Let me illustrate what I mean by this by giving an example of what it would be. We have a very large number of memories, and the question arises of what properties of the brain make this possible—of what explains this aspect of memory. The standard answer is that the brain is a hugely complex system, consisting of millions of interconnected neurons, and there are more than enough discrete states of the brain to account for the number of memories we can store. This explanation seems to me entirely adequate: we know perfectly well how it is *possible* for the brain, as we now understand it, to harbour as large a memory store as it does—there is no problem of *principle* about this. It would be different if the brain were just a simple lump with no internal articulation; then it *would* be a problem how it could house all those memories. But, as it is, the brain has enough complexity to account for the sheer *number* of memories we have. This explanation works because the number of memories is *identical* to the number of (a subset of the) brain's states—if it were bigger, we would again have a problem.[11] But nothing like this works for the

[10] For a recent defence of this view see David Chalmers and Frank Jackson, 'Conceptual Analysis and Reductive Explanation', *Philosophical Review* (July 2001). I come to a similar conclusion in a somewhat different way in 'How Not to Solve the Mind-Body Problem', in *Physicalism and Its Discontents*, (eds.) Carl Gillett and Barry Loewer (Cambridge University Press, 2001).

[11] Another psychophysical problem in which we can see how to close the explanatory gap (i.e. there is no such gap) is accounting for the limits of the visual field. Clearly, the boundedness of the visual field results from the anatomy of the eye (and the laws of optics). Thus there is no profound problem of explaining why visual experiences have the kind of perimeter they have in terms of facts about the

fact that the brain generates sentience: there is no property in the brain that just *is* sentience, in the way that the number of memories corresponds to the number of neural states in the brain. Similarly, the fact that thoughts occur in temporal sequence can be explained by the fact that the underlying brain processes occur in temporal sequence: no explanatory gap there either. That property of thoughts is simply identical to a property of the corresponding neural processes—viz. temporal sequence. We know that brain processes have this property quite independently of the fact that thoughts have it—just as we know that neural states have the property of being very large in number quite independently of knowing that memories do. But in the case of consciousness we have nothing like this: there *is* no (known) property of the brain, which we have independently ascertained to be instantiated, which is simply identical to the property of consciousness. This is really why analytic functionalism *would* close the explanatory gap if it were true: we know that brain states have causal roles independently of knowing that they correspond to conscious states, and causal roles are said to *be* conscious states. The reducing theory has the explanatory materials *before* any 'bridge laws' are set up to match the two theories. In any case, any adequate solution must properly close the explanatory gap. A priori entailments do that, and only they do it; which is why we need them.

Connectedly, the correct theory must deactivate the intuitions of contingency that surround our thinking about the relation between mind and body.[12] And if the theory delivers a priori entailments, then this will certainly follow, since we will have more than mere a posteriori statements of correspondence (purporting to be identity statements). If it is a priori true that if p then

body. Contrast explaining why we have visual experiences *at all* in terms of facts about the body.

[12] Those intuitions that Saul Kripke so effectively exploited in his resuscitation of one of Descartes' arguments for dualism: see *Naming and Necessity* (Harvard University Press, 1980).

q, then we will not find ourselves conceiving of cases in which p holds but q does not. Thus an adequate theory must close down the intuitions that Kripke invoked to undermine the identity theory, on pain (!) of not delivering conservative emergence. In consequence, an adequate theory must exclude dualism as an option: once we see how the brain generates consciousness we will have no inclination to think that mind and brain are separate entities, with the mind capable of existing independently of the brain. A successful reduction of water to H_2O does not leave open the option that water and H_2O might yet be separate substances; it is not interpretable as merely stating a correlation. In the same way any adequate reduction of consciousness must make dualism a non-starter—as silly as insisting that heat is merely correlated with molecular motion without *being* it. Again connectedly, the solution must vindicate supervenience: it must explain just why the mental supervenes on brain states, so that this is no longer just a matter of faith or philosophical ideology. If two bodies of water are in exactly the same state of molecular agitation, and one of them is boiling, then we can see that it is simply impossible for the other not be boiling, in the light of what we know boiling to be: and we need something comparable for mental supervenience.[13]

I can put these requirements by saying that an adequate solution needs to remove the *philosophical* problem—the problem of choosing between materialism and dualism, the sense of magic that surrounds the emergence of consciousness, the ceaseless wrangles. What the theory has to do is specify some property of the brain from which it follows a priori that there is an associated consciousness, as well as specific properties that entail specific types of conscious state. A priori entailments are what would do the trick—transparent necessitation, with no recourse to stipulated identities and the like. There would be no need for appeals to Occam's razor—to the effect that it is just simpler to opt for

---

[13] Here I am simply following what others have argued; I am not attempting to argue the position afresh—so I am not aiming to convert the unconverted.

materialism rather than dualism (or vice versa). No, the theory needs to *demonstrate* that conscious states are reducible to something that can be known independently to be true of the brain, with nothing left out. In other words, an adequate theory must mirror the kinds of reduction with which we are familiar—water to H_2O, heat to molecular motion, etc. What it certainly cannot be is a mere statement of correlations, since this leaves dualism as an option, does not close the explanatory gap, invites intuitions of contingency, and makes any claim of emergence look radical not conservative; nor must it be merely a correlation theory *hyping* itself as a genuine reduction. Of course, a theory of that correlational type is much easier to achieve than the far more ambitious theory I am saying is needed, and I have no desire to deny that such a theory is humanly attainable. What I doubt is that a theory of the strong type I am specifying will ever be found—that is, a genuinely reductive theory (though I don't doubt that consciousness *is*, as a matter of knowledge-independent fact, reducible).

Before I turn to my reasons for maintaining this view I want to make some remarks about the doctrine known as 'physicalism', which many today take to be already the solution we seek. As several writers have pointed out, it is unclear what this doctrine really comes to—unclear what 'physicalism' *means*.[14] Let me distinguish *narrow* and *wide* physicalism. Narrow physicalism asserts that consciousness is reducible to the properties *now* described in books of neurophysiology and physics—whatever is currently known of the brain and matter in general. The trouble with this, obviously, is that it leaves no room for the idea that the relevant sciences might expand in the future, speaking of new properties and laws. Then 'physicalism', in the narrow sense, will turn out to

[14] I associate this view particularly with Noam Chomsky: see, e.g., his entry in *A Companion to the Philosophy of Mind*, (ed.) Samuel Guttenplan (Basil Blackwell, 1994). See also the entry in the same volume by Tim Crane for a similar scepticism: 'Physicalism(2)'. There is an excellent defence of this view in Max Deutsch's Rutgers doctoral dissertation (2000).

be empirically false, for uninteresting reasons. Presumably no philosophical physicalist intends this kind of narrow physicalism; the idea is rather that the mental is reducible to the physical in some broader sense. But what is that sense? Let wide physicalism be the doctrine that the mental is reducible to what would feature in an ideal theory of the world (don't say *physical* world, because that raises the same question). But that is totally vacuous: *of course* the mental is so reducible, even if mental terms themselves figure in that ultimate theory. That final theory might invoke very different kinds of entities and principles from those we speak of today, just as our physics goes substantially beyond what was contemplated in Newton's time. Just how different we cannot really say, though we will probably keep calling the new constructs 'physical' for boring institutional reasons. The problem is that there seems to be no position intermediate between narrow and wide physicalism (so-called); and as a consequence we really don't know what we mean by 'physical' (or 'material'). So it is completely unclear what the doctrine of 'physicalism' is. Obviously, it is no use speaking of what *physicists* talk about, since they talk of many things—and who is to count as a 'physicist' anyway? This raises the same dilemma of narrow and wide definitions that I just spelled out: the resulting doctrine is either too restrictive or too liberal.

It might be thought that the concept of *space* will help us out here: the physical is to be defined as the spatial. But there are several problems with this. First, it presents the same dilemma as before: do we mean space as it is *now* conceived or space as it would be conceived in the ideal theory? Clearly the former is no use, but the latter is again open to trivialization, since the mind *is* presumably spatial in that capacious sense—it fits somehow into the world that contains objects in space.[15] Maybe the ultimate theory of space will be one in which our current conception of space will be radically revised, and we might not even use the word 'space' any

<hr />

[15] See my 'Consciousness and Space' in *Conscious Experience*, (ed.) Thomas Metzinger (Schoningh, 1995); also *The Mysterious Flame*, ch. 4.

more; but the mind will presumably be related intelligibly to this space, no matter what its nature turns out to be. If 'physicalism' is the doctrine that the mind is spatial in this very elastic sense, then it is vacuously true. But surely that is not what people who call themselves 'physicalists' have intended; indeed, they might even deny that they are committed to the spatiality of the mind, on the grounds that the physical might turn out not to be spatial in any interesting sense (are quanta 'spatial'?). Besides, empty space is spatial, but physicalists don't want to identify the mind with empty space; they want to identify it with what *occupies* space— but then we need to know what kinds of things are being considered as potential occupants. I won't pursue this further, because I think it is clear how the dialectic is going to go; the lesson is that defining 'physical' is a lot harder than people imagine.

Narrow physicalism does not give us a priori entailments—that much is clear. So it fails our conditions of adequacy. But what should we say about wide physicalism? Here the answer must surely be that it *does* give us a priori entailments, since after all it is by stipulation the correct and ultimate reductive theory of the mind. But this is just to say that the correct theory has the form of any correct theory—the notion of the 'physical' has been stripped of all content by this time. If black-and-white Mary were to know *this* theory, then she would know all there is to know about the mind, since epistemically transparent necessitations are what this theory is all about.[16] But by the same token there is no content to the claim that this theory is 'physicalist', except what is given by the trivial assumption that it will speak of the brain and its properties (where these properties might be very different from anything currently envisaged). I recommend dropping the term 'physical' from all discussions of the mind-body problem; its survival depends on a systematic tendency to veer from the narrow to the wide interpretations, whereby it contrives to sound both

---

[16] On the epistemic powers of Mary see Frank Jackson, 'What Mary Didn't Know', *Journal of Philosophy*, 83: 291–5.

substantive and not obviously false.[17] If you imagine the issue arising three hundred years ago, when the scope of the sciences was much more restricted than now, you will see how susceptible the doctrine of 'physicalism' is to this dilemma. (Of course, dualism is equally ill-defined, given that it is the claim that the mental is *not* physical; so my criticism of 'physicalism' is in no way a brief for 'dualism'—which now also needs its apologetic scare-quotes.)

I myself think it is obvious on the basis of our knowledge by acquaintance of consciousness that narrow physicalism (including narrow functionalism) is false—we know that consciousness does not have an essence so specified (neurons spiking at such and such a rate, chemical concentrations of so and so amount, etc.)—and so-called wide physicalism is so unspecific that we have no idea what to say, except that if it is the true theory of the mind then of course that is precisely what it is. So I do not regard something called 'physicalism' as a candidate solution to the mind-body problem.

Let us return to the question of in-principle solubility. I said that an adequate theory needs to contain a priori entailments, statements of the form 'P if and only if Q' that can be known a priori: that is, there has to be a conceptual bridge spanning the biconditional. The concepts have to be a priori connectable in virtue of being the concepts they are. Analytic functionalism aimed to provide just this, so at least it was a theory that tried to meet the necessary requirements. But there is a clear obstacle to achieving such a priori connections, namely the vastly different concepts that figure on either side of the biconditional. On almost anybody's view, we have here a deep conceptual dualism—these are just not

[17] I am sometimes described as a mysterian physicalist, i.e. as someone who holds that there are unknowable *physical* properties of the brain. That, however, is not my position: I would not describe the unknowable properties of the brain that explain consciousness as 'physical', since I am suspicious of the whole notion of the physical. For the same reason, of course, I am not a dualist, if that means someone who believes that the mind is 'non-physical'. All such categories are ill-defined, as I see it. If anything, I am a mysterian property *pluralist*: I think there are many kinds of properties that pose various kinds of explanatory questions, some soluble, some not.

the same *kinds* of concept. Consider the concepts *pain* and *C-fibre stimulation*. The first concept is subjective (in Nagel's sense), acquaintance-dependent, and introspectively ascribed; the second concept is objective, acquaintance-independent, and perceptually ascribed. I shall focus here on the last of these contrasts, and I shall abbreviate the point by saying that concepts like *pain* are introspective concepts while concepts like *C-fibre stimulation* are perceptual concepts. I take it that this distinction bears on the *kind* of concepts we are dealing with and not merely on extrinsic facts about how they are applied. It is presumably because these are such different concepts that we have no a priori entailments between them, with all the consequences of this that I enumerated above. So, clearly, we are not going to solve the mind-body problem simply by inserting *these* concepts into our reductive biconditional: that is where we languish today, with no transparent connections between mind and brain. What we need is some new type of concept that will mediate between the two sides, somehow dissolving the conceptual dualism that is the origin of the problem.

In an earlier paper[18] I introduced property P as the property that will solve the problem—so let us say that we need a concept *P* that will provide the needed a priori entailments. P will bridge the explanatory gap because *P* will bridge the conceptual gap. So, it might be thought, all we need to do is come up with *P*. But now we are faced with a dilemma: either *P* will be an introspective concept or it will be a perceptual concept—since those are the two types of concepts that fall within our conceptual repertoire. But if so, it will be suspectible to the same problem we started with—the conceptual dualism that caused the original problem. So *if* our best attempts at *P* fall into one or other of these categories, we will not be able to provide what is needed. Such concepts will always give rise to intimations of dualism, thus failing a critical test of

[18] See my 'Can We Solve the Mind-Body Problem?' in *The Problem of Consciousness*.

adequacy; and the reason is that they will not supply the right a priori entailments, on account of the conceptual dualism that creates the problem in the first place. The point can be made vivid by bringing in space. If we agree that mental concepts represent mental states as non-spatial (in the narrow sense), while concepts like *C-fibre stimulation* (notice I don't say 'physical' concepts!) represent their referents as spatial, then we can see just why we cannot expect a priori entailments between them: for how could there be such entailments between concepts that differ so radically? But then *P*, if it is of one or the other kind, will just raise the same problem again.

The question then is whether we have any other way of generating concepts that will not create the same problem. We need a type of concept that belongs to neither category, yet links the two. Here two problems loom. First, even if we could come up with such a concept, how will it do the necessary linking, since we still have the same conceptual dualism inherent in our current introspective and perceptual concepts? The problem is generated by these concepts, but they are still there, uneasily linked to the putative *P*. At the least these concepts would need to be replaced or revised. But now, second, do we really have any other conceptual faculties that might come to our aid? Aren't these two great categories of concept *exhaustive*? Our thinking about the world is either perception-based or introspection-based—we just don't *have* anything else to go on (but see below). Those are the two faculties through which we apprehend the empirical world; we don't have anything else to try. We obviously cannot just will concepts into being (try willing yourself to have the concept of a bat's experience!); they have to be grounded in our actual cognitive faculties. But the only faculties we have are the *source* of the problem. Therefore we aren't going to solve the mind-body problem, as we are currently cognitively constituted.

It is instructive here to recall Nagel's notion of 'objective phenomenology', designed to bridge the conceptual and explanatory gap between mind and brain.[19] This purports to be a way of conceiving mental states that represents them objectively, and so equips us to reduce them to objectively conceived brain states. Here the conceptual dualism is agreed to be the underlying problem and an attempt to impose a conceptual monism is offered as a potential solution (or way forward). This is all exactly as I have been requiring—it has the same basic form as analytic functionalism, in terms of the methodology of the theory. Concepts of 'objective phenomenology' would be genuinely bridging concepts. But I think it is obvious on reflection that such a concept is not coherent, or at least will not do what it is designed to do. It is true that mental states have objective descriptions—for example, temporal and causal descriptions—but what we need is an objective description of their *intrinsic essence*. That means we need to be able to specify what it is like to have them using purely objective terms; but we have no idea what this might be. It would be like trying to convey our concepts of colour to a blind man by using geometry. Our concepts of consciousness are acquaintance-based, but any objective descriptions of conscious states are not—so the latter can never adequately capture the former. The idea of 'objective phenomenology' is as problematic as that of 'subjective physiology' as a way forward. Concepts are either accessible from a single point of view, or they are accessible from many points of view: but that is (partly) what, by Nagel's own showing, creates the problem. Those straddling concepts are harder to come by than you might suppose.

Suppose we had no faculty of introspection (like most animals), and yet we needed a concept that was introspection-based. Then, clearly, we could not acquire that concept without an enhancement of our basic cognitive faculties: we would need to acquire a full-blown faculty of introspection. I am saying that this is the *kind* of position we are in with respect to *P*: we need a new basic faculty,

[19] See Nagel's 'What Is It Like to Be a Bat?' *Philosophical Review*, 83: 435–50.

not just a new concept drawn from our present faculties. For those faculties, and the concepts tied to them, are what produce the problem in the first place: we conceive of mind and brain in such a way that we cannot now find a way to bring them together. What might such a new faculty be like? Here it is heuristically helpful to consider the God's eye view of the universe. God obviously does not apprehend the world by directing his senses towards it—seeing it, hearing it, smelling it, etc. Nor does he infer our mental states from our behaviour. There is no process of divine theory construction, confirmation, induction, inference to the best explanation, and so on. God doesn't need to employ the scientific method. Somehow, we are to understand, God's omniscience takes in everything, in an instant, and with extraordinary clarity and directness: he just 'intuits' the totality of reality. Perhaps his knowledge of the universe most resembles our a priori knowledge of the abstract world, where we too employ a faculty that is neither perceptual nor introspective—a kind of direct 'intuition' of how things are, and must be. So perhaps God understands the mind-brain relation in somewhat the way we understand geometry (in any case, that is my personal epistemological theology); specifically, he does not employ anything like our introspective and perceptual concepts. God's faculties do not deign to wield such sublunary human concepts; he has his own Transcendent Conceptual Scheme. For God, then, there is no mind-body problem, given the nature of the divine concepts: all is lucid a priori entailment for God's penetrating intellect. Our problem is that *our* a priori concepts don't extend as far as God's; they hardly get any grip on the empirical world at all—only the abstract world. So there is no future in mining our store of a priori concepts in hopes of coming up with the concepts necessary to solve the mind-body problem—what is needed here is an empirical theory of the concrete world. We are accordingly limited to the conceptual faculties associated with perception and introspection, and they are what produce the philosophical problem—the conceptual dualism that keeps intimating ontological dualism (despite our principled resistance to it). We cannot even *conceive* of concepts that would not give rise to these dualistic leanings—however much we set ourselves to resist them. What would a concept of consciousness be like that was not acquaintance-based, that did not require *being* conscious in order to possess it? What kind of concept of experiencing red would it be that allowed this concept to be possessed without ever having experienced red? For these are the kinds of concept we would need if we were to overcome the conceptual dualism that defines the problem. And how could we conceive of the brain except in terms of concepts that trace back to the idea of the brain as a perceptible object in space? Our 'phenomenal world' (to use Kantian terminology) is shaped by our introspective and percep- tual modes of apprehension, along with the concepts proper to these faculties; we cannot step out of this world into a brand new conceptual landscape. But such stepping out is what the mind- body problem demands of us. We need to remember that our concepts are just human constructs, constrained by biology, the contingent tools of finite beings; there is no guarantee that they can reach into every corner of the universe that created us.[20]

It might be said that there have been 'paradigm shifts' before, revolutions of theory that overthrow earlier ways of conceiving the universe—so why can there not be such a paradigm shift in the understanding of consciousness? True, it may be admitted, we need a conceptual revolution, but such revolutions have occurred before—aren't they even part of 'normal' scientific progress? But past theoretical shifts have never required us to go outside of our current cognitive *faculties*, merely to create new concepts and theories within our present faculties. What we need is a *perspective* shift, not just a paradigm shift—a shift not merely of world-view, but of ways of apprehending the world. We need to become another type of cognitive being altogether. A creature devoid of

[20] See the works cited in n. 8 and many passages in Chomsky's writings.

psychological concepts, but possessing concepts of the external world, needs more than a mere paradigm shift in order to grasp ordinary folk psychology; she needs an entirely new cognitive perspective—a new conceptual faculty (as would a creature with the converse conceptual repertoire). No amount of paradigm-shifting will teach us what it is like to be a bat, or teach a blind man what it is like to see, since these deficiencies go deeper than that. Given the way we form our concepts, and the kinds of concepts we employ, we need more than a paradigm shift to solve the mind-body problem; we need to become different cognitive beings.

I have argued that we know by means of introspective self-consciousness that there is a mind-body problem. But I have also argued that this very way of knowing is what blocks us from solving it (along with the way we know about the brain). It is almost as if we have been *designed* to be struck by a problem that we are constitutionally unable to solve: the very self-consciousness that makes us aware of the problem is (part of) what prevents us from solving it, because of the concepts that are generated by such self-consciousness. I can imagine a type of God for whom this would be an amusing irony—even an irresistible temptation. Let's build a thinking being whose very way of thinking about itself made it opaque to itself; but let's not make this too obvious to our creation. If that is what God set out to do, then I think he achieved his aim perfectly.[21]

[21] Of course, what makes us opaque to ourselves—our empirical concepts—makes the rest of the world (relatively) transparent to us; so God wasn't being entirely mischievous, I suppose.

2

How Not to Solve the Mind-Body Problem

I

The conclusion I aim to establish in this chapter is this: the solution to the mind-body problem cannot take the form of an empirical identity statement but must rather consist in an analytic identity statement. That is, to solve the problem we would need to provide a conceptual reduction of consciousness, not an a posteriori reduction. It is not that I know what this conceptual reduction would look like—far from it. My thesis is merely that there is a general argument that shows that the solution must take this form. I shall also be concerned to spell out the consequences of this thesis for the prospects of solving the mind-body problem, and to indicate how my conclusion bears upon certain arguments that have been given to undermine physicalism.

II

The logical analysis of identity statements has proved crucial in assessing the claims of physicalism, and so it will be in this chapter.

Early identity theorists, notably J. J. C. Smart, observed that not all true identity statements are conceptual truths, following Frege's precedent[1]. This opened the way to claiming that there might be true identity statements linking mental and physical properties that could not be certified to be true on conceptual grounds alone. It was thus not incumbent on a physicalist to provide any analysis of mental concepts in order to claim to possess a complete physical reduction of mental properties. This liberalization of the conditions of adequacy upon a physicalist theory brightened the prospects for that theory considerably, and it established a paradigm for what a solution to the mind-body problem might look like. We could say that pain is C-fibre stimulation in the same spirit in which we say that heat is molecular motion. The key is to recognize that true identities do not have to link synonyms. All at once a host of familiar objections, of a generally epistemic nature, fall away. In particular, the physicalist is under no obligation to say that I *know* my C-fibres are firing when I know I am in pain.

The next step came from Saul Kripke: although identity statements could be empirical and true, they could not be contingent and true.[2] All identities are necessary, though some are a posteriori. So if we have good reason to think that psychophysical identity statements are not necessary then we have good reason to think they are not true. This spelled trouble for the identity theory, because such statements do appear contingent. The appearance of contigency has to be explained away if we are to accept the truth of the identity theory.

I want to focus on the informativeness of psychophysical identity statements. The argument I shall defend is not unfamiliar, but its power and ramifications have not been properly

[1] J. J. C. Smart, 'Sensations and Brain Processes', in D. Rosenthal (ed.), *The Nature of Mind* (Oxford: Oxford University Press, 1980).

[2] Saul Kripke, *Naming and Necessity* (Cambridge, Mass.: Harvard University Press, 1990).

appreciated.[3] In fact, the argument occurs quite plainly in Smart's original paper, and his response to it strikes me as basically correct, at least as to its general form. Smart writes:

Even if objections 1 and 2 do not prove that sensations are something over and above brain processes, they do prove that the qualities of sensations are something over and above the qualities of brain processes. That is, it may be possible to get out of asserting the existence of irreducibly psychic processes, but not out of asserting the existence of irreducibly psychic *properties*. For suppose we identify the Morning Star with the Evening Star. Then there must be some properties which logically imply that of being the Morning Star, and quite distinct properties that entail that of being the Evening Star. Again, there must be some properties (for example, that of being a yellowish flash) which are logically distinct from those in the physicalist story.... Now how do I get over the objection that a sensation can be identified with a brain process only if it has some phenomenal property, not possessed by brain processes, whereby one-half of the identification may be, so to speak, pinned down.[4]

In a footnote Smart says: 'I think this objection was first put to me by Professor Max Black. I think it is the most subtle of any of those I have considered, and the one which I am least confident of having met.'[5] Smart's response to Black's objection is immediately to concede its force—the phenomenal property is indeed distinct from any brain property. He thus abandons the kind of type-identity theory based upon the usual scientific paradigms. But he works to retain a general materialism by offering a topic-neutral analysis of those residual mental properties—an analysis of basically functionalist cast. The result, though Smart does not have the apparatus to put it this way, is token identity materialism combined with analytic functionalism about mental properties. The processes that instantiate mental properties are brain processes,

[3] The only discussions I know of are Stephen White, 'Curse of the Qualia', *Synthese* 68 (1986): 333–68 and Christopher Hill, *Sensations* (Cambridge: Cambridge University Press, 1991), 98–101.

[4] Smart, 172.

[5] Ibid. n. 13.

while the properties are analysed in topic-neutral functional terms. Thus mental properties are *not* held to be identical with brain properties, but rather with topic-neutral functional properties. In effect, Smart in this paper introduces type-identity theory and then abandons it before the paper is finished. Some readers have been puzzled by his strategy: why not stick with type-identity theory and forgo the implausible topic-neutral analysis? But I think Smart's reasoning is impeccable, and the underlying predicament he uncovers is genuine. The point is that Black's objection refutes type-identity theory and the only way to go in saving materialism is to offer a conceptual reduction of the mental. What is absolutely crucial here is that any empirical identity theory will face the question of what makes its characteristic identity statements informative, and the only way out of this problem is to provide a nonempirical identity theory. Only conceptual reduction can block the resurgence of those 'irreducibly psychic properties' Smart is so anxious to avoid. I shall now spell out the basic argument more rigorously than Smart does, so that its full force can be appreciated.

III

Everyone will agree that the informativeness of an identity statement depends upon there being two senses corresponding to a single reference. More controversial is the question of what distinguishes distinct senses—in particular, how epistemic or mentalistic the notion of sense should be. I shall put forward a schema intended to capture distinctness of sense and hence explain what identity informativeness consists in. If 'A' and 'B' are codenoting terms, then 'A = B' is informative if and only if 'A' connotes a property F that is numerically distinct from the property G that is connoted by 'B'. Connotation is not the same relation as denotation: 'A' and 'B' denote an entity that is not identical to either of the properties connoted by the terms; so there are three items at play here, two connoted, one denoted. This schema is intended to hold for any kinds of terms and any kinds of denotation. In effect, the idea is that when we learn the truth of an informative identity proposition we learn that two properties are coinstantiated: the connoted properties converge on a single object. According to this schema, we can say that an identity statement is never 'barely informative', in the sense that there is no explanation of its informativeness in terms of coinstantiated connoted properties. Distinctness of sense is distinctness of connotation, and connotation consists in properties expressed. The fact that we come to know when we learn that A = B is the fact that F and G are coinstantiated. Let me now illustrate how the schema works in application to particular identity statements.

Take 'the evening star = the morning star', where the flanking descriptions really are descriptive terms not disguised proper names. The denotation of both descriptions is Venus, so the statement is true. The connotations are, however, quite distinct: one description connotes the property of being (uniquely) an evening star, the other connotes the property of being (uniquely) a morning star. The statement tells us that these two properties are possessed by a single object: the proposition we come to know is that the property of being (uniquely) a morning star is coinstantiated with the property of being (uniquely) an evening star. (Ignore the fact that both descriptions are strictly improper. Think of them as short for 'the first star to appear in the morning/evening'.) It seems entirely clear that exactly the same account should be given for all identity propositions involving descriptions; the predicates in the descriptions serve to express the connoted properties on the distinctness of which the informativeness turns.

I think the same is true of names, though it is a matter of controversy whether the properties involved belong to the senses of the names. The descriptions that express these properties may be merely reference-fixing descriptions, and they may vary from speaker to speaker. Still, what is learned by learning the truth of, say, 'Marilyn Monroe = Norma Jeane Baker' is that certain properties are coinstantiated—as it might be, that the property of being (uniquely) a platinum-haired actress in *Some Like it Hot* is coinstantiated with the property of having once been a rather plain brunette in such-and-such high school. What other kind of thing could make the identity statement informative? As we know from Frege, it certainly cannot be the denotation of the two names, because this is the same while the senses differ.

Similarly with demonstrative and indexical identity statements. Consider 'that elephant = that elephant' said while pointing successively to the tusks and tail of a partly occluded pachyderm. That could be informative, but only because the recipient learns that the property of being thus tusked is coinstantiated with the property of being so tailed, and these are quite distinct properties (tusks not being tails). We learn in effect that property diversity masks uniqueness of instantiating objects. Objects have many properties, and we sometimes discover that these distinct properties occur in the same entity. To be true, an identity statement must refer to a single entity, but to be informative it must express divergent properties. Or again, consider 'I am Colin McGinn', learned after I wake from amnesia and discover that I wrote the book I am reading. Here again what I discover is something similar to this: the person with the property of having these mental states also has the property of having written this book. Two modes of presentation of me have been discovered to be such, as when my doctor remarks to me, 'You know, you wrote that book.' (I reply: 'Oh, then it is a lot better than I thought.')

Same for natural kind identities. Following Kripke, we can say that 'heat = molecular motion' is informative because 'heat' connotes the property of causing the sensation of heat in people while 'molecular motion' does not, connoting instead the property of being molecules in motion.[6] We accordingly learn that what has

[6] Kripke, 131

the former property also has the latter property, in other words what causes the sensation of heat is what has high molecular motion, where these are distinct properties of heat (which is why in some possible worlds molecular motion does not cause the sensation of heat). A single property or kind has two distinct properties, and we learn that these are coinstantiated, something that cannot be inferred from knowledge of the identity of the properties. Sometimes, as with 'heat', the connoted property involves the kind of mental state the natural kind in question produces in us.

Now we can move to putative psychophysical identities. Consider the double-aspect token-identity theory, which asserts such propositions as 'this pain is identical to that C-fibre firing'. Supposing such statements to be true, they fit our schema perfectly: a single token event is said to have two distinct properties, and this is informative because there is no a priori or analytic link between the concepts of the two properties. On another occasion, indeed, the property of pain might be coinstantiated with D-fibre firing or whatever. The case is, logically, exactly the same as the evening star and the morning star. But what of putative type-identities, the crucial case? Here we are saying that the properties are identical, so we cannot appeal to their distinctness to explain the informativeness of 'the property of pain = the property of C-fibres firing'. That statement is certainly informative—superinformative we might say—but it cannot be so in virtue of the denoted properties. So what else is there to explain the informativeness? On the face of it, the statement can be true only if uninformative, but it is informative, so it is not true. That is, this holds on the assumption that the properties connoted by the terms are those of pain and C-fibre firing. It begins to seem that we are mistaking a mere correlation of distinct properties for an identity, as is shown by the informativeness of bringing them together. That was Black and Smart's original point: the two properties connoted have to be distinct, but they seem to be nothing other than the properties of pain and C-fibre firing, so the identity theory is false. Accordingly, we need an account of what pain is that does not lead to this proliferation problem; and because it cannot take the form of an empirical identity statement, it must be an uninformative analytic or a priori identity statement. This appears to spell a swift demise for empirical type-identity theory, and pointed out by someone widely believed to espouse that theory.

Let me make a couple of observations on what this argument establishes, if it is sound, before I turn to replying to objections to it. First, it is not specifically an argument against materialism; the same point would apply to an empirical identity statement linking mental terms with terms for the states of a Cartesian immaterial substance. What is shown is that no kind of solution to the mind-body problem can take the form of an empirical identity statement, and substance dualism is no way out of that. The same point applies to versions of functionalism that offer empirical identity-based reductions. But the point does not apply to analytical functionalism, because that theory does not offer empirical identities but a priori or conceptual ones. Neither is the argument applicable solely to identity theories concerning the mind. It applies to any attempt to empirically identify one property with another. We always need to ask whether the connoted property needed to explain informativeness is actually just the denoted property, thus undermining the identity assertion. Thus, suppose we took a fancy to the idea of empirical phenomenalism, holding that material object properties such as squareness are really possibilities of sensation, this being an a posteriori claim. There would then be the objection that 'square' must denote something other than sensation possibilities, because the putative identity statement is held to be informative, and there is nothing but squareness to be the connotation of the term. (Actually, of course, phenomenalists have always been of the analytical persuasion, which shows some savvy on their part—ditto the logical behaviourists.) Or consider attempts to identify the Good with some naturalistic property on a posteriori grounds: the question arises whether the informativeness is consistent with the claimed identity, as 'good' will have to connote a property distinct from any property connoted by the naturalistic term in question. The challenge is always to find some extra property to be the connoted property, where this diverges from the denoted property. And the problem is that this seems none too easy a thing to do. Later I shall consider some ways to try to meet this challenge in the case of psychophysical identity theories and show why they fail. But first I want to bring to bear a cognate line of thought that casts doubt on the very structure of the standard type-identity picture that shows a deep internal tension in the position.

IV

Presumably all will agree that the appearance of pain is nothing like the appearance of C-fibres firing: the way pain seems from the inside (or indeed from the third-person point of view) is nothing like the way C-fibres appear when you look into a person's brain. It is precisely this fact that makes the identity theory surprising and informative—that these vastly different appearances are nevertheless appearances of a single property or kind. Who would have thought that one thing could give rise to such different appearances? And one's naive suspicion has always been that the appearances are actually too different to be consistent with the purported identity; hence the sense that one has to do some serious swallowing in order to accept the claim of identity. Now I want to argue that this natural response—so often dismissed as simply confused (can't you distinguish sense from reference?)—is actually soundly based. The point is that we cannot explain the distinction between the appearances in a way that is consistent with the identity claim. The way we explain distinctions of sense accompanied by sameness of reference in ordinary cases is to draw attention to the gap between the sense and the reference, because if there were no such gap, the unity of reference would give rise to a unity of sense; thus we need to show some distance between reference and sense— some degrees of freedom, some failure of determination. If we could not do that, then a distinction of sense would imply a distinction of reference.

Consider the appearances of pains and tickles. These appearances are totally distinct. But is it conceivable that they are nevertheless appearances of the same sensation? Someone might say that it is conceivable, because reference never determines sense. It is epistemically possible that only one sensation property underlies these admittedly divergent appearances. But this is crazy, and the reason is obvious: we cannot pull apart appearance and reality in this case. Given the relation between the appearance of pains/tickles and the actual pains/tickles, namely identity (or at least containment), and given the difference of the appearances, the realities *cannot* be the same. So sometimes it is valid to argue from appearance distinctions to reality distinctions, depending upon how intimately appearance and reality are related. I would argue that we can do this for perceptual appearances too—say, of colours and shapes. It is not conceivable that visual perceptions of red and green, or round and square, should correspond to one property that appears differently: the property represented can be inferred from its perceptual appearance and vice versa. (I don't mean that an object with one colour or shape might not appear to have two such. I mean that the colour or shape perceptually represented cannot admit of such divergent appearances, because that property determines the appearances.) So what now of pain and C-fibre firing?

Well, the appearance of pain clearly coincides with pain itself, so there is no exploitable gap there to play with. Given the identity between them, we can immediately infer that the (perceptual) appearance of C-fibres is not identical to pain, because it is not identical to the appearance of pain. But that in itself is nothing to worry about for the identity theorist, whose claim is not that the way C-fibre firing looks is identical to pain but that C-fibre firing itself is. If we could identify C-fibre firing with the way it looks, then we could indeed derive the non-identity, just as we did with pains and tickles, but that hardly seems plausible. Yet there is still the question whether we can explain the distinction of appearances here given the slender materials available. For all we really have to go on is the gap between C-fibres and their appearance. Is this gap big enough to capture the difference between the appearance of pain (i.e. pain) and the appearance of C-fibre firing? I suggest that it is not. Intuitively, the problem is that the gap between C-fibres and their appearance is too small to be parlayed into the enormous gulf separating the appearance of pain and the appearance of C-fibre firing. Imagine staring at someone's firing C-fibres under a microscope: the content of your visual experience would be specified by saying that it is *C-fibre firing* that you are experiencing. The property enters into the very content of what you experience (or at least it could). But the appearance of pain is totally different from such an appearance of C-fibres. So how do we explain this difference, given that the gap between C-fibres and their appearance is so narrow? We simply don't have enough properties in play to explain the appearance distinctions that indubitably exist. If we started out agnostic on the question of identity, I think we would find it persuasive against identity that the appearances cannot be squared with the claim of identity. We would take it that there have to be two properties—pain and C-fibre firing—in order to account for the distinction of appearances. The problem, intuitively, is that we are driven to ascribe two aspects to a (putatively) single thing, but then we have given up the claim of property identity, because an aspect is just a property. Hence the internal tension: how can we have two appearance-fixing aspects of what is meant to be an indissoluble unity? The statement of property identity can be informative, again, only if it is not true. It is indeed highly informative to be told that these are appearances of the same thing, namely a brain state, but then we cannot find the resources with which to capture the conditions of the possibility of this informativeness, namely, the radical distinction of appearances. The question then is whether we can capture the needed distinction by appealing to something other than the distinctness of pain and C-fibre firing; to this I now turn.

V

The argument as presented so far relies on the assumption that the sense of 'pain' is the property of pain and the sense of 'C-fibre firing' is the property of C-fibre firing—that these properties are the proper connotations of the terms in question. Equivalently, the conceptual distinctness of the concepts *pain* and *C-fibre firing* consists in the ontological distinctness of the associated properties of pain and C-fibre firing. That is the overwhelmingly natural view to take, I think, but it is not the only conceivable view. As far as I can see, there are two alternative views that might be proposed to block the argument: one view accepts the requirement that some property be found that distinguishes the senses of the terms,[7] the other view rejects this requirement and proposes that we can explain conceptual distinctness without invoking property distinctness.[8] Let us consider these in turn. Is it possible to hold that the property that constitutes the sense of 'pain' is not pain but some other property? Well, we cannot say that this extra property is something like the appearance of pain, because that is not distinguishable from pain. We might try saying that it is the property of causing certain sorts of behaviour, the kind that pain typically causes. That is certainly a distinct property from pain (unless you are a behaviourist), so that it has the potential to constitute the

---

[7] This is Hill's strategy (1991, 100).
[8] This type of position is advocated by Brian Loar, 'Phenomenal States', *Philosophical Perspectives* 4: 81–108.

informativeness-generating concept we need. But the trouble is that it is implausible to suggest that this is really the sense of 'pain'. The reason is that 'pain = the cause of such-and-such behaviour' is potentially informative, which it shouldn't be if the two terms have the same sense. Note that we cannot save the identity theory by identifying pain with such a behavioural property because then it will be false that pain = C-fibre firing, as the latter is not a behavioural property. No, we have to be saying that pain is a property distinct from the behavioural property that constitutes its mode of presentation, so that pain = C-fibre firing while the behavioural property does not. Logically that would do the trick in responding to the Smart–Black style of argument, but it is not just not credible that 'pain' means what it would have to for the response to succeed. I certainly do not think of my pains under such a description when I self-ascribe 'pain', and it is entirely consistent to say 'it might turn out that pain does not cause such-and-such behaviour'.

It might be thought that I am here begging the question against the thesis that 'pain' does just mean 'the cause of such-and-such behaviour', but that is not what is going on. My point, remember, is that the Smart–Black argument shows that in the end we have to give a conceptual analysis in physical or topic-neutral terms of mental concepts if we are to avoid the problem of residual mental properties. The behaviourist response in question concedes this point. Now it is true that I have no sympathy for this kind of behaviourist analysis for reasons not discussed in this chapter, but the point I am making now is that such an approach agrees with the upshot of the Smart–Black argument. Later I shall be discussing another way out and urging its merits.

On the other hand, if we suggest a mentalistic mode of presentation for 'pain'—say, 'the sensation I dislike the most'—then we are still left with a mental residue, which is what we are trying to avoid. It may be analytic that pain is the sensation I dislike the most, but that is no help if the new mode of presentation is a mental property, because the same problem will arise for an empirical identity theory of it. So, although I have not exhausted every possible property that might be suggested as the mode of presentation of pain, I think it is pretty clear that this route will not work: the plain fact is that it is pain itself that constitutes the mode of presentation of pain—the connotation and denotation of 'pain' coincide. And this is not meant to be a point solely about the first-person perspective; 'pain' is univocal in first- and third-person uses, and its sense is given by the property of pain in both uses. The sense of 'pain' is not the place to look for that fugitive extra property over and above the property of pain.

It might then be thought more promising to focus on the other term of the identity statement. Thus it might be suggested that 'C-fibre firing' connotes the property, not of C-fibre firing, but the property of looking a certain way or the property of being responsible for such-and-such observations. The idea might be that this is a theoretical term and that such terms have modes of presentation that diverge from their denotations. I think there are at least three problems with this. First, if we allow ourselves mentalistic modes of presentation, as with how C-fibres *look*, then we generate a vicious regress, because then we will have to give an identity theory of these mental properties with the same problem arising. Clearly we do not avoid the problem of the mental residue by introducing a mental property in connection with the physical term 'C-fibre firing'! Second, the proposal is implausible for the same reason the comparable move for 'pain' was, namely that it is informative to be told that C-fibre firing looks such-and-such a way. It is not analytic that C-fibre firing looks this way, and it might have turned out not to, so the sense of the term 'C-fibre firing' cannot consist in such a description. Nor is this a remotely plausible idea independently of trying to respond to the argument at issue. It sounds similar to one of those bad old positivist distortions, that theoretical terms have to be definable in terms of observations. Third, we surely do not want to generate an a priori proof that mental states cannot be identical to *observable* features of the brain on the grounds that if they were we would not be able to reply to the argument by invoking the alleged 'theoreticalness' of terms such as 'C-fibre firing'! In fact, I think it is quite clear that the way of thinking of C-fibre firing that is associated with 'C-fibre firing' is simply that of having the property of C-fibre firing—and not, say, the property expressed by 'the brain state most discussed by philosophers'. As it were, the term gives you the property it denotes—it connotes what it denotes. But if that is right then both terms connote what they denote, so that there is no room to capture informativeness by means of property connoted that is consistent with the claimed identity. The case is totally unlike those favoured paradigms beloved of identity theorists—'heat = molecular motion' and the like. For in these cases we always have a property such as 'cause of the sensation of heat' to invoke to capture informativeness, this description introducing a distinct property from any connoted by the term 'molecular motion'. The crucial disanalogy is that such identity assertions don't care if they invoke an unreduced mental property, because they are not in the business of trying to tell us what the sensation of heat is, only what heat is. But in the case of pain that is precisely what we are trying to do, which is why we cannot perform the analogous trick. So the analogy breaks down at exactly the point at which it needs to work most. The problem arises because we do think of heat under such a mental mode of presentation, and this is quite distinct from heat. In the case of pain the first part of this is true, but not the second (Kripke was tapping into the same point). Pain cannot be peeled off itself.

The second kind of response seeks to distinguish concepts by something other than property connoted. This response implicitly abandons externalism about meaning. It finds semantic distinctions that have no world-oriented counterpart. An externalist would say that two concepts C_1 and C_2 differ in their content if and only if there are properties P_1 and P_2 such that C_1 connotes P_1

and C2 connotes P2 and P1 is not identical to P2. One motivation for this is that a concept is a way of thinking of something, and a way of thinking of something is a way something is taken to *be*, in other words a property it is taken to have. Thus if two ways of thinking differ, then they differ in how the world is taken to be, in the properties that are taken to be instantiated. If I think of something as red, then I think of it precisely as having the property of redness—that is what this way of thinking consists in. To hold otherwise is to shift what belongs to the intentional object of the concept onto the mental vehicle of the concept. That is to psychologize sense in such a way as to detach it from how the world is taken to be. But, according to the line we are considering, there is no distinction in what properties the world is taken to have when one thinks of it as containing pain or C-fibre firing. Exactly the same state of affairs is represented when one thinks of propositions involving these two concepts. The concepts differ purely psychologically, purely 'internally'; there is no difference in their intentional objects.

Now I have general misgivings about this approach to conceptual identity, because I am an externalist about content,[9] but the point I want to make now is peculiar to the case at issue. The point is that this response to the Smart–Black argument leads to a vicious infinite regress. To see this, first consider an analogous proposal, namely that the identity theory applies to pain and not to the appearance of pain. Thus, pain is C-fibre firing but the appearance of pain is not—that is just the way pain presents itself to the subject. And we are not interested in an identity theory of appearances but only of realities. Now we are already familiar with the problem that pain and its appearance cannot be severed in this way, but there is another problem too: surely, even if we grant the distinction between pain and its appearance, the identity theorist needs an account of the appearance of pain also, because that itself

---

[9] See my *Mental Content* (Oxford: Blackwell, 1989).

is something mental. If we now propose an identity theory of this—say, that the appearance of pain is identical to D-fibre firing—then we face the question as to why this is not the way the appearance of pain appears. It is no use at this point to speak of the appearance of the appearance of pain because the same problem arises for that, with the same threat if we introduce a new physical property—say, E-fibre firing—to be identical with that higher-level appearance. We cannot keep peeling off the appearances at each new level in the hope of explaining the apparent distinction between the mental and physical property at the next level down. Put it this way: the way pain appears is the way pain really appears—it is an aspect of mental reality—so we need to give a materialist account of it if we are aiming to capture everything real. But then we always have a mental residue each time we identify an appearance with a physical property. This shows that we cannot explain why pain does not seem similar to C-fibre stimulation by shifting the distinction onto the appearance of pain—on pain of vicious regress (so to speak).

Now consider this: suppose the concepts of pain and C-fibre firing are distinct, even though the denoted properties are identical; there is still the property of satisfying one or other of these concepts. So consider the property of satisfying the concept *pain*, or the property of applying that concept to a subject, possibly oneself. That is a real property, quite distinct from the property of satisfying the concept *C-fibre firing*; and it is plainly a mental property. So I may have only one property when I am in pain, because pain is identical to C-fibre firing, but I have two properties in virtue of self-ascribing the concept *pain* and the concept *C-fibre firing*, because these are admitted to be distinct concepts. (I could have one of these properties without the other, as I might lack the latter concept.) Then the question is what sort of property this is: is it identical to some new physical property? If it is not, then there is a mental property that is not physical, which abandons the identity theory. If it is, then we can form a suitable identity statement for the property, as it might be, 'the property of applying the concept *pain* = Z-fibre firing'. But this is an informative empirical identity statement, so there has to be a cognitive distinction between its two terms. If we explain the distinction by invoking distinct connoted properties, then again we have a mental property left dangling, thus conceding the argument. Suppose then that we explain the distinction by saying that the concepts differ not in virtue of any distinct properties but in virtue of being irreducibly distinct concepts. Then we can form a new property in turn—the property of satisfying this new concept (the concept of the property of satisfying the concept *pain*). But then again we need to find a physical property for this mental property to be identical with, and the cycle begins again. Each time we find a new concept to explain the informativeness we can form the property of satisfying this concept, and this property needs its corresponding physical property. The regress arises because concepts generate extra properties, the properties of satisfying or applying them. If no new property came in the wake of distinguishing the concepts, then there would be no regress, because all the properties in the world would be accounted for at the first level. But once we admit that there is a property of satisfying or applying the concept *pain* then that property cries out for explanation, and the regress is set to begin—for there is always a new property one step ahead of the proposed explanation of informativeness. Logically, it is the same as with the regress of appearances: distinguishing the appearance of pain from pain to explain informativeness leaves the appearance dangling, and once it is identified with a new physical property we have the same problem again. At bottom the difficulty is simple and predictable: we are trying to shove the apparent distinction between pain and C-fibre firing off onto a distinction in the concepts, but that in turn gives us a further mental property, and once this is identified with some physical property the cycle starts up again. The proposal only seemed as if it could work as an alternative to the property explanation of informativeness because we forgot to ask what the property of satisfying the concept consists in.

It may help if I put the point in terms of Frank Jackson's Mary thought experiment.[10] In brief, Mary learns all of physics in a black-and-white room, then leaves it one day to be confronted with her first experience of red. She seems to learn a new fact thereby, while by hypothesis she knew all the physical facts already. Therefore experiencing red is not a physical fact. One popular reply to Jackson is that the same properties or facts are brought under new concepts when Mary emerges from the room, so that the argument fallaciously conflates facts and their conceptual representation. Mary knew all the facts; she simply didn't know all the *descriptions* of the facts. But, I reply to this reply, applying the concept *experience of red* to oneself is just another property one has. So if Mary knew all the properties before she left the room, she must have known this one; but she did not. If we try to say that she knew this property under another description, then there is the further property of applying that description, but this produces the same problem. The difficulty is that a mode of presentation of a fact is *itself a fact*—the fact that something has that mode of presentation. So if Mary knows all the facts in virtue of knowing all the physical facts, then she must already know that her internal states have every mode of presentation they actually have, so she must know that one of her brain states has the mode of presentation 'an experience of red' (she certainly must know that her brain state satisfies that linguistic string). If we now say that she knows about this mode of presentation but only under some other mode of presentation, then (a) this is crazy and (b) it just raises the same question again. She must know all the conceptual distinctions there are, because these are just one species of fact. So she must know the facts that constitute applying the concept *experience of*

[10] Frank Jackson, 'What Mary Didn't Know', in Rosenthal, 392–4.

red. But how can she know this without knowing what it is like to see something red, which by hypothesis she does not know while still in the room? Compare the appearance version of this strategy again: she knows all the realities but not the way those realities appear—specifically, how her experience of red will appear. But that is just one more fact about the world, so she ought to know how experiences of red appear too. Yet she doesn't. If we say that she knows how experiences of red appear but not how these appearances appear, then (a) this is crazy and (b) it leads to an obvious regress. The problem is that the distinctions that are offered as alternatives to factual distinctions are really just another kind of factual distinction—only now at the level of appearances. Similarly, conceptual distinctions are just factual distinctions about how we represent the world, so we need to know what kinds of facts they are. In short, there isn't the kind of distinction between the ontological and the epistemological that the response we are considering relies on there being.

This problem is quite general and seems to me to undermine the second line of resistance to the Smart–Black argument. It also seems very peculiar and ad hoc that only psychophysical type identities should call for this kind of explanation of their informativeness, while every other identity statement (including token identity without type identity) should be explicable in the familiar property style. Is it that externalism about concept identity works in every case but this one? How surprising to find that type-identity theory is defensible only if externalism is (locally) false! Is that a consequence we envisaged when we found ourselves attracted to materialism?

I conclude, then, that neither line of resistance to the Smart–Black argument succeeds. It therefore looks as if either property dualism is true or that there is some kind of analytic version of the identity theory in the offing. Which of these is correct?

VI

It may seem at this point as if we have argued ourselves into a very nasty corner, because neither property dualism nor the standard sorts of analytical reduction are attractive options. I certainly find neither of these views palatable. But let us take stock: all we have really argued so far is that an account of mental properties must not take the form of an empirical identity statement. There is no argument yet for either of those unpalatable positions. Is there then a third option to consider here? I suggest that there is.

Someone could conclude from the argument so far that no *identity* statement can be made about mental properties of such a kind as to solve the mind-body problem; but I think this would be the wrong conclusion to draw. For any solution to the mind-body problem should tell us the nature of mental properties, and in such a way as to connect them explanatorily to the brain. The solution should not leave open what pain is. That is the problem with simple property dualism: in not telling us what mental properties are, it leaves them unconnected explanatorily to the brain. Thus it is hard to see how we can avoid couching our solution in the form of an identity statement. The right lesson, as I have already indicated, is that we need an account of mental properties that is conceptually true. The identity statement that solves the mind-body problem must be analytic. Only then do we have a genuine *reduction*, in contrast to empirical identity theories. An analytic identity statement is not empirically informative, so it does not force us to introduce or recognize an unreduced mental property. This is what Smart saw quite clearly, and he tried to offer a theory that would meet this condition of adequacy.

So should we embrace analytical functionalism, which is essentially what Smart does? Are we driven to embrace that theory by the argument so far, because there is nothing else left in logical space? I hope not, because I find analytical functionalism quite unacceptable, for reasons I cannot go into here. The threat then is that we have shown that there is no answer to the mind-body problem after all. What I want to suggest, however, is that there is a third type of position, which I shall describe as 'analytical central-state materialism'. According to analytical central-state material-ism, mental properties are brain properties of some sort, and there are analytic identities linking mental terms and brain terms (these brain terms need not correspond to anything recognized in current neurophysiology). It is not a bit surprising that this position has been neglected, because it seems ruled out from the very start by the content of mental concepts—these concepts have no a priori links with concepts of the brain. The two principal theories have been varieties of analytical behaviourism that claim a priori connections between mental concepts and behavioural concepts, these connections being apparent to a master of mental concepts; and varieties of empirical materialism, which shun a priori connections between mind and brain, on the sensible ground that we know nothing about the brain just by having mastery of mental concepts. How can there be room for analytical materialism, granted that mental concepts contain nothing about the cerebral basis of mental states? At least in the case of analytical behaviour-ism ordinary masters of mental concepts are cognizant of the behaviour that is apt to go with having a mental state; but the ordinary user of the concept *pain* has no idea what is going on in his brain when that concept applies to him.

The answer is that we need to introduce new concepts for mental properties, concepts that do provide the needed conceptual link to the brain. Thus suppose we introduce the new concept PAIN that refers to pain but does not have the sense of our word 'pain'; this concept reveals the essence of pain in such a way as to display analytic connections to concepts of the brain. The argument of this chapter so far can be construed as an existence proof with respect to this concept: there has to be such a concept as no other option is feasible. Because it is highly unlikely that our current concepts of the brain are sufficient to explain the mind, we will also need new concepts of the brain. On empirical grounds C-fibres look to be the correlates of pain, so we can assume that C-fibres have some property * such that * is what entails the presence of pain in the subject. Now we can form the identity statement 'PAIN = * (C-fibres)'. This statement identifies pain (the property) with a property, namely *, that C-fibres have, and it does so by identifying these properties under descriptions that render the statement conceptually necessary. It will thus be possible to infer a priori from someone's having * that he is in pain and from his being in pain to infer a priori that he has *. Logically, this statement plays the role that analytical functionalists hoped that their psychofunctional identity statements would play, namely, to provide a conceptual reduction of mental properties. But, unlike that theory, our statement is central-state and conceptually innovative. The analytic links hold between concepts not in our current conceptual repertoire.

I suggest that this idea is not incoherent and, in the light of our earlier argument, is really the only way to think about the correct form of an identity theory. This is what the solution to the mind-body problem has to look like. What we have argued so far, in effect, is that there is no solution to the mind-body problem within the limits of our current concepts of mind and brain: for the solution must be a conceptual identity, by the Smart–Black argument. Yet our current concepts yield no such identities; therefore the correct solution requires new concepts. And because I believe it is independently plausible that major conceptual innovation is required, I take this to confirm the general argument we have been making so far.

What does the analytic status of 'PAIN = * (C-fibres)' imply? It clearly implies transparent necessary conceptual links between brain and mind. These generate epistemic consequences: that if we had the solution we could know that our brain had * just by knowing we were in pain; that I could deduce your mental states from your brain states, thus solving the problem of other minds; and that there is a sense in which we could *see* consciousness in the brain, assuming that we could see the brain to have * (but see the following text). Thus the upshot of possessing this form of solution is vastly more dramatic than what is envisaged under the empirical identity paradigm, where the whole point of the exercise is to avoid commitment to these epistemic consequences (hence the great play made with the nonsynonymy of 'pain' and 'C-fibre firing'). There is indeed no analytic link between 'pain' and 'PAIN', because otherwise we could infer * a priori from our present concept of pain, which palpably we cannot do. That is why we need a radically new concept, though one that is demonstrably a concept *of pain* (there is no point in just inventing a concept that applies to the neural correlates of pain and then merely declaring or stipulating that this concept refers to pain). Clearly, possessing the concept PAIN would transform our understanding of both mind and brain, by essentially unifying them. It would completely close any 'explanatory gap', rid us of puzzlement about how matter could give rise to consciousness in the course of evolution, make dualism seem wildly unnatural, and turn psychophysical causation into regular science. Presumably too it would radically alter our conception of the physical world, by showing how matter has the right properties to entail consciousness. The concept *PAIN*, unlike our present concept *pain*, would connote precisely those properties of pain that render its connection to matter and the brain entirely perspicuous.

All this may prompt the question: how distant are we from acquiring such a marvellous concept? More pointedly, don't these utopian consequences show that this whole approach has to be wrong, because nothing we might discover could have such revolutionary consequences? Well, I do think an adequate solution to the mind-body problem would have to have these strong consequences, but I also think we are unlikely to discover anything with such consequences.[11] These are consistent beliefs: the reconciling

[11] See my *The Problems of Consciousness* (Oxford: Blackwell, 1991), and *Problems in Philosophy* (Oxford: Blackwell, 1993).

thought is that such a solution exists but is not discoverable by us. I have not claimed to demonstrate the latter thesis in this chapter, but the effect of what I have argued is to raise the bar for anyone trying to solve the problem. If we think we need only seek empirical identities, then we set the conditions of adequacy quite low, and we make it easy to elevate mere empirical correlations into genuine theoretical reductions (which is exactly what I think has happened with the likes of 'pain = C-fibre firing'). But if I am right, discovering empirical correlations between mental and physical concepts is never enough to entitle us to assert psychophysical identities; and the extra needed is not Occam's razor but rather a set of convincing *conceptual* necessities linking mind and brain. This sets the requirements on a solution much higher than we have been taught to expect under the influence of the natural kind model exemplified by 'heat = molecular motion' and the like. In fact, I think that once it is appreciated how high the bar must be set it becomes difficult to see how we could clear the bar: where are we supposed to find a concept PAIN that is analytically linked to concepts of C-fibres in such a way as to close the psychophysical gap? The very idea seems to boggle the mind.

The point I am making is that my pessimism about solving the mind-body problem might look unduly gloomy if we are fixated on the empirical identity paradigm, because that makes the demands on a solution look relatively minimal and permits empirical correlations to be promoted to the status of theoretical reductions. But once we see that any solution has to take the form of an analytically true psychoneural identity statement, where this calls for radical conceptual innovation of a kind of which we have not even an inkling, then my pessimism starts to look more reasonable. To be sure, these adequacy conditions do not entail such pessimism, but they do show how hard it would be to come up with what is necessary. To put it bluntly, how likely is it that we are going to come up with psychoneural identity statements with the semantic status of 'bachelors are unmarried males'?

VII

I now want to indicate briefly how this position bears upon some standard discussions of these matters. What I am suggesting, basically, is the existence of (humanly) unknowable conceptual connections between mind and brain. The implicated concepts are not ours, obviously. They belong in Frege's realm of sense, items that may or may not be grasped (or be graspable) by *human* minds. Heuristically, we can think of them as the contents of God's thoughts. So the idea is that God grasps the truth of 'PAIN = * (C-fibres)' and thus enjoys all the epistemic benefits thereof. God can see right into the conceptual necessities whose existence we can only gesture at. In his mind supervenience is a species of logical entailment.

This bears directly on all the modal arguments that have been given for dualism.[12] These are all unsound because they assume that conceptual entailments should be epistemically transparent to us. When a psychophysical connection strikes us as contingent, that could be a reflection merely of our ignorance of the concepts and identity statements that secure the underlying conceptual entailments. Our modal faculty naturally goes haywire in the conceptual vacuum generated by our ignorance. If we had the concepts of PAIN and *, then we would not be tempted by these stampeding modal intuitions. But we are so cognitively distant from them (to the point of unreachability) that we cannot feel their necessity-conferring force. We certainly cannot argue for property dualism on the basis of these intuitions, because they can be otherwise explained as stemming from conceptual poverty. I am not saying that we know for sure that our present concepts of the brain form an adequate supervenience base that guarantees sameness of mental states across all possible worlds. What I am saying is that such a supervenience base exists, possibly in an

---

[12] For example, Kripke, 144–55, and David Chalmers, *The Conscious Mind* (Oxford: Oxford University Press, 1996).

extension of our present concepts, and that the supervenience holds as a matter of conceptual necessity. There is no conceptually possible world in which C-fibres have * and people are not in pain (i.e. PAIN applies to those people). Nor will multiple realization of mental states by (suitable) neural properties really be possible, though it will strike us as possible in our epistemic predicament: there is no world in which someone is in pain and their C-fibres are not *. Analytic identity statements give us as tight a modal connection as could be wished.

Then there are the knowledge-based arguments.[13] These turn out to be soundly based in terms of their argumentative strategy but not to lead to the conclusions commonly drawn from them. If Mary knows that John's C-fibres are *, then she knows a priori that he is in PAIN. So if she can know that * is instantiated before coming out of the room, then she knows all the facts about pain and will learn nothing new when she experiences her first pain. But can she know propositions involving the concept * before she comes out into a world of pain? Could she know propositions about the *-like property that entails experiencing red while living in a black-and-white room? I have no idea. Maybe the cognitive faculties necessary require more than this, maybe they require having experiences of red. The point is that Jackson sounded right when he claimed that all the physical facts can be known by Mary in her room if we assume that these facts are just the kind currently spoken of in physics. But if we allow for radically new kinds of properties, then it becomes quite unclear what the cognitive conditions for grasp of these properties might be. I have no idea what it would take to grasp the concept PAIN and hence whether Mary could in principle grasp that concept while still pain free. What I do know is that if she grasps that concept while in her room (and this may be impossible), *then* she will already know what property pain is. She will say when she first feels pain 'Ah, just

<hr/>

[13] Thomas Nagel, 'What is it Like to be a Bat?', *Mortal Questions* (Cambridge: Cambridge University Press, 1979). Jackson, cited in n. 10.

the way I expected pain to feel!' Similarly for Nagel's bats: if we could grasp the concepts of the bat brain that analytically entail their experiences, *then* we would know what it is like to be a bat, but whether we could grasp these concepts as we are now constituted is another question. Maybe we need to have bat experiences ourselves in order to grasp the * property that entails those experiences. It is quite true that none of our present brain concepts gives us the entailments we would need, so those concepts do not enable us to know what it is like to be a bat. But of course it does not follow that no brain concepts could confer this kind of knowledge. I believe such concepts exist, though I don't believe we can grasp them; so the impossibility in question is entirely epistemic.

What I would especially emphasize here is that these kinds of epistemological arguments tacitly rely upon the kind of position I have defended in this chapter, notably the conception of concept identity I have argued for. For without that they are immediately vulnerable to the charge of trading illicitly upon an opaque context. The underlying issue about concept identity thus needs to be made explicit and brought to the fore in these arguments. Once it is, we see that it is doing all the heavy lifting in giving the arguments whatever plausibility they have. We can only derive a conclusion about property distinctness from premises about concept distinctness if we accept that concept distinctness ultimately depends upon property distinctness.

VIII

I need to say something finally about the relation between the two concepts expressed by 'pain' and 'PAIN'. Consider this objection: 'pain = PAIN' is informative, so the two concepts must connote distinct properties—which reinstates the dualism we are striving to avoid. We cannot say that this is an analytic statement, because clearly we cannot infer PAIN from our current concept *pain*. Yet we also want this identity statement to be truly assertible, or else we cannot claim to be giving an account of pain. So what is its status? I think this is quite a difficult question and I am not sure I have a complete answer to it. I know what one wants to say here, and I know that it is something we do say in other areas; but as to quite what the correct analysis of the statement comes to, that is trickier. The thought clearly is that PAIN is a kind of successor concept to *pain*, something that replaces it in a scientific picture of things. Analogies are the relation between *weight* and *mass* or our old earth-centred concept of motion and the relativistic notion now used in physics. What should we say about the analysis of 'weight = mass' and 'motion = MOTION'? These statements are not empirically discovered synthetic identities such as 'heat = molecular motion', but neither are they analytic identities such as 'bachelors = unmarried males'. What they tell us, intuitively, is that an old concept has morphed into a new concept as our theory of the world has matured. They preserve the core of the concept while deepening it and shedding its erroneous associations. That is what I want to say about *pain* and *PAIN*: the latter concept will transform the former but will recognizably be a concept of the same thing. It will operate as a natural conceptual descendant of our present concept. This relation of descendancy fits neither the paradigm of two distinct senses of the same referent nor the paradigm of straight conceptual identity (analyticity). It belongs in a class of its own, and one that is not well understood. In any case, I do not think there is any sound objection to my final position that can be derived from reflection on 'pain = PAIN', because this will not count as a case of same referent with two empirically associated senses, which is what threatened to resurrect the very objection we are trying to avoid.

IX

My conclusion then is twofold: the solution to the mind-body problem must take the form of a conceptually true identity statement, not an empirically true identity statement; and such an identity statement will contain concepts far removed from our current concepts of mind and body, calling for radical conceptual innovation. The overall thrust of the chapter is to make the conceptual innovation thesis mandatory. Whether we are capable of such innovation I have not discussed, though I believe the prospects are dim. The present point is that the conceptual and theoretical conservatism inherent in standard empirical identity theories is misguided.[14]

[14] I am grateful to the following people for helpful discussions: Thomas Nagel, Michael Tye, Brian Loar, Brian McLaughlin, Ned Block, and Galen Strawson.

3

Solving the Philosophical
Mind-Body Problem

I

I began my 1989 paper, 'Can We Solve the Mind-Body Problem?',
with this quotation from Thomas Huxley, writing in 1886: 'How it
is that anything so remarkable as a state of consciousness comes
about as a result of irritating nervous tissue, is just as unaccount-
able as the appearance of the djinn when Aladdin rubbed his lamp
in the story.'[1] That succinctly states the essence of the philosophical
problem about mind and body, about consciousness and the brain:
something 'remarkable' seems to result from something unre-
markable, and in a way that is unprecedented in nature. The
problem can be put this way: if you rub most physical objects,
even lamps, you do not usually get a djinn to appear; yet Aladdin's
lamp has the power to do just that—and it seems not to differ in
any fundamental way from the objects that fail to harbour djinns.
So how does it happen that *this* physical object manages so unique

---

[1] The paper originally appeared in *Mind* 98, no. 891 (July 1989), and is reprinted in
my *The Problem of Consciousness* (Oxford: Blackwell, 1991). In that paper I misattrib-
uted the quotation from Thomas Huxley to Julian Huxley, for uninteresting reasons,
as Nicholas Humphrey first pointed out to me.

a feat? Analogously, if you 'irritate' most physical objects, even organs of the body, no conscious state appears; yet the brain has the power to generate conscious states—and it seems not to differ in any fundamental way from objects that fail to harbour consciousness. So how does it happen that *this* physical object manages so unique a feat? What underlying difference explains this difference of generative power between brains and other physical objects? Indeed, what explains the difference between states of the brain that do yield conscious states and states that do not? All brain states look much the same, physically speaking, yet some are 'associated with' consciousness and some are not: how is this marked difference consistent with the evident similarity manifest at the neural level? It seems no more intelligible that neurons should produce conscious states than that kidney cells should, or sawdust for that matter. We seem to be confronted with a kind of spontaneous generation in which a deep ontological gulf is miraculously bridged. The question then is whether this impression of miracle can be removed—whether, that is, the djinn of consciousness can find a naturalistic place in the lamp of the brain. And the problem is hard because it is so atrociously difficult to see how the fit is supposed to work. Brain states cause conscious states—that is what observation suggests: but the question is how such a thing is so much as *possible*.

Consider, as a thought experiment, the following imaginary scenario. The brain is actually not the real basis of consciousness but acts merely as an interface between the real basis and bodily behaviour. The real basis lies elsewhere, perhaps up in the sky, perhaps underground, and the whole system works by transmitting signals from the basis to the brain and hence controlling behaviour. Thus conscious states are really located roughly where the real basis is located, since the location of the mind is parasitic on the location of its physical basis. (Don't ask how such an odd set-up could have resulted from evolution—this is meant to be an imaginary thought experiment designed to make a certain conceptual point, not a genuine empirical possibility.) Now the crucial point is that the real basis is actually totally different in structure and composition from the brain; in fact, it is like nothing else we have ever encountered in nature, running by means of principles unique to it. Moreover, we can suppose that were we to discover this basis its relation to conscious states would strike us as transparently intelligible—unlike the organ that actually sits in our heads. Nevertheless, there are systematic correlations between brain states and conscious states, as one would expect given that the brain acts as a kind of transmitter of signals from the real basis. States of the basis cause conscious states, which are in turn correlated with brain states, as the body is remotely controlled from the basis. So there is a kind of illusion an investigator would be subject to, in that it would be natural (though false) to conclude that the brain is the basis of consciousness, despite the fact that (by hypothesis) it is quite incapable of acting as the origin of consciousness. An investigator would naturally take the brain to be the basis of consciousness, not knowing about the strange way things are really arranged, and would therefore frame questions along these lines: how is it possible for the brain to be the cause of consciousness when it looks incapable of being so, in view of its similarity to other physical systems that have not a hint of consciousness in them? And the point is that this question is misconceived in view of the true situation, since the brain is unable to act as the basis of consciousness. No doubt some thinkers in this imaginary world would assert manfully that conscious states just are brain states, though in our stipulated set-up they are not; while others might opt for Cartesian dualism or eliminativism or behaviourism or whatever. But we know better, having stipulated the case, correctly locating consciousness in another physical object of a radically different, and more suitable, design.

The lesson I want to draw from this thought experiment is that our epistemic situation with respect to mind and brain is significantly analogous to this strange story. It is as if the brain *appears* to us be a mere mediator of conscious states and not their ultimate origin, given our knowledge of its operations. In fact, if we simply shift the real basis in our imaginary case from outside the brain to *inside* it we get a precise analogue to our current epistemic predicament. Suppose then that the real basis is hidden somewhere inside the observable brain, perhaps too microscopic to be accessible to us; it actually sits at the precise midpoint of the reticular formation, say (again, remember this is an imaginary thought-experiment). Then again we would be quite wrong in assigning to the gross brain the role of causal basis of conscious states—the brain simply transmits messages from the real miniature basis whose properties are radically different from those of the observable brain. And now we can take one more step towards the probably actual situation and suppose that the real basis of consciousness lies not in the properties of nerve cells as currently conceived but rather in some new properties that serve to distinguish cells that yield conscious states from cells that do not. The mind-body problem then is the problem of finding out what these special distinguishing properties are. In the thought-experiment we set it up so that the properties in question were not regular neural properties, but this only serves to highlight the epistemic situation in which we stand in the actual world; and it acts as a warning against those who opt for more conservative responses to the problem stated so trenchantly by Huxley—since such responses would be false by hypothesis in the imaginary case. The challenge posed by the thought-experiment is simply this: if the standard responses are wrong in that case, why are we so sure that they are sensible in the actual case, in which much the same problem is presented by the observed phenomena? In any case, the philosophical problem can be formulated as the problem of identifying the real basis of consciousness, given that the ordinary neural properties of the brain are inadequate to do the job. What, that is, is the nature of the *epistemically* remote basis of consciousness? What is inside the brain lamp such that it can produce a consciousness djinn when you rub it?

In my 1989 paper I answered the question that forms its title ('Can we solve the mind-body problem?') with the words 'No and Yes'. No, in that we cannot identify the real basis of consciousness, so we cannot explain what it is about the brain that yields conscious states; but Yes, in that we can nevertheless solve the philosophical problem generated by the mind-brain nexus. Critics and expositors have focused on the negative part of my position, wondering whether my pessimism is warranted; but there has been very little discussion of the positive aspect of my position—the philosophical good news, as it were. This is unfortunate because I took the negative part to be a piece of an overall position with a positive message: it was not intended as pessimism for its own sake, but rather as a stepping-stone to ridding ourselves of intractable philosophical perplexity. So in this paper I will accentuate the positive and set out my reasons for supposing that my position actually *solves* the philosophical mind-body problem. I will not attempt to defend my cognitive closure thesis here but instead dwell upon its role in dissolving philosophical perplexity. Part of my point here is that the label 'mysterian' as applied to my position can be misleading, since there is also a strongly anti-mysterian component to the view; indeed the mysterian element is invoked to advance an anti-mysterian agenda.[2] I am really just another kind of naturalist (though this label too can be misleading), not a purveyor of thrilling quasi-mystical doctrines. This paper could have been subtitled 'Why I am not a Mysterian' and not be wildly wide of the mark.

Clearly, if my answer to the question whether we can solve the mind-body problem is 'No and Yes' I must be supposing that there

[2] The label 'mysterian' was first introduced by O. Flanagan in *The Science of Mind* (Cambridge, Mass.: MIT Press, 1984) to describe the views of Thomas Nagel, myself, and others. Actually, Nagel has never advanced the strong unknowability thesis I defend and is quite sceptical about it. The label is strictly speaking quite accurate in describing my position, since I do regard the mind-body problem as an insoluble (epistemic) mystery, but the connotations of anti-naturalism are misleading, so I do not use it self-referentially.

are two distinct questions here, on pain of self-contradiction; and one of these questions cannot be answered while the other can. We cannot answer the question of what the basis of consciousness is, but we can answer the question of how to respond to the philosophical perplexities raised by this difficulty. Using some earlier terminology, I want to distinguish between a 'constructive' and a 'non-constructive' solution to the mind-body problem: to give a constructive solution would be to *produce* the property or theory that explains how the brain causes consciousness; but a non-constructive solution requires only that we find reason to suppose that such a property or theory *exists*, whether we can produce it or not. If we had reason to believe such a property to exist, and reason to believe that we could not identify it, then we would have an explanation of why we find the problem so hard and why we tend to go in for unsatisfying constructive solutions for it. Put simply, the aim is to remove the suspicion that the world is behaving very strangely—almost paradoxically—when conscious states are generated by the brain, without having to produce the theory that explains how things are actually working. We want to save common sense without having to come up with a theory of how the brain operates to yield consciousness. Let me now sketch the way this non-constructive solution is intended to dissolve our perplexities—what intellectual work it does for us.

II

It is of prime importance to recognize that what makes the mind-body problem philosophical is not simply that we have not yet identified the basis of consciousness—that we have an unsolved problem on our hands. For this does not distinguish a philosophical problem from a merely scientific one: our problem is more fundamental, more conceptual. Compare the problem of what caused the dinosaurs to go extinct. Here we have an array of possible explanations, each of which has the right form to explain the extinction of a species, yet we cannot settle by empirical means which of these is the true explanation. There were dinosaurs, they did go extinct—but was it the result of a meteor impact or changing climate or increased competition from other species or alien intervention? Each of these *would* explain the extinction, but the evidence for selecting one theory over another is lacking. But this is precisely what is not the case with respect to the question of what causes the existence of consciousness: we do not have a plethora of theoretically adequate options from among which we cannot empirically choose; rather, nothing that we can think of has a chance of explaining what needs to be explained. We don't know what a possible explanation of consciousness would even *look like*—hence the feeling of deep conceptual intractability. Instead, we have a range of characteristically philosophical 'positions' (*attitudes*) that are offered in response to the manifest lack of understanding. These positions display a typical form, and it is this form that signals the existence of a philosophical problem: I call this form the DIME shape. So the idea is that the philosophical mind-body problem leads to the DIME shape, which constitutes a set of variously unsatisfactory responses to the explanatory problem we face.[3]

The DIME shape comprises the following options: 'D' stands for deflationary reductionism; 'I' stands for outright irreducibility; 'M' stands for eerily magical; 'E' stands for ontological elimination. I will not discuss this taxonomy of philosophical responses in any depth here, having done so elsewhere; but I think it is clear enough that this is precisely the set of responses that cluster around the mind-body problem. Thus we have reductive materialism or behaviourism or functionalism; we have claims of *sui generis* irreduci-

---

[3] For an extended discussion of the DIME shape, see. my *Problems in Philosophy: the Limits of Enquiry* (Oxford: Blackwell, 1993). My general thesis in that book is that there are a range of other philosophical problems that display the same form as the problem of consciousness.

bility; we have supernatural dualisms of various forms; and we have the suggestion that there is no such thing as consciousness after all. Now my point is that it is the presence of the DIME shape that makes the mind-body problem specifically philosophical; and it does so because none of these options can command any consensus—the topic is permanently controversial. We have nothing like this with respect to the problem of dinosaur extinction: we don't find some theorists holding that dinosaurs are really some other species in disguise, where that species does have a known explanation for its extinction (as it might be, Dodos); other theorists who claim that the extinction has no explanation but is just a brute fact about nature; others who maintain that it was some supernatural event that caused the extinction (God got tired of dinosaurs one day and zapped them with a divine ray); and yet others who sincerely assert that there were not any dinosaurs after all, which is why we are having so much trouble explaining how they went out of existence. All such positions would seem ludicrously extreme in respect of the dinosaur problem, but they are exactly the positions that insinuate themselves when we ask what causes consciousness. The essence of the philosophical problem, then—what makes the mind-brain relation so conceptually perplexing—is that we seem impaled on the DIME shape. In other words, none of the available options is intrinsically appealing; all seem more or less desperate responses to a deep explanatory conundrum. In particular, we feel under pressure either to accept ontological peculiarities in the world or to deny the very existence of consciousness. What I am calling the philosophical mind-body problem is the problem of getting out from under this pressure, so that we can acknowledge that consciousness is both real and non-miraculous. The task is to show how consciousness is *possible*, despite the appearances. So when I say that the philosophical problem can be solved, I mean to be speaking of *that* problem— escaping the clutches of the DIME shape, not succumbing to the pressures it creates. And my suggestion is that we can do that without constructively solving the problem, i.e. without actually identifying the objective basis of consciousness.

III

Is consciousness mysterious? The core of my position is that this question is seriously ambiguous: does it ask whether consciousness has an occult non-natural *nature*, or does it ask simply whether we do or can *understand* the nature of consciousness? The first reading is ontological or metaphysical, the second is purely epistemo-logical. My thesis is that consciousness is not mysterious in the first sense but it is in the second sense. I am an ontological anti-mysterian and an epistemological mysterian. The key point is that I think the sense of deep mystery we have, which naturally expresses itself in ontological rhetoric, is really entirely epistemic; the mystery is *relative* to the human intellect as it attempts to come to terms with the problem. This is, if you like, a deflationary view of the issue, since it locates the apparent oddity of consciousness entirely in the eye of the beholder. The world itself is as smoothly natural and seamless as one could wish; it is just that we lack the conceptual resources with which to discover its objective linea-ments. And this perspective gives us a way both to escape the DIME shape and to explain its seeming compulsoriness. Con-sciousness indubitably exists, yet it is not magical, nor irreducible, nor reducible to the usual kinds of physical basis. It only *seems* magical because we have no grasp of what explains it; it only *seems* irreducible because we cannot find the right explanation; it only *seems* as if physicalism is the only possible naturalistic theory because that is what we are conceptually limited to; and it only *seems* to invite elimination because we can find no explanation for it from within our conceptual scheme. We solve the philosophical problem by diagnosing how it arises and asserting that conscious-ness is not non-natural despite all appearances to the contrary. It is because we cannot in principle discover the constructive solution that we find ourselves under so much philosophical pressure; but we can relieve this pressure by accepting our theoretical limitations. That is what I mean by solving the philosophical mind-body problem. The negative 'mysterian' part of my position thus serves to underpin the positive 'naturalist' part. Wittgenstein spoke of the 'unbridgeable gulf' that seems to separate conscious states from the brain,[4] and he correctly diagnosed this as the source of the philosophical problem; my answer to the problem consists in rendering the gulf ontologically innocuous, by locating it entirely in our cognitive biases and limitations. Objectively, there *is* no such gulf—the gulf is a kind of illusion resulting from cognitive closure.

Let me present an analogy to illustrate how this solution is meant to work. We all have the notion of an unperceived object, i.e. an object that exists while not being an object of sensory observation. This is a basic element in our general picture of the world; it is part of what we mean by the objectivity of physical objects. How do we form this conception? The answer is obvious enough: we have a conception of space in which objects and our own bodies are located, and we conceive of independent objects in terms of their being located at a point in space at which our sense-organs are not directed, and which therefore do not exert causal influence on our sensory state. Thus our notion of independently existing objects—of objects that persist while not being observed—involves conceiving of them in spatial and causal terms. If we are asked how unperceived existence is possible, then we reply with the spatial story just adumbrated. But now consider a race of beings who perceive physical objects but who lack the conceptual framework of space and its causally active occupants: they don't

---

[4] Wittgenstein writes: 'The feeling of an unbridgeable gulf between consciousness and brain-process: how does it come about that this idea does not come into the considerations of our ordinary life? This idea of a difference in kind is accompanied by slight giddiness,—which occurs when we are performing a piece of logical sleight-of-hand. (The same giddiness attacks us when we think of certain theorems in set theory.)' *Philosophical Investigations* (Oxford: Blackwell, 1953), §412.

have the conceptual resources with which to conceive of the objects of their experience in terms of their relative locations in space, including their own located bodies, along with the causal concepts that enable us to explain the possibility of unperceived objects. They are cognitively closed with respect to this spatial-cum-causal theory. When they have a visual experience of a red sphere, say, the object is presented to them as phenomenally 'outer', but they do not have the concepts and theoretical capacity that would make this appearance intelligible. They thus do not know how unperceived existence is possible, though we may suppose them to have raised the question to themselves. They ask themselves whether objects could exist without being perceived, but they lack the concepts that are necessary to answering that question. Perhaps they are convinced that reality consists of such unperceived objects, but they are at a loss to understand the nature of that reality. They accordingly find themselves in deep philosophical perplexity over the question.

I conjecture that the philosophers among these cognitively limited beings will find themselves in thrall to an array of unsatisfactory DIME options. The deflationary position might be that objects are really nothing but potentialities for sensation, so that to say that an object exists unperceived is just to say that certain counterfactuals are true about the course of their experience; or perhaps so-called unperceived objects are really nothing but ideas in the mind of God. The irreducibility position will be that the notion of unperceived existence admits of no explanation, being just a brute fact with no further conceptual articulation. The magical position, prompted no doubt by the weaknesses of the first two positions, might be that the object somehow springs out of the sense-impression by a sort of miracle (rather like the djinn springing out of the lamp)—that it is a kind of ghost of the sense-impression that persists when the impression ceases. Maybe God performs this miracle every time they close their eyes. This may make them take an attitude of unusual reverence towards unperceived objects, even arguing to the existence of God on the strength of what needs to be assumed in order to explain such a remarkable thing (compare the attitude of some human beings towards consciousness). Finally, sterner souls may seek to sidestep the entire controversy, with all its handwaving and denunciations and intellectual sleights-of-hand, and declare roundly that objects do not exist unperceived at all—that there is really nothing in the world save sense-impressions and the minds that house them. Loftier commentators may wonder how they could have found themselves locked into these unsatisfactory options and hunger for some new perspective to relieve their intellectual cramps. In any case, *we* can see, no doubt with some wry condescension, that each of these DIME options is mistaken, arising as they do from a limited and distorted view of the nature of the objects of perception. It is apparent to us that their perplexities arise from a cognitive deficit on their part—not understanding how objects are located in space and so on. We can also see that they are not condemned to enslavement to the DIME, since it is open to them to hold that their perplexities spring from a conceptual blindspot. Their mistake in cleaving to the DIME options is basically that of overestimating their cognitive powers, trying to force unperceived objects into the conceptual categories they have available. If they could only acknowledge that the nature of objects exceeds their conceptual resources, then they could hold that objects do exist unperceived without benefit of miracle and in a fully robust sense, but in virtue of having properties they are prohibited from conceiving. Thus they could solve their philosophical problem, by relieving the pressure to accept what is not rationally acceptable. It only *seems* to them that objects call for these bizarre and revisionary theories because they lack a proper conception of their underlying nature as spatial entities.

I say it is like this with us and the mind-body problem. Consciousness and the brain do have a nature that renders their union perspicuous and natural, but we are blocked from grasping this nature, so we are apt to pin ourselves to the DIME shape. If this is correct, then we have the resources with which to dissolve the philosophical problem—construed as the problem of avoiding those perennially unappealing options. Consciousness exists, it is not non-natural, it is not something else in disguise, and it has an explanation: it is just that its nature is deeply hidden to us. This diagnosis explains the appeal of the DIME options and also provides an alternative to them. We can thus relax in the face of the explanatory vacuum and not feel forced to interpret it in terms we cannot really live with. The basic expression of this relief is the recognition that consciousness is nothing extraordinary after all— that it is not a glitch in the natural order. As I like to put it, consciousness is no more remarkable to God's mind than digestion is to ours—though that truth is something we will never be able properly to absorb, given the way the psychophysical nexus strikes us.

Let me give one more analogy, this time of a more scientific sort. Consider the correlation between the temperature of a gas and its pressure, and compare this to the correlation between brain states and conscious states. In the gas case, there seems no a priori reason for such a correlation to exist—it is scarcely a conceptual truth about 'pressure' and 'temperature'. Rather, it is an empirically established law that such a correlation exists. This correlation naturally prompts the question *why* it obtains—what is it about gases that makes their temperature and pressure correlate in this way? What unites these apparently distinct magnitudes? The answer, we now know, lies in the molecular conception of gases: the rapid movement of molecules gives rise *both* to the pressure of the gas and to its temperature, since pressure is the result of the molecules striking the interior of the container and temperature is just the mean kinetic energy of molecules. In this way we explain the correlation and render it 'unmiraculous'. But if you had a mind that was prevented from forming the idea of constituent molecules and their movements, this explanation would be closed to you, and you would find yourself faced with a brute correlation. My claim is that this is essentially our predicament with respect to psychophysical correlations: we lack the unifying underlying theory, so we are deeply puzzled about the observed correlations. But this is not in itself a reason to beat our heads against the DIME shape; we need simply to accept our deep ignorance. Then we will see that what strikes us as unintelligible might have an objectively straightforward explanation.

IV

I regard this as a demystifying answer to the mind-body problem; for it takes the mystery out of the mystery, so to speak. The impression that consciousness arises from the brain in the miraculous way the djinn emerges from the lamp is given a deflationary account: it is an artefact of our cognitive gaps, not a veridical indication of ontological oddity. I also intend the view to stem from a naturalistic conception of human cognitive powers: the human mind is an evolved collection of biologically driven mechanisms and strategies, responsive to the usual evolutionary pressures. No doubt human reason is a remarkable product of evolution, permitting all sorts of adaptation-transcendent feats of thought; but that is not to exempt it from all biological constraint and bias. As Chomsky points out, the human language faculty is also a remarkable cognitive achievement, conferring all sorts of powers on our minds, but it is a biologically structured natural faculty with intrinsic biases and limitations nonetheless.[5] Our minds have certain epistemic strengths and weaknesses, most apparent in perception and memory, but also present in the so-called higher cognitive functions. So my thesis of cognitive

[5] Cf., for example, N. Chomsky, *Reflections on Language* (New York: Pantheon, 1975). Language, like reason, confers creativity, but only because it has its own fixed structure. The mistake is to think that creativity requires the myth of the *tabula rasa*, the inherently featureless cognitive receptacle.

inaccessibility with respect to the mind-brain link is intended as just one more limitation on human cognitive capacity, not fundamentally different in kind from our inability to remember more than eight digit sequences. We should always remember that intelligence is just one form of biological adaptation, recently evolved, and no doubt set to evolve further, so that it is subject to the same kinds of architectural and functional limitations as any other evolved trait; it is not something that somehow elevates us to the level of epistemic gods. So if I am a mysterian about the mind-brain link, it is because I am a naturalist about the human mind; indeed, since consciousness appears essential to scientific and philosophical understanding, I am a mysterian about consciousness precisely because I am a naturalist about it. Our conscious thinking has its natural limits and that is why it is a mystery to us. Nagel sees correctly into the spirit of my position when he remarks that it is too demystifying for him: he finds it hard to believe that the sense of profundity we feel about problems of mind could be simply a result of naturally based cognitive lacks.[6] And anyone who feels that the world is a more intrinsically mysterious place than I am willing to recognize will brand me unacceptably anti-mysterian. This response seems to me far more apposite than the usual one, namely that I am a pedlar of revamped religious mysteries; indeed, part of my point is to block the way to all such religious metaphysical outlooks. Certainly, I myself find the startling aspect of my view to be the suggestion that the profundity of the mind-body problem is a kind of projective illusion; this is the aspect I have to repeat to myself over and over again with shocked incredulity, and I am not a bit surprised if people find it hard to accept. In comparison the thesis of terminal cognitive closure seems like a mild and banal claim, and I find myself puzzled at the vehemence with which it is often rejected. It is the hard-core naturalism that should take one's breath away, not the soft-core mysterianism.

[6] Cf. Th. Nagel, *The Last Word* (New York: Oxford University Press, 1997), 131, n. 9.

It might be helpful to compare my view with Wittgenstein's general metaphilosophical outlook. He recognizes that it is a mark of a philosophically interesting concept that intimations of the 'queer' and 'occult' and 'sublime' should surround our thinking about that concept. Thus meaning and reference are apt to strike us in this way—we naturally suppose that something extraordinary is involved in these things.[7] He also appreciates the dialectic that is apt to spring up around such intimations—misplaced reductionism, eliminativism, radical dualism. His view, of course, is that all this flows from certain identifiable sources of philosophical error—particularly, misunderstandings of our ordinary language for speaking about meaning and reference. Now my position clearly does not agree with Wittgenstein's diagnostically, but there is agreement over the role of those intimations of supernaturalism and over the conceptual deformations they are likely to produce. Where Wittgenstein thinks we can dispell the philosophical clouds by reminding ourselves of our actual language-games, I think we should do so by acknowledging our cognitive limitations. Where he thinks nothing is hidden, I think hiddenness is exactly the problem. Nevertheless, at a certain abstract level, I am agreeing with Wittgenstein's conception of the form of a philosophical problem, and I am likewise proposing a deflationary response to the perplexities generated. We both think that *ontologically* there is nothing 'funny' going on; nothing is 'queer' *de re*. Consciousness, I say, is really just a particular biological phenomenon, and quite a primitive one at that, found quite far down the phylogenetic scale (remember that by 'consciousness' we simply mean 'conscious states' and these include such humble items as simple perceptual experiences of the environment). It is a great mistake to suppose just because consciousness is especially problematic that it must

[7] Cf., for example, §38 of *Philosophical Investigations*. It should be obvious that Wittgenstein's use of 'occult' and similar terms is not intended to be equivalent to 'non-physical' (whatever that may mean); he is clearly not advancing a materialist programme in invoking these notions. My own use of 'non-natural' is similarly not confined to that which flouts 'physicalist' scruples.

therefore belong to what we deem the highest of human faculties; on the contrary, quite lowly species—bats, reptiles, birds—have consciousness in an equally problematic way, since they are conscious of their environment, feel pain, and so on. There would be a deep philosophical problem of consciousness even if evolution had never progressed beyond the dinosaurs. To my mind, this strongly suggests that our inability to solve the mind-body problem is the result of a quite specific *bias* in our faculties of comprehension: we are cognitively targeted away from understanding consciousness and towards some quite different kind of entity, namely physical objects in space. But the point I am making now is that the refractoriness of the problem of consciousness is no sure guide to its ranking in terms of objective complexity or biological sophistication, since that reflects our cognitive slant as much as the nature of reality.

The general upshot is that the negative part of my position should not be seen as pessimism for its own sake but rather as a component of an overall position that is intended to ease our philosophical perplexities about consciousness. When we have the right explanation for our failure to solve the problem we see why it is that the DIME options are not forced upon us, and thus we are relieved of the philosophical pressure they seem to exert.

V

I said just now that our minds are biased away from arriving at an understanding of the mind-brain link. What kind of bias might this be—where might it stem from? We can only be speculative about this question, but I think that the role of physical space in our thinking must be at least part of the story. As I have argued elsewhere, conscious experiences are not aptly conceived in ordinary spatial terms, as extended occupants of space with the standard spatial properties.[8] Yet the neural processes with which experiences are correlated are *bona fide* spatial entities. This puts an obstacle in the way of theories that attempt to assimilate conscious states to brain states of the standard type, since this would require doing violence to the very essence of consciousness; so materialist reduction looks misguided granted the non-spatiality of the mind. Because of this we cannot conceive of conscious states as combinatorial products of brain constituents, since that would be to try to derive the non-spatial from the spatial by mere combination or aggregation. The underlying problem here is that our spatial methods of understanding the world fail to yield the right relation between consciousness and the brain: higher-level phenomena are standardly conceived as complex combinatorial emergents, but this mode of understanding is inadequate to explain how conscious states emerge from brain states—since conscious states are not themselves spatial entities. So our cognitive bias towards spatial modes of understanding lets us down in the present case. The combinatorial paradigm cannot subsume the mind-brain relation. But this is no reason to suppose that anything non-natural is afoot: that *we* think in combinatorial spatial terms is not a reason to think that nature itself must always operate in those terms. There must be non-combinatorial principles that link conscious states to brain states, since that is how nature appears to be working here; it is just that our bias towards the spatial prevents us from gaining insight into these principles.[9]

These remarks are just a summary of my diagnosis of the source of cognitive closure with respect to the mind-body problem; they are intended to illustrate the *kind* of explanation that might exist for the negative part of my position, and to show how it feeds into

[8] Cf. my 'Consciousness and Space', in *Conscious Experience*, ed. Th. Metzinger (Paderborn: Schöningh/Imprint Academic, 1995).

[9] For discussion of the combinatorial paradigm, cf. my *Problems in Philosophy*, cited in n. 3. In that book, I call this the CALM format—combinatorial atomism with lawlike mappings.

the positive part. The DIME shape tempts us because of our deepseated spatial combinatorialism about the natural world, but we can break its hold on our thinking by recognizing that nature may not always work by means of forms of spatial aggregation. In the case of the mind there is really no reason to suppose that the mode of thought that works so well for the non-mental world should carry over to the mental world. Here, bias leads inevitably to distortion. The way out is to recognize the bias and draw the appropriate epistemic conclusion.

It is instructive to compare the problem here with an opposite problem faced by some forms of idealism. Suppose we hold that only minds are real and that minds are non-spatial substances in the style of Descartes. Then a question arises about the nature of ordinary objects like tables and chairs: they seem to have spatial qualities, but how is this possible if nothing is spatial? Perception presents these objects to us as spatial, but the assumed metaphysics has no room for the spatial. The question here is the converse of the question posed by mental states for a materialist metaphysics: since everything is spatial according to that metaphysics, what are we to make of the apparent non-spatiality of the mind? The idealist, for her part, is faced with some unpalatable choices when it comes to ordinary objects: she can either say there are no tables and chairs after all, since they would have to be spatial and nothing is spatial, or she could try to maintain that there are tables and chairs but they are not spatial, thus convicting perceptual experience of a radical form of error. Better, perhaps, to question the revisionary idealist metaphysics. In the same way, a materialist might try to maintain that experiences only seem non-spatial but are really spatial, thus convicting introspection of a form of radical error. Just as the idealist has trouble finding room for ordinary objects in her non-spatial world of pure minds, so the materialist has trouble finding a place for conscious states in his purely spatial world. Seeing this analogy can help to encourage appreciation for the problem posed for materialism by the apparent non-spatiality of conscious states. Against an idealist background of universal non-spatiality, ordinary objects are an anomaly that prompts revisionary manoeuvres; against a materialist background of universal spatiality, conscious states are an anomaly that prompts comparable revisionary manoeuvres. We are much more accustomed in this century to the latter kind of manoeuvering, but it is worth remembering that in periods of thought of idealist cast the converse would have seemed far more reasonable. The right response, in both cases, is extreme chariness about the kinds of tendentious revisionism enforced by the metaphysical outlooks in question.

VI

I began this paper by recalling Huxley's formulation of the mind-body problem; I can now summarize my response to the problem thus posed. If we did come across a lamp that produced a djinn when rubbed, we would be justified in concluding that it had properties going far beyond any that are apparent to us—it could not be simply a *lamp*. Not knowing these properties, we might be tempted to reduce the djinn to a mere puff of innocuous smoke (go reductionist about djinns), or to declare that we are up against a primitive inexplicable natural law linking (some) lamps and djinns (opt for radical irreducibility), or to concede that there are miracles out there after all (accept the magical and supernatural), or simply to deny that anything comes out of the lamp at all (embrace eliminativism). None of these responses would be reasonable, I maintain; the right response is that there is more to some lamps (and their djinns) than meets the eye. If there were not, then indeed we would have a problem, since there would then be no escaping the DIME options with all their discomfort—we would *have* to accept a deflationary reduction of djinns on pain of miracles or elimination. But once we have accepted that reality exceeds our grasp here we can carry on rubbing lamps and getting djinns out of them without fearing that we will be engulfed in philosophical perplexity. Djinns exist, as we can see, and they have a natural explanation; it is just that the lamps that produce them have properties that lie outside of our ken.[10] We thus solve the philosophical djinn–lamp problem—while accepting that we cannot explain the djinn–lamp link. Nature has solved the djinn–lamp problem, though we cannot see how; and that is all we really need to know.

[10] Just for the record, I do not of course believe in djinns! I am speaking metaphorically.

4

What is it not Like to be a Brain?

1. Introduction

Materialism is the thesis that facts about the mind are entirely reducible to facts about the brain. To be in pain, say, is to have one's C-fibres firing or for this brain state to realize a physically defined functional role. The usual objection to materialism, expressed in many different forms, is that it fails to do justice to the nature of the mind; it omits or distorts the distinctive character of mental phenomena. In this paper I shall *not* be pressing this objection to materialism. Instead, I shall invert the standard objection and argue that materialism fails to do justice to the nature of *matter*; it omits or distorts the distinctive character of physical phenomena. The symmetry of identity will play a crucial role in this argument.

2. The mental and the physical

Let me begin by listing a familiar set of characteristics commonly ascribed to mental phenomena which are held to set the mind apart from the physical world. (By 'mental phenomena' I shall primarily mean conscious states and processes.) The list is eclectic and not uncontroversial; my intention is not to supply a full defence of it, but only to provide a foil for my own argument. The mind is held to be:

1. Unobservable—in the sense that mental states are not perceptible by means of the senses.
2. Asymmetrically accessible—in the sense that the owner of a mental state has a kind of immediate access to it that other people do not.
3. Subjective—in the sense that its nature is knowable only from a single 'point of view' (Nagel 1979, 1986).
4. Non-spatial—in the sense that mental states do not take up a well-defined region of space.[1]
5. Subject-dependent—in the sense that mental states only exist for a subject of awareness.[2]

The usual claim, then, is that physical phenomena, such as brain states, do not exhibit these features, and hence cannot satisfactorily reduce mental states. Suppose the materialist maintains that pain is identical to C-fibre firing, so that there is nothing more to the state of being in pain than having one's C-fibres fire. The firing of C-fibres has the following characteristics: it is observable by means of the sense organs; it is accessible to oneself and others in the same way; it is objective in that it can be grasped from any point of view, not necessarily that of a pain-feeler; it is spatially defined; it could in principle exist without being experienced by a subject. The objection, accordingly, is that C-fibres are just the wrong kind of thing to identify with pain. If there were really nothing more to pain talk than C-fibres firing, then there would be no pain after all,

[1] I discuss the non-spatiality of the mind in my essay in T. Metzinger (ed.), *Conscious Experience* (Imprint Academic, 1995).
[2] John Searle expresses this point by saying that conscious states have 'first-person ontology' in *The Rediscovery of the Mind* (Cambridge, Mass.: MIT Press, 1992).

since pain is defined by the opposite set of characteristics. The putative reduction would amount to a form of elimination. Of course, this line of argument would be disputed by a materialist at various points, but prima facie it would seem that the anti-reductionist at least has a case that needs to be answered. The distinctive character of the mental certainly appears to be lost under such a reduction. It needs to be explained why it is that the reduction does not omit or distort the intrinsic nature of the mental. Let me summarize this objection by saying that materialism makes the subjective too objective. I shall take it that this is a familiar story, in one or another version.

3. The symmetry of identity

The logical properties of identity statements have played a significant role in the defence and criticism of materialism. Thus the epistemic contingency and metaphysical necessity of identity statements such as 'pain = C-fibre firing' have figured heavily in these debates.[3] I want to draw attention to the least controversial property of the identity relation: its symmetry. This property allows us to say that if pain = C-fibre firing, then C-fibre firing = pain. And just as the truth of such an identity statement licenses us to say that there is nothing more to pain than C-fibre firing, so it licenses us to say that there is nothing more to C-fibre firing than pain. For C-fibre firing simply *is* pain, neither more nor less. If A = B, then there is nothing more to A than B *and* vice versa. C-fibre firing is not anything over and above pain. It has no properties not possessed by pain. It reduces to pain, collapses into it. It consists of pain. It has no reality beyond that of pain. C-fibre firing is

---

[3] On the epistemic contingency of psychophysical identity statements see J. J. C. Smart, 'Sensations and Brain Processes', *Philosophical Review* 67: 141–56. On the metaphysical necessity of identity statements see S. Kripke, *Naming and Necessity* (Cambridge, Mass.: Harvard University Press, 1980).

constituted by pain. Pain is what C-fibre firing turns out to *be*. The *essence* of C-fibre firing is pain.

But surely this sounds wrong: one wants to say that such an identification fails to do justice to the objectivity of C-fibre firing. If C-fibre firing were really nothing but pain, then it would not be observable, symmetrically accessible, conceivable from many points of view, spatial and subject-independent. The identification makes the objective too subjective. It has the flavour of an elimination, not a reality-preserving reduction. If the reduction were correct, then C-fibre firing would not be an objective property of the world after all, contrary to the appearances. The case is quite unlike, say, the identification of molecular motion with heat: here there is no strain in saying that molecular motion amounts to nothing but heat, since heat is not itself a subjective phenomenon. The objectivity of molecular motion is preserved in this reduction, whereas in the case of identifying C-fibre firing with pain we have an attempt to characterize an objective property in subjective terms.

Thus the inversion permitted by the symmetry of identity results in an implausible reduction of the objective to the subjective—a loss of objectivity in the property we started out with. It might be thought that this argument works only on condition that the reductionism takes the form of an identity claim. What if the reduction is formulated in terms of composition?[4]

Suppose we say that water is composed of H_2O molecules; we cannot then symmetrically say that H_2O molecules are composed of water—yet such a claim permits a thesis of reduction of water to H_2O molecules. Thus we might analogously maintain that pain is (wholly) composed of the firings of C-fibres without committing ourselves to the converse claim. This certainly avoids the simple move from symmetry that I made against the identity formulation of reductionism, but I think that parallel problems beset the

---

[4] Thomas Nagel suggested that I consider this line of defence.

composition formulation too. First, if water is composed of H_2O molecules, then H_2O molecules are constituents or parts of water; equally C-fibre firings must be constituents or parts of pain if they compose pain. But how could something be literally a *part* of pain without being itself subjective? Consider a more familiar part–whole relation in respect of pain: I experience a complex pain resulting from banging my elbow against something hot. We might say that the resulting pain has both a collision component and a burn component; but these parts of my complex pain are clearly themselves subjective. If anything is a part of a subjective state, and not merely part of the neural correlate of that state, then it has to be subjective too. The claim is that pain is composed of nothing but C-fibre firings, but then C-fibre firings have to be the very elements that constitute pain, and hence must share its subjectivity. Just as a part of something objective must be objective, so a part of something subjective must be subjective. We would never allow that a putatively objective property might be wholly constituted by subjective elements, so why dispense a comparable leniency in the other direction?

Secondly, we can always derive an identity statement from a claim of composition. If X is composed of Fs, then there is some Y that is an aggregation of Fs such that $Y = X$. If water is composed of H_2O molecules, then there is an aggregation of those molecules such that that aggregation is identical to water. Water is not merely composed of H_2O molecules singly considered; it also *is* a collection of such molecules: it is identical to the aggregate of the elements that compose it. But then pain must be identical to the aggregate of the C-fibre firings that compose it, which is to say that that aggregate is identical to pain. This implies that (suitable) aggregates of C-fibre firings are as subjective as pain. When you put the C-fibre firings together you get something that is nothing over and above a pain. But surely an aggregate of objective elements should itself be an objective entity. Composition is not symmetrical, but it generates a symmetrical relation via the operation of aggregation. Again, the objective is collapsing into the subjective. So composition does not help the reductionist escape the argument. From now on, then, I shall persist with the simpler identity formulation.

4. Mentalism and reduction

A good way to get a feel for what I am arguing is to consider an imaginary school of philosophers who adopt a wholesale reduction of the objective to the subjective. These philosophers, call them 'mentalists', are troubled by the notion of objectivity; they find it hard to understand how there can be irreducible objective physical facts. Perhaps they think that the idea of such facts requires an 'absolute conception' that abstracts totally away from their specific sensory point of view, and they cannot see how we could acquire such transcendent concepts.[5]

Objectivity requires a 'view from nowhere', and they cannot conceive of such a detached view of the world. In any case, they find the idea of objective facts problematic, for whatever reason. Yet they are not eliminativist, at least not officially: they agree that there really are objects that are square and electrically charged and made of neurons. They agree too that such facts can obtain whether or not they are being perceived by us (or by God); the mentalists are not idealists. What they insist is that every such fact is identical to a subjective fact. When an object is square, for example, they hold that this consists in the object's having a certain conscious state: there is something it is like to be square *for* the object. So-called objective properties are reducible to subjective properties, by way of suitable identity statements. They may not

[5] On the availability of the 'absolute conception' see B. Williams, *Descartes: The Project of Pure Enquiry* (Harmondsworth: Penguin Books, 1978); T. Nagel, 'What is it Like to be a Bat?', repr. in *Mortal Questions* (Cambridge: Cambridge University Press, 1979); and C. McGinn, *The Subjective View* (Oxford: Oxford University Press, 1982).

always know *which* subjective property a given objective property reduces to, but they are confident that there always is one. Every physical property is identical to a *quale* of some sort, known or unknown. This mentalistic metaphysics is different from panpsychism: panpsychism says that every object has some mental property, in addition to its physical properties; mentalism says that every physical property of every object is itself mental. There is no fact there is not something it is like to have.

What should we say about this startling mentalist doctrine? The obvious objection to it is that it is a reduction that signally fails to do justice to the objective physical world as we ordinarily understand it. If such a reduction were correct, then physical properties like being square or electrically charged would turn out to be unobservable, asymmetrically accessible, subjective, non-spatial, and subject-dependent—given that mental states have these defining characteristics. Such properties would turn out to have all the proprietary features of the mental: they would be unobservable inner states of a subject of consciousness, not the publicly accessible objective properties we naively take them to be. And that is objectionably eliminativist, no matter what the official line of the mentalists may be. (One can imagine all the fancy footwork they would have to do in order to fend off the objection that we can *see* that being square is not an unobservable mental state just by looking at a square object. Compare the objection that we can see that a pain isn't C-fibre firing just by introspecting our pains.)

But if global mentalism of this kind is guilty of denying the objectivity of the physical, then surely local mentalism is too, albeit more narrowly. It is just as implausible to suggest that *some* physical properties are really mental as that all are. The global mentalists in effect treat physical terms as if they are natural kind terms for properties that will turn out to have a subjective essence—analogously to the way materialists take mental terms to be natural kind terms for properties that will turn out to have an objective essence. But local mentalists are really no better off: they take some physical terms—those for (some) brain states—to be natural kind terms for properties that will turn out to have a subjective essence. But this involves an implausibly subjectivist interpretation of an objective property, sacrificing all the objective features we naively ascribe to such properties. The subjectivist sin is not any less because it is localized. (Compare: some moral 'oughts' are reducible to naturalistic facts and some are not.) But local mentalism is the *same doctrine* as materialism, by the symmetry of identity, since materialists precisely hold that some physical properties can be identified with subjective properties. They hold, for example, that C-fibre firing in the brain is identical to a sensation of pain felt by a conscious subject, and has no characteristics beyond those of pain. They hold that a physical property consists in a property defined by what it is like for its owner.

The trouble with materialism, ironically enough, is that it is not materialist enough about matter. It makes some pockets of matter too subjective in nature. It has essentially the same fault as global mentalism—a failure to respect the intrinsic objectivity of physical properties.

5. A problem for localized materialism

Let me incidentally note how odd the localized character of materialism is when seen for what it is. Offhand one might have thought that all physical properties are on a par, none having a fundamentally different essence from the others. But according to materialism some physical properties have a subjective essence while some do not. And it is not merely that physical states of the kidneys don't have a subjective essence while states of the brain do; some states of the brain itself have a subjective essence while some do not—despite the fact that all brain states consist of neurons and their firings. Not every brain state has a 'correlated' mental state. Whence this strange violation of the uniformity of nature? Induction would suggest that all neural states have a purely objective essence, since so many do; but when we come to a particular subset of them we allegedly find that they have a subjective essence. It is like discovering that some molecular motion is heat and some is not, despite the uniformity of the molecules and their motions. That would seem arbitrary and miraculous. But materialism finds itself countenancing something equally arbitrary and miraculous— the fact that some physical states but not others reduce to mental states. At the very least we need to be told what it is about this remarkable subset of physical states that makes them alone reducible to subjective states. Once we permit a robust notion of subjectivity this must seem a pressing question.

6. Parallels with arguments surrounding materialist reduction

I now want to briefly consider some instructive parallels with the usual arguments surrounding materialist reduction.

1. *What it is like.* Thomas Nagel argued that there is something it is like to undergo conscious experience, and that this something is accessible only to those beings who enjoy similar experiences (Nagel 1979, 1986). He then argued that brain states are not defined in such terms; they are accessible from a variety of experiential standpoints. Hence the claim of reduction is flawed: we cannot find a place for the subjective in our objective conception of the world, including the brain. Inverting this, I insist that it is part of the very definition of a physical state of the brain that it is objective, in the sense that it is knowable by beings with the right intelligence irrespective of the particular types of experience they enjoy, so that we cannot reduce such states to states bearing the marks of subjectivity. Just as it is important that there is something it is like to be a bat, so it is important that there is nothing it is like to

have a bat's brain: that is, it is important that bat brain states are objective properties of the world. We do not want to collapse bat brain states into purely inner processes. Indeed, if we did we would not know what properties the bat's brain has, since we do not know what kinds of experience it has—which is absurd. If facts about bat brains are identical to facts about what it is like to be a bat, then such facts are not knowable without sharing the subjectivity of a bat—i.e. they are subjective facts. But they are not subjective facts, since the neurophysiology of bats is knowable by beings other than bats. Thus the objectivity of a bat's brain is just as inconsistent with materialist reduction as the subjectivity of its experience is. Either we deny the subjectivity of the experience in order to sustain the reduction to brain states, or we deny the objectivity of the brain in order to conform to the subjectivity of experience. If Nagel is right about the inherent subjectivity of experience, as I think he is, then materialism results in a denial of the objectivity of matter. The B-fibres that are identified with the bat's subjective experience will turn out to have all the subjectivity of those experiences, and nothing more.

2. *The knowledge argument.* Frank Jackson's Mary is said to know all the physical facts without being thereby apprised of all the facts about the mind; she cannot deduce subjective facts from her comprehensive knowledge of objective facts (Jackson 1982, 1986). When Mary emerges from her black-and-white room armed with complete knowledge of neurophysiology she learns something new when she first enjoys an experience of red. So what she learns was not prefigured in what she already knew. Hence materialism is not a complete theory of the mind. Now consider Maisie: she knows all the phenomenal facts—all the facts about her own mental states and their interrelations. She spends the early years of her life floating in a vat enjoying her own phenomenology, thinking about her experiences, classifying them, revelling in them. There is little outside distraction from her inner world; specifically, she is taught

no physics, including neurophysiology. One day she is removed from her phenomenological vat and forced to learn physics. In the course of her studies, at which she proves remarkably adept, she learns all about her brain, including the correlates of the phenomenal states she knows so well. Does she thereby learn anything new? She used only to know what experiences of red were like; now she also knows all about the R-fibres that underlie these experiences. Well, it certainly seems like she learns a new fact—that she has R-fibres that correlate with her familiar old experience of red. Moreover, she learns a fact of a new kind—an objective fact, as distinct from a subjective phenomenal fact. Therefore R-fibres cannot be identical with experiences of red. Just as subjective facts cannot be deduced from objective facts, this creating a knowledge gap, so objective facts cannot be deduced from subjective facts, this also creating a knowledge gap. The gap is as large whichever direction you approach it from. Maisie is as ignorant as Mary before both their life-styles change. (Of course, there are replies to the knowledge argument, which I will not go into here,[6] and replies to these replies, but my point is just that the argument cuts both ways.)

3. *What God had to do*. Saul Kripke maintains that when God created pain he had to do more than create C-fibre firing—whereas to create heat it sufficed to create molecular motion (Kripke 1980). At least that is our strong intuition. If the intuition is correct, then the mind is not necessarily supervenient on the brain. Pain must be something over and above C-fibre firing. Accordingly, zombies are conceivable: beings in some possible world who share our physical properties but differ from us in having no mental states at all.[7] There is a modal and ontological gap between C-fibres and pain, marked by the tasks God had to perform to make a world like ours.

[6] I make a few remarks about one standard reply below. For a much fuller discussion see my 'How not to Solve the Mind-Body Problem', in C. Gillett and B. Loewer (eds.) (Cambridge: Cambridge University Press, 2001).

[7] See David Chalmers, *The Conscious Mind* (Oxford: Oxford University Press, 1996), in which the alleged conceivability of zombies plays a pivotal role.

But it is no less intuitive to make the opposite point: in order to create C-fibres it was not enough for God to create pain—he had some additional work to do in order to bring C-fibres into the world. Accordingly, mental states do not logically determine physical states: there is a lack of supervenience here, and disembodiment seems logically conceivable. That is, after having created pain it was up to God (i) *what* physical state to correlate with it and (ii) whether to correlate *any* physical state with it. There is thus a modal and ontological gap between pain and C-fibres, marked by the extra effort involved in producing the latter after producing the former. The arguments are exactly parallel.

Now it is not that I myself subscribe to either of these arguments: I actually believe that the connections here are necessary despite our modal intuitions to the contrary.[8] What I am saying is that the arguments are exactly parallel, so that anyone who accepts them one way round has to ask whether to accept them the other way round. In particular, those who believe in the possibility of zombies need to ask whether they also believe in the possibility of disembodied minds.

4. *The epistemic interpretation.* A standard reply to the above anti-reductionist arguments is that they confuse ontology with epistemology.[9] Our *concepts* of pain and C-fibre firing may indeed be distinct, but it does not follow that they denote distinct *properties*; and mental properties may be reducible to physical properties without the concepts that denote them being reducible to physical concepts. The idea is that 'subjective' and 'objective' are predicates that apply to properties or facts only under certain descriptions or concepts. A property P might be subjective under the description

---

[8] On the idea of hidden necessary connections see my *The Problem of Consciousness* (Oxford: Blackwell, 1991), esp. 19–21, and my review of Chalmers (1996) in my *Minds and Bodies* (New York: Oxford University Press, 1997).

[9] For example, P. Churchland, 'Knowing Qualia: A Reply to Jackson', repr. in P. M. Churchland and P. S. Churchland, *On the Contrary* (Cambridge, Mass.: MIT Press, 1998).

'pain' and objective under the description 'C-fibre firing'. The ontological gap that seems to separate the subjective from the objective is really just an epistemic gap between the *concept* of pain and the *concept* of C-fibre firing, not a gap between the properties themselves.

Now a lot can be said about this form of reply, but I want to make only one point relevant to the argument of this paper.[10] The epistemic reply to the claim that materialist reduction fails to do justice to the nature of the subjective is that pain is only subjective as so described; it is subjective *de dicto* but not *de re*. When we redescribe pain as C-fibre firing we can see that it is really an objective property in itself (*de re*). The characteristics I listed at the beginning as distinctive of the mind belong to it only under a mental description—they apply to pain only *de dicto*. In effect, they all generate opaque contexts. But if this is true of the subjective it must also be true of the objective: properties are only objective under certain descriptions, and never *de re*.

When I redescribe C-fibre firing as pain it ceases to be objective, save relative to that physical description. C-fibre firing is only objective under a description and not in itself. And similarly for any other apparently objective property: we cannot say that having an electrical charge is objective *de re* but only that it is objective *de dicto*, since the notion of objectivity is being interpreted merely epistemically. If I think of an electrical charge under the description 'that which causes pain in humans', then I consign it to the class of subjective facts. According to this view, it makes no sense to attribute objectivity (or subjectivity) to states of affairs in themselves. We cannot even say that a universe in which there are no minds contains purely objective facts, unless reference is made to our current concepts. This seems very odd. Surely it is an inherent intrinsic *de re* fact that physical states in general are objective states,

---

[10] The obvious question is what *makes* concepts different if not the properties they express: see my 'How not to Solve the Mind-Body Problem' (n. 6 above).

in the sense I spelled out at the beginning. It is not that they *become* objective only when we decide to describe them in a certain way. It is absurd to suggest, say, that physical objects are only spatial under a description and not in themselves. It is in the very nature of physical facts that they are objective.

The point I am making is that materialists implicitly adopt an invidious attitude towards the subjective and the objective: they are only too happy to assert that properties are subjective only under a certain description, but the parallel move for objectivity looks distinctly unappealing once its implications are appreciated. Yet it is this move that is necessary if we are going to object to my argument by saying that C-fibres can be objective under that description but not under the description 'pain'. That is no way to protect the robust objectivity of physical facts. The plain truth is that if pain is allowed to be robustly subjective, in the *de re* sense, then identifying C-fibre firing with pain results in divesting this physical process of its vaunted objectivity. This objectivity cannot be plausibly restored by retreating to the thesis that C-fibre firing is objective only *de dicto*—on pain of making all objective facts similarly weakly objective. So the epistemic interpretation fails to deliver a robust notion of objectivity, just as it fails to provide a robust sense of subjectivity. The latter is tolerable to a materialist, given his ontological biases; but the former is surely highly unpalatable to the materialist.

There are three options here: (i) the characteristic marks of subjectivity or objectivity are not possessed at all, so that we end up with eliminativism either about the subjective or the objective; (ii) these characteristics are possessed only in the *de dicto* sense, so that we end up denying that anything can be subjective *or* objective in itself; (iii) we allow that properties can be subjective or objective *de re*, so that we end up either distorting the nature of the subjective *or* (the plaint of this paper) distorting the nature of objectivity. Assuming that we want to avoid eliminativism, we have the result that you cannot be an identity theorist who respects the robustness of subjectivity *and* respects the robustness of objectivity. If you identify a physical property with a genuinely mental property, then you cannot avoid an unacceptable subjectivization of the objective. The trouble with materialism is that it does not take the objectivity of matter seriously enough, despite its overt intentions.

7. Conclusion

What should we conclude from this discussion? I think we can conclude that classic type-identity materialism is false, either the central state version or physicalistic functionalism (and behaviourism). But I do not think we can conclude either that mental states are irreducible or that there are merely contingent connections between mental states and brain states. Maybe mental states are reducible to something that does not have the marks of full-blown objectivity, unlike C-fibre firing and its kin. Maybe new properties could be discovered that both reduce mental states and are not themselves objective; and even if they could not be discovered they might nevertheless exist.[11]

And there may be necessary connections between pain and C-fibre firing even though it is not possible to *identify* the two; these may be distinct properties that are non-contingently connected. The nature of the necessary links might be hidden and not be inferable from our current concepts, but they might exist anyway (McGinn 1991, 1997). So nothing I have said entails a rejection of supervenience or an acceptance of irreducibly mental properties. The correct view of the mind-body relation is left open by what I have argued. All I have contended is that the usual kinds

[11] I believe, for reasons not entered into in this paper, that the most likely hypothesis is that the properties that are needed to solve the mind-body problem are in principle inaccessible to the human mind; my present point is just that a reduction *might* exist that we shall never discover. See my *Problem of Consciousness* (n. 8 above).

of materialistic identity theory are committed to an unacceptably subjective conception of the physical world. As Kripke remarked after presenting his own modal argument against the identity theory, the mind-body problem is 'wide open and extremely confusing'.[12]

[12] S. Kripke, *Naming and Necessity* (Cambridge, Mass.: Harvard University Press, 1980), 155, n. 77.

5

Consciousness and Space

I: The Location of Consciousness

Descartes famously held that, while the essence of body is spatial extension, the essence of mind is thought. Thought is taken to be the defining attribute of incorporeal substance—substance that is non-spatial in nature. He writes: 'For if we ... examine what we are, we see very clearly that neither extension nor shape nor local motion, nor anything of this kind which is attributable to a body, belongs to our nature, but that thought alone belongs to it.'[1] The mental and the spatial are thus mutually exclusive categories.

It is hard to deny that Descartes was tapping into our ordinary understanding of the nature of mental phenomena when he formulated the distinction between mind and body in this way—our consciousness does indeed present itself as non-spatial in character. Consider a visual experience, E, as of a yellow flash. Associated with E in the cortex is a complex of neural structures and events, N, which does admit of spatial description. N occurs, say, an inch

[1] J. Cottingham, R. Stoothoff, and D. Murdoch (eds.), *The Philosophical Writings of Descartes*, vol. 1 (Cambridge: Cambridge University Press, 1985), 156.

from the back of the head; it extends over some specific area of the cortex; it has some kind of configuration or contour; it is composed of spatial parts that aggregate into a structured whole; it exists in three spatial dimensions; it excludes other neural complexes from its spatial location. N is a regular denizen of space, as much as any other physical entity. But E seems not to have any of these spatial characteristics: it is not located at any specific place; it takes up no particular volume of space; it has no shape; it is not made up of spatially distributed parts; it has no spatial dimensionality; it is not solid. Even to ask for its spatial properties is to commit some sort of category mistake, analogous to asking for the spatial properties of numbers. E seems not to be the *kind of thing* that falls under spatial predicates. It falls under temporal predicates and it can obviously be described in other ways—by specifying its owner, its intentional content, its phenomenal character—but it resists being cast as a regular inhabitant of the space we see around us and within which the material world has its existence. Spatial occupancy is not (at least on the face of it) the mind's preferred mode of being.

No doubt this is connected with the fact that conscious states are not *perceived*. We perceive, by our various sense organs, a variety of material objects laid out in space, taking up certain volumes and separated by certain distances. We thus conceive of these perceptual objects as spatial entities; perception informs us directly of their spatiality. But conscious subjects and their mental states are not in this way perceptual objects. We do not see or hear or smell or touch them, and a fortiori do not perceive them as spatially individuated.[2] This holds both for the first- and third-person perspectives. Since we do not *observe* our own states of consciousness, nor those of others, we do not apprehend these

[2] Obviously I am not denying that there is a sense in which we can perceive persons, by perceiving their bodies; my point is that we do not perceive the psychological subject *qua* psychological subject. If you like, we do not perceive the *I* of the Cogito.

states as spatial. So our modes of cognition of mental states do not bring them under the kinds of spatial concepts appropriate to perceptual acquaintance. Perceptual geometry gets no purchase on them. And this is not just a contingent fact about the mind.[3]

Nor do we think of conscious states as occupying an unperceived space, as we think of the unobservable entities of physics. We have no conception of what it would even *be* to perceive them as spatial entities. God may see the elementary particles as arrayed in space, but even He does not perceive our conscious states as spatially defined—no more than He sees numbers as spatially defined. It is not that experiences have location, shape, and dimensionality for eyes that are sharper than ours. Since they are non-spatial they are in principle unperceivable.

This is I think what people have in mind when they aver that 'consciousness is not a thing'. The thought expressed here is not the trivial one that to refer to consciousness is to invoke a category of events or states or processes and not a category of objects or continuant particulars. Our intuition that conscious states are not spatial is not the intuition that no *state* is an *object*. For ordinary physical states and events are spatial entities in the intended sense: we apprehend events as occurring *in* space, and states are features *of* spatially constituted objects. So it would be wrong to offer a deflationary interpretation of our non-spatial conception of consciousness by insisting that it comes to nothing more than a recognition that talk of consciousness is talk of events and states—just like talk of explosions and motions and electric charge. The non-spatial nature of consciousness, as we conceive it, is much more radical than that diagnosis suggests. Descartes was not committing the simple howler of failing to notice that conscious phenomena are not objects at all and hence not spatial objects. In

[3] We see an echo of this in two doctrines of Wittgenstein's: that self-ascription is not based upon observation; and that the notion of inner ostension (pointing) is ill-defined. In this respect, at least, Wittgenstein and Descartes converge on the same fundamental insights. I think, in fact, that a good deal of Wittgenstein's philosophy of mind is based upon a repudiation of a spatial model of the mind.

fact, even when we do speak of something that belongs to the category of continuant object, namely the *subject* of consciousness, we still insist upon its non-spatial character.[4] The self is not a 'thing' either, in the intended sense. The mental realm is just not bound up in the world of objects in space in the way that ordinary physical events are so bound up. So, at any rate, our pretheoretical view assures us.

That may seem exaggerated, at least under one interpretation of the idea of connectedness to the spatial world. For, it might be said, we do in point of fact locate conscious events in the spatial world— not very precisely perhaps, but at least in a fairly systematic way. Thus we take each subject of consciousness to be somewhere in the vicinity of a distinguished body, and we locate conscious events in the approximate neighbourhood of the physical object we call the brain. We certainly do not suppose that I am in some *other* place than my body, and we locate my thoughts nearer to my head than to my feet. So, perhaps we do grant spatial characteristics to consciousness, at least of a rudimentary sort.

I think this point should be granted, at least so far as it goes: but it does not go very far in undermining the intrinsic non-spatiality of the mental. How do we actually make the locational judgements about consciousness that we do? Not, clearly, by perceiving that conscious events occupy particular places; rather, by trading upon certain *causal* considerations. Events in particular physical objects are directly causally involved in changes of mental state, and we locate the mental change roughly where those causally proximate physical objects are. I am where that body is whose physical states bear most directly on my mental state; and my states of consciousness are situated in the vicinity of that brain whose activity is most directly implicated in the causal relations controlling my mental life. For example, my visual states are in the whereabouts of the

---

[4] I am assuming that the conscious subject is not simply identical with the body. But my overall position does not depend upon this, since the point applies equally to conscious states themselves.

eyes and brain that produce them, and not somewhere in (say) the Grand Canyon (unless my eyes and brain happen to be there). But this kind of causally based location of the mental should be taken for what it is. First, it is parasitic on a prior location of physical objects; there is no independent route on to mental location, since that is based solely on bearing causal relations to things that *can* be nonderivatively located. If we imagine abrogating these causal relations, by considering a world in which there are no psychophysical causal connections, but only intra-mental ones, then we see that in such a world no form of spatial location would be available for mental events. They would not be tied down to any location at all, no matter how vague. Locating mental events as we do in the actual world is merely 'theoretical'—a sort of courtesy location. Considered in themselves, intrinsically, we do not regard mental events as having location. The imprecision of our locational judgements here is a mark of this. Second, to allow that consciousness can be roughly located is not to grant it the full panoply of spatial predications. We still do not get predications of shape, size, dimensionality, etc. And this shows that such spatiality as we do allow to mental matters is of a second-class and derivative nature. Descartes himself might readily have allowed this kind of causally based location of the mental while still insisting that concepts of extension have no proper application to the mental.

It might be objected that there are some mental events that do permit precise location, and that this is based on something like immediate perception. Thus I feel a pain to be in my hand, and that is indeed exactly where it is. Isn't this just like seeing the physical injury to my hand that produces the pain? Well, it is true enough that the pain presents itself as being in my hand, but there are familiar reasons for not taking this at face value. Without my brain no such pain would be felt, and the same pain can be produced simply by stimulating my brain and leaving my hand alone (I might not even have a hand). Such facts incline us to say, reasonably enough, that the pain is really in my brain, if anywhere, and only appears to be in my hand (a sort of locational illusion takes place). That is, causal criteria yield a different location for the pain from phenomenal criteria. Anyway bodily pain is an unusual case and does not generalize to other mental phenomena (perhaps this is why we ordinarily speak of pain as a bodily state rather than a mental one).

It is instructive to consider the notion of spatial exclusion in relation to the mind. A well-known metaphysical principle has it that no two material objects (of the same kind) can occupy the same place at the same time. It is in the very nature of space and objects that there should be this kind of necessary exclusion. And analogous principles can be formulated for material events, states, and processes. Now ask whether this principle applies also to mental items. Can two subjects of awareness occupy the same place at the same time? Can two thoughts be spatio-temporally coincident? Can two bodily sensations? The questions seem misconceived, since the issue does not really *arise* for mental things. We want to say: 'Well, *if* mental things had location and other spatial properties, *then* there might be such exclusion; but since they don't it is not clear what to say. Maybe, for all we know, they can be spatio-temporally coincident, since nothing in their intrinsic nature rules it out.' The fact is that the question is too much like asking whether two numbers can be at the same place at the same time. We just do not conceive of these things in ways that bring them within the scope of the principle of spatial exclusion. This is a way of saying that the notion of *solidity* has no application to mental phenomena. If the essential mark of the spatial is competition for space, as the metaphysical principle records, then the mental lacks that essential feature.

In view of the above considerations there is something highly misleading about the popular suggestion that mental phenomena have the same sort of conceptual status as the posits of physical science: that is, that both are unobservables postulated to make the best sense of the data. Apart from the obvious point that we also know about our mental states 'from the inside', there is a crucial disanalogy here, which underscores the *sui generis* character of the mental case. While we think of the unobservables of physics as existing in space and hence in spatial relation to the things we do observe, we do not think of the mental states that explain behaviour in this way. Explanatory posits they may be, at least from the third-person perspective, but they are not the reassuring spatial entities that other explanatory posits are. It is thus far more puzzling how they relate to behaviour, especially causally, than is the relation of atomic events to the macroscopic behaviour of material bodies. In the physical case, we have notions of contact causation and gravita-tional force acting across space, but in the mental case it is quite unclear how these causal paradigms are supposed to apply. *How* do conscious events cause physical changes in the body? Not by proximate contact, apparently, on pain of over-spatializing con-sciousness, and presumably not by action-at-a-distance either. Recent philosophy has become accustomed to the idea of mental causation, but this is actually much more mysterious than is gener-ally appreciated, once the non-spatial character of consciousness is acknowledged. To put it differently, we understand mental caus-ation *only* if we deny the intuition of non-spatiality. The standard analogy with physical unobservables simply dodges these hard questions, lulling us into a false sense of intelligibility.[5]

I conclude, then, from this quick survey of somewhat familiar terrain that consciousness does not, on its face, slot smoothly into the ordinary spatial world. The Cartesian intuition of unextended-ness is a firm part of our ordinary conception of the mental. In advance of theoretical reconstruction consciousness is not spatially well-behaved. We shall next look at some consequences of this, inquiring what theoretical response should be made to it.

[5] Of course, it is a presupposed materialism that permits the usual insouciance over mental causation. I am simply pointing out that *without* materialism the claim of mental causation, though no doubt correct, is burdened with severe problems of intelligibility. Once materialism is questioned all the old problems about mental causation resurface.

II: The Origin of Consciousness

If consciousness is not constitutionally spatial, then how could it have had its origin in the spatial world? According to received cosmology, there was a time at which the universe contained no consciousness but only matter in space obeying the laws of physics. Then the evolution of life began and matter started clumping together in novel ways, driven by the mechanism of natural selection. Soon, in cosmic time, neural nuclei appeared, leading to brains of various sizes and structures—and along with that (as we think) came consciousness. Evidently, then, matter fell into ever more complex and ingenious arrangements and as a result consciousness came into the world. The only ingredients in the pot when consciousness was cooking were particles and fields laid out in space, yet something radically non-spatial got produced. On that fine spring morning when consciousness was first laid on nature's table there was nothing around but extended matter in space, yet now a non-spatial stuff simmered and bubbled. We seem compelled to conclude that something essentially non-spatial emerged from something purely spatial—that the non-spatial is somehow a construction out of the spatial. And this looks more like magic than a predictable unfolding of natural law. Let us call the problem of how this is possible the 'space problem' with respect to consciousness.[6]

Notice that this problem has no parallel in the evolution of life forms *per se*. These are indeed cosmic novelties, but they do not essentially transcend the mechanisms of spatial aggregation, and we have a good theory of how the novelty is generated. There is no space problem in explaining the emergence of organisms as such; that problem only begins to bite when conscious states enter the scene. To put it in Descartes' terms: how can something whose essence is to be non-spatial develop from something whose essence

[6] There are some suggestive remarks on the spatiality of organisms and the non-combinatorial nature of the mental in T. Nagel, *The View from Nowhere* (Oxford: Oxford University Press, 1986), 49, 51.

is to be spatial? How can you derive the unextended from the extended? Note too that this problem has no parallel in the relation between the abstract and the physical, since, though non-spatial, the abstract is not supposed to have *emerged* from the material. The problem arises from a specific clash between the essence of consciousness and its apparent origin.

We might be reminded at this point of the big bang. That notable occurrence can be regarded as presenting an inverse space problem. For, on received views, it was at the moment of the big bang that space itself came into existence, there being nothing spatial antecedently to that. But how does space come from non-space? What kind of 'explosion' could create space *ab initio*? And this problem offers an even closer structural parallel to the consciousness problem if we assume, as I would argue is plausible, that the big bang was not the beginning (temporally or explanatorily) of all existence.[7] Some prior independent state of things must have led to that early cataclysm, and this sequence of events itself must have some intelligible explanation—just as there must be an explanation for the sequence that led from matter-in-space to consciousness. The brain puts into reverse, as it were, what the big bang initiated: it erases spatial dimensions rather than creating them. It undoes the

[7] Here I am raising highly controversial issues. Let me just say that all the arguments I have heard for supposing the big bang to be the beginning of everything take the form of inferring an ontological conclusion from epistemic premises—to the effect that since we can't *know* anything about any earlier state we should suppose there to *be* no such state. But that, I assert, is an idealist fallacy. Sometimes it is suggested that time began with the big bang, because of its supposed internal connection with space. I find such arguments unconvincing. But, actually, my point is consistent with allowing time to start with the big bang, since we could always introduce a notion of explanation that did not require temporal priority. I myself see no good reason to rule out a picture of the universe in which radically new realities come into existence as a result of other realities. Just as it took gravity to convert the gaseous early state of the universe into the clumpy galaxies we now take for granted, so the big bang may have been just one episode in which the universe underwent a radical transformation. In general, I think people are too ready to suppose that nothing antecedent to the big bang could have existed, usually on shaky philosophical grounds—ultimately of an anthropocentric nature. (No doubt I shall get into trouble for poking my nose into cosmologists' business here!).

work of creating space, swallowing down matter and spitting out consciousness. So, taking the very long view, the universe has gone through phases of space generation and (local) space annihilation; or at least, with respect to the latter, there have been operations on space that have generated a non-spatial being. This suggests the following heady speculation: that the origin of consciousness somehow draws upon those properties of the universe that antedate and explain the occurrence of the big bang. If we need a pre-spatial level of reality to account for the big bang, then it may be this very level that is exploited in the generation of consciousness. That is, assuming that remnants of the pre-big bang universe have persisted, it may be that these features of the universe are somehow involved in engineering the non-spatial phenomenon of consciousness. If so, consciousness turns out to be older than matter in space, at least as to its raw materials.[8]

However that may be, we are still faced with the space problem for consciousness. How might it be dealt with? There are, historically, two main lines of response to the problem, commonly supposed to be exclusive and exhaustive. One response denies a key premise of the problem, namely that mind sprang from matter. Instead, mind has an autonomous existence, as independent of matter as matter is of mind. Perhaps mind has always existed, or maybe came about in some analogue of the origin of matter, or owes its existence to a direct act of God. In any event, mind is no kind of out-growth of matter but an independent ontological category. Thus we have classical dualism, Descartes' own position. In effect, dualism takes the space problem to be a *reductio* of the

---

[8] Clearly, there are many large assumptions here: not merely that reality did not begin with the big bang, but also that the prior reality has somehow persisted into the post-big bang state of the universe, presumably by virtue of some sort of conservation principle. These seem to me pretty plausible assumptions, though how to establish them is another question. I should note also that the speculation in the text pertains only to the non-spatiality of consciousness; I am not suggesting that all the features of consciousness could be explained by pre-big bang properties. In this paper I am leaving on one side questions about the subjectivity of consciousness, qualia and so on.

emergence hypothesis. Mind and matter may causally interact (let us not inquire how!) but it is absurd, for dualism, to suppose that mind could owe its very *being* to matter. That is simply metaphysically impossible, according to dualism. You can no more derive the unextended from the extended than you can derive an ought from an is.[9]

A second response questions what we have been assuming so far, namely that consciousness is inherently non-spatial. We may grant that we ordinarily *conceive* of it in this way, but we should insist that that mode of conception be abandoned. Here we encounter, it may be said, yet another area in which common sense misconceives the true nature of reality. In fact, conscious states are just as spatially constituted as brain states, since they *are* brain states—neural configurations in all their spatial glory. Thus we have classical materialism, the thesis that consciousness is nothing over and above the cellular structures and processes we observe in the brain.[10] Since these admit of straightforward spatial characterization, so, by identity, do conscious states. The case is analogous to the following: to common sense physical objects appear solid, but science tells us that this is an illusion, since they are really made up of widely spaced particles in a lattice that is anything but solid. Somewhat so, the materialist insists that the appearance of non-spatiality that consciousness presents is a kind of illusion, and that in reality it is as spatial (even solid!) as the cell clusters that constitute the brain.[11] It is Descartes' assumption of

[9] In my 'Consciousness and Cosmology: Hyperdualism Ventilated', in *Consciousness*, ed. M. Davies and G. W. Humphreys (Oxford: Blackwell, 1993), I give dualism the best defence I can, though it is not a position I subscribe to.

[10] Functionalism and allied doctrines should be included here, since they are broadly materialist. Computationalism is harder to classify because of tricky questions about the ontology of computer programs. On one natural interpretation computer programs are constituted by abstract objects, so they are non-spatial. This may or may not be a good way to capture the non-spatiality of consciousness (actually not), but the view is clearly no longer materialist.

[11] This is an unspoken assumption of large tracts of contemporary philosophy of mind. Even those who recognize that consciousness poses problems for materialism

unextendedness that is mistaken, according to materialism, not the emergence hypothesis.

Now it is not my intention here to rehearse any of the usual criticisms of these two venerable positions, beyond noting that both have deeply unattractive features, which I think we would be reluctant to countenance if it were not for the urgency of the problem. These are positions we feel driven to, rather than ones that save the phenomena in a theoretically satisfying way. My purpose is to identify a third option, and to explore some of its ramifications. The point of this third option is to preserve material emergence while not denying the ordinary non-spatial conception of consciousness. The heart of the view, put simply, is this: the brain cannot have merely the spatial properties recognized in current physical science, since these are insufficient to explain what it can achieve, namely the generation of consciousness. The brain must have aspects that are not represented in our current physical world-view, aspects we deeply do not understand, in addition to all those neurons and electro-chemical processes. There is, on this view, a radical incompleteness in our view of reality, including physical reality. In order to provide an explanation of the emergence of consciousness we would need a conceptual revolution, in which fundamentally new properties and principles are identified. This may involve merely supplementing our current theories with new elements, so that we need not abandon what we now believe; or it may be—as I think more likely—that some profound revisions are required, some repudiation of current theory. Consciousness is an anomaly in our present world-view and, like all anomalies, it calls for some more or less drastic rectification in that relative to which it is anomalous.

in virtue of its phenomenal character seldom acknowledge that its non-spatiality is also a major stumbling-block for materialism—despite the fact that Descartes took it (and not qualia) to be critical.

Some ideal theory T contains the solution to the space problem, but arriving at T would require some major upheavals in our basic conception of reality.

I am now in a position to state the main thesis of this paper: in order to solve the mind-body problem we need, at a minimum, a new conception of space. We need a conceptual breakthrough in the way we think about the medium in which material objects exist, and hence in our conception of material objects themselves. That is the region in which our ignorance is focused: not in the details of neurophysiological activity but, more fundamentally, in how space is structured or constituted. That which we refer to when we use the word 'space' has a nature that is quite different from how we standardly conceive it to be; so different, indeed, that it is capable of 'containing' the non-spatial (as we now conceive it) phenomenon of consciousness. Things in space can generate consciousness only because those things are not, at some level, just how we conceive them to be; they harbour some hidden aspect or principle.

Before I try to motivate this hypothesis further, let me explain why I think the needed conceptual shift goes deeper than mere brain physiology, down to physics itself. For, if I am right, then it is not just the science of matter in the head that is deficient but the science of matter spread more widely.[12] A bad reason for insisting that the incompleteness reaches down as far as physics is the assumption that physiology *reduces* to physics, so that any incompleteness in the reduced theory must be reflected in the reducing theory. This is a bad reason because it is a mistake to think that the so-called special sciences—geology, biology, information science, psychology, etc.—reduce to physics. I will not rehearse the usual arguments for this, since they have been well marshalled

---

[12] Penrose (1989) also takes consciousness to challenge the adequacy of current physics.

elsewhere.[13] If that were the right way to look at the matter, then physics would be *highly* incomplete and defective on many fronts, since all the special sciences have outstanding unsolved problems. But it is surely grotesque to claim that the problem of how (say) the dinosaurs became extinct shows any inadequacy in the basic laws of physics! Rather, the intransitivity of problems down the heirarchy of the sciences is itself a reason to reject any reductionist view of their interrelations. So it is certainly an open question whether the problem of consciousness requires revisions in neuro-physiology alone, or whether those revisions will upset broader reaches of physical theory. It depends entirely on what is the correct diagnosis of the essential core of the problem. And what I am suggesting is that the correct diagnosis involves a challenge to our general conception of space. Given the fact of emergence, matter in space has to have features that go beyond the usual conception, in order that something as spatially anomalous as consciousness could have thereby come into existence. Somehow the unextended can issue from matter in space, and this must depend upon properties of the basis that permit such a derivation. It therefore seems hard to avoid the conclusion that the requisite properties are instantiated by matter prior to its organization into brain structure. The brain must draw upon aspects of nature that were already there. According to our earlier speculation, these aspects may be connected to features of the universe that played a part in the early creation of matter and space itself—those features, themselves pre-spatial, that characterized the universe before the big bang. Consciousness is so singular, ontologically, and such an affront to our standard spatial notions, that some pretty remarkable properties of matter will be needed in order to sustain the assumption that consciousness can come from matter. It is not likely that we need merely a local conceptual revolution.

[13] See, for instance, J. Fodor, 'Special Sciences', 1974, *Synthese* 28: 77–115.

III: The Nature of Space

Let us perform an induction over the history of science. There is what might be called a 'folk theory of space', a set of beliefs about the general nature of space that comes naturally to human beings in advance of doing any systematic science. It probably develops, in part, out of our perceptual systems and it serves to guide our behaviour; we might think of it as a visuo-motor space. No doubt it would be difficult to describe this mental representation of space in full detail, but I think it is fair to report that it encodes a broadly Euclidean geometry and that it regards motion as relative to the position of the earth. It also has some firm ideas about what it is for something to *be* somewhere. Now it is a platitude of the history of science that this folk theory has come under successive challenges, which have substantially undermined and reformed it. Indeed, most of the big advances in physics and astronomy have involved revising our folk theory of space. Let me mention, sketchily, a few of these, to give flavour to what I am building up to. First, of course, there was the replacement of the geocentric view of the universe with the heliocentric one, and then the replacement of that with an a-centric view. The Newtonian scheme takes the earth to be just one body in space among others, subject to the same laws of motion; our earthly position does not define some privileged coordinate with respect to which everything else must be measured. We must also recognize the existence of a new force, gravity, which acts across space without benefit of a mechanical medium. Thus space has a hitherto unsuspected power—which Newton himself regarded as dubiously 'occult'. Later, and just as famously, the developments surrounding relativity theory called for the abandonment of a Euclidean conception of physical space, to be replaced by geometries that are counter-intuitive to the folk theory of space. Curved space-time was the upshot, among other exotica. Quantum theory also prompts serious questions about the nature of space: particles have no unique location, and various 'non-locality effects' upset our usual ideas about physical things and their causal dependence. What it is to be *in* space becomes obscure. Then we have such speculations as string theory and twistor theory and the many-worlds hypothesis, in which further 'hidden' dimensions are introduced. Our folk theory of space has been regularly hung out to dry. From the point of view of the divine physicist, space must look to be a very different creature from that presented to the visuo-motor system of human beings.

All this is suggestive of a certain diagnosis of the problem with respect to consciousness. For here too we have a phenomenon that puts pressure on our ordinary conception of space. Conscious phenomena are not located and extended in the usual way; but then again they are surely not somehow 'outside' of space, adjacent perhaps to the abstract realm. Rather, they bear an opaque and anomalous relation to space as currently conceived. They seem neither quite 'in' it nor quite 'out' of it. Presumably, however, this is merely an epistemological fact, not an ontological one. It is just that we lack the theory with which to make sense of the relation in question. In themselves consciousness and space must be related in some intelligible naturalistic fashion, though they may have to be conceived very differently from the way they now are for this to become apparent. My conjecture is that it is in this nexus that the solution to the space problem lies. Consciousness is the next big anomaly to call for a revision in how we conceive space—just as other revisions were called for by earlier anomalies. And the revision is likely to be large-scale, despite the confinement of consciousness to certain small pockets of the natural world. This is because space is such a fundamental feature of things that anything that produces disturbances in our conception of it must cut pretty deeply into our world-view.

No doubt this is all very mind-stretching and obscure; and it is of course not a theory but an indication of where the correct theory might lie. There is a rather Kantian ring to it, what with noumenal space containing all the answers that phenomenal space cannot provide. But I am not really distressed by the lack of transparency of the conjecture, because I think that it is quite *predictable* that our intellects should falter when trying to make sense of the place of consciousness in the natural order.[14] And here the bitter pill beneath the sweet coating begins to seep through. For to suggest that we need a radically new conception of space is not to imply that we *can achieve* any such conception, even in principle. It may be merely to point to the place at which we are incurably ignorant. To explain what I mean let us back up for a while to consider the question of human epistemology—the question of what we can and cannot know.

IV: The Limits of Human Knowledge

It is easier not to know than to know. That truism has long had its philosophical counterpart in rueful admissions that there are non-trivial limits on what human beings can come to grasp. The human epistemic system has a specific structure and mode of operation, and there may well be realities that lie beyond its powers of coverage. Chomsky, in particular, regards our cognitive system as a collection of special-purpose modules that target specific areas of competence, and fail to target others.[15] The language faculty is one of these, which itself breaks down into a number of sub-modules. It is targeted away from certain possible languages as a by-product of its positive targeting: human languages, yes; Martian languages, no. Chomsky adopts essentially the same conception of what he calls our 'science-forming' faculties: they too are just a collection of contingent cognitive structures, biologically based, that have arisen in us over the course of evolution. They have a phylogeny and an ontogeny, and they operate according to certain specific principles,

[14] See n. 9 above and my *Problems in Philosophy* (Oxford: Blackwell, 1993).
[15] N. Chomsky, *Reflections on Language* (London: Fontana, 1976) and *Language and Problems of Knowledge* (Cambridge, Mass.: MIT Press, 1988).

these being realized by machinery in the brain. They are as natural as any organ of the body. Given this, there is absolutely no reason to believe that the faculties in question are capable, at this period in our evolution, of understanding everything there is about the natural world. Viewing the matter in a properly naturalistic spirit, with the human species counted as just one evolved species among others, the overwhelming probability is that we are subject to definite limits on our powers of understanding, just as every other species is. We hardly suppose that the bipedal species who preceded us, traces of which sometimes show up in the fossil record, were themselves as intellectually advanced as we are, with our massively protruding frontal lobes and impressive manual dexterity. We just need to project ourselves into the position of the species that might succeed us to see how contingent and limited our capacities are.

This general viewpoint makes one open to the possibility that some problems may simply exceed our cognitive competence. But I think something more specific is suggested by our discussion so far: namely, that our troubles over space and consciousness arise from certain deep-seated features of the way we represent space to ourselves. We are, cognitively speaking as well as physically, spatial beings *par excellence*: our entire conceptual scheme is shot through with spatial notions, these providing the skeleton of our thought in general. Experience itself, the underpinning of thought, is spatial to its core. The world as we find it—the human world—is a pre-eminently spatial world. This is a line of thinking powerfully advocated by P. F. Strawson, who focuses particularly on the role of space in our practices of identification.[16] The guiding Strawsonian thesis is that the distinction between particular and universal, and hence between subject and predicate, is founded on the idea, or experience, of spatial distinctness. We regard x and y as distinct

[16] See P. F. Strawson, *Individuals* (London: Methuen, 1959) and *Subject and Predicate in Logic and Grammar* (London: Methuen, 1974).

particular instances of the same universal P just in so far as we acknowledge that x and y are *at distinct places*. That is what the non-identity of particulars fundamentally consists in for us. Without that spatial resource we should not be able to frame the conception of multiple instances of a single property. This implies that the very notion of a proposition presupposes the notion of spatial separation, and hence location. At root, then, our entire structure of thought is based upon a conception of space in which objects are severally arrayed; though once this structure is in place we can extend and refine it by means of analogy and relations of conceptual dependence.

Now consider thought about consciousness. The non-spatiality of consciousness presents a prima facie problem for our system of thought: how, if the Strawsonian thesis is right, do we contrive to think about consciousness at all? It ought to be impossible. The answer lies in those analogies and dependencies just mentioned. We go in for spatializing metaphors and, centrally, we exploit relations to the *body* in making sense of numerically distinct but similar conscious episodes. We embed the mental in the conceptual framework provided by matter in space. We don't *reduce* it to that framework; we appeal, rather, to systematic relations that the two realms manifest. But—and this is the crucial point for me—this is to impose upon conscious events a conceptual grid that is alien to their intrinsic nature. It is as if we must resort to a spatial scheme because nothing else is available to us, given our *de facto* reliance on spatial conceptions. It is not that this scheme is ideally fitted to embed the target subject-matter. Thus we get a kind of partial fit in which location is causally based and notions of extension find no purchase at all. Consciousness comes out looking queasily quasi-spatial, a deformed hybrid. Deep down we know it isn't just extended matter in space, but our modes of thought drag it in that direction, producing much philosophical confusion. We represent the mental by relying upon our folk theory of space because that theory lies at the root of our being able to represent at all—not because the mental itself has a nature that craves such a mode of representation.[17]

To represent consciousness as it is in itself—neat, as it were—we would need to let go of the spatial skeleton of our thought. But, according to the Strawsonian thesis, that would be to let go of the very notion of a proposition, leaving us nothing to think with. So there is no real prospect of our achieving a spatially non-derivative style of thought about consciousness. But then, there is no prospect of our developing a set of concepts that is truly adequate to the intrinsic nature of consciousness; we will always be haunted by the ill-fitting spatial scheme. No doubt this lies behind the sense of total theoretical blankness that attends our attempts to fathom the nature of consciousness; we stare agape in a vacuum of incomprehension. Our conceptual lens is optically out of focus, skewed, and myopic, with too much space in the field of view. We can form thoughts *about* conscious states, but we cannot articulate the natural constitution of what we are thinking about. It is the spatial bias of our thinking that stands in our way (along perhaps with other impediments). And without a more adequate articulation of consciousness we are not going to be in a position to come up with the unifying theory that must link consciousness to the world of matter in space. We are not going to discover what space must be like *such that* consciousness can have its origin in that sphere. Clearly, the space of perception and action is no place to find the roots of consciousness! In that sense of 'space' consciousness is not spatial; but we seem unable to develop a new conception of space that can overcome the impossibility of finding a place for consciousness in it.[18]

[17] The inadequacy of spatially-based identification of conscious particulars is my contention, not Strawson's; he seems far more sanguine that the spatial scheme is satisfactory for talk of the mental.
[18] Cf. cognitive beings who have mastered Euclidean geometry but who constitutionally lack the mathematical ability to develop non-Euclidean geometry. An instructive parable on cognitive limitation, with special reference to space and

I am presupposing here a robust form of realism about the natural world. The constraint to form our concepts in a certain way does not entail that reality must match that way. Our knowledge constitutes a kind of 'best fit' between our cognitive structure and the objective world; and it fits better in some domains than others. The mind is an area of relatively poor fit. Consciousness occurs in objective reality in a perfectly naturalistic way; we just have no access to its real inner constitution. Perhaps surprisingly, consciousness is one of the more knowledge-transcendent constituents of reality. It must not be forgotten that knowledge is the product of a biological organ whose architecture is fashioned by evolution for brutely pragmatic purposes. Since our bodies are extended objects in space, and since the fate of these bodies is crucial to our reproductive prospects, we need a guidance system in our heads that will enable us to navigate the right trajectory through space, avoiding some objects (predators, poisons, precipices) while steering us close to others (friends, food, feather beds). Thus our space-representing faculties have a quite specific set of goals that by no means coincide with solving the deep ontological problems surrounding consciousness and space. Many animals are expert navigators without having the faintest idea about the true objective structure of space. (The eagle, for one, still awaits its sharp-beaked Newton.) There is no good reason to expect our basic forms of spatial representation to lead smoothly to the ideal theory of the universe. What we need from space, practically speaking, is by no means the same as how space is structured in itself.

I suspect that the very depth of embeddedness of space in our cognitive system produces in us the illusion that we understand it much better than we do. After all, we *see* it whenever we open our eyes and we *feel* it in our bodies as we move. (Time has a similar

geometry, is E. A. Abbott's, *Flatland: A Romance of Many Dimensions* (New York: Signet Classic, 1884). I am saying that we too are Flatlanders of a sort: we tend to take the space of our experience as the only space there is or could be.

status.) Hence the large cognitive shocks brought about by the changes in our view of space required by systematic science. We are prone to think that we *can't* be all that wrong about space. I have been arguing that consciousness tests the adequacy of our spatial understanding. It marks the place of a deep lack of knowledge about space, which is hard even to get into focus. No doubt it is difficult to accept that two of the things with which we are most familiar might harbour such intractable obscurities. Irony being a mark of truth, however, we should take seriously the possibility that what we tend to think completely transparent should turn out to transcend altogether our powers of comprehension.

6

Consciousness, Atomism, and the Ancient Greeks

Atomism about matter was not always the entrenched and incontestable theory it is today. Originally, it was a bold and virtually groundless speculation—a sheer stab in the dark.[1] Only much later did it receive serious confirmation (and elaboration). The basic idea of atomism is that the physical substances that we observe, in all their immense variety, might be composed of imperceptible units, relatively few in number, whose various combinations give rise to observed reality. The properties of these hidden units explain the behaviour and interactions of the manifest substances, so that we may derive descriptions of the macroscopic world from information about the microscopic world. Since the atomic units themselves are not observed, they are initially introduced as theoretical posits, justified by their explanatory power. By definition, they are simple—that is, not composed of more elementary parts—and hence have no further explanation in terms of

---

[1] See Anthony Gottlieb, *The Dream of Reason* (W. W. Norton: 2000), ch. 8, for a lively account of the early days of atomism. This book is also my main source for the ideas of the Greek philosophers I discuss later; indeed, it was reading (and reviewing) this book that prompted the idea for the present paper.

composition. They exist in some sort of medium—space or 'the void'—and they are subject to certain sorts of adhesive force—that which holds them together into the stable forms that we observe. Thus atomism is a *reductive* theory, in that it seeks to account for apparent natural variety in terms of relatively homogeneous elements; the world is more parsimonious than it appears, more uniform. Atomism views the manifest world as a series of variations on a small number of themes—with the themes not apparent to the naked eye. It decomposes the variety of the world into simpler unobserved units.

In this paper I want to explore the possibility that atomism might also be true of the mind, specifically of consciousness. I do *not* mean by this the idea that the mind might be composed of the *same* atoms that matter is composed of; my question is not whether *materialistic* atomism might be true. My question is more abstract: might *some* version of atomism be true of consciousness? That is: might the mind be composed of unobservable units, relatively few in number, that combine to produce the richly varied phenomenology that we find in mental life? Might there be a reduction of the varieties of consciousness to the properties of these atoms, where these properties would permit a derivation of the manifest properties of consciousness—an explanatory theory analogous to our atomic theory of matter? Whether these atoms of mind are 'physical' or 'mental' (or whether these are useful or meaningful categories) is not my chief concern; I am concerned with the *structure* of the theory—whether it fulfils the abstract description of atomism so far presented. The question is whether consciousness might have an *analysis* (in roughly the chemist's sense) into atomic elements that combine to generate its manifest qualities—whatever the nature of these elements turns out to be. In other words, is anything *analogous* to the atomic theory of matter true of the mind?

In order to pursue this question, I propose that we revisit the ancient Greeks. My reason for proposing this is that I believe that the current state of understanding of the mind resembles pre-Socratic understanding (or the lack of it) of the material world, so that we can derive some valuable lessons by comparing our own state of knowledge to theirs. Of course, *they* had no appreciation of how primitive their theories were—those theories no doubt impressed their proponents as the height of sophistication; and I believe that we too have an overly rosy perspective on the adequacy of our present understanding of consciousness.[2] Indeed, there are striking parallels between the theories contemplated then—and no doubt maintained with great seriousness and vehemence—and our contemporary theories of the mind. This, then, is to be a lesson in humility—or historical perspective (which may be the same thing). Atomism, I shall suggest, is the best bet in the current state of knowledge, i.e. ignorance. It is not that we can *know* atomism to be true, but as stabs in the dark go it is a pretty good one—about as good as the stabs of the ancient atomists.

When Democritus first hit upon the atomic theory it was totally speculative, with almost no empirical support or explanatory success; it was a theory schema, pulled from thin air, an overreaching hunch. It is said that he noticed motes of dust in the air and conceived the idea that all of matter might be composed of such tiny parts, only tinier.[3] The level of explanation was along the lines of postulating sharp spikes on the atoms composing certain foods to explain their bitter taste—that is, wholly false. But Democritus did, crucially, have the idea that there ought to be *some* explanation of this form—some account of the macro in terms of the micro. He sensed that the observable world might conceal its own workings—the right level of explanation might go beyond anything that we can observe. This was his central insight—an idea about the

---

[2] Of course, since I believe that the mind-body problem is insoluble (within the scope of our present conceptual faculties) I certainly think that we overestimate our current grip on the problem.

[3] *The Dream of Reason*, 99.

form of the correct theory. The theory was, of course, widely dismissed in the ancient world, even ridiculed; but as we all know it was spectacularly confirmed some two millennia later, though in a form that Democritus could hardly have envisaged. It was the best theory in the ancient world, though it didn't look like it then; it was just too bold, too distant from common observation.[4] Less ambitious theories looked better to ancient thinkers. My conjecture is that the same is true of atomism about consciousness now: it looks wild, unfounded, counter-intuitive, but it will turn out to be the best theory—better than its contemporary rivals, for all their seeming sanity. Let me then recall those ancient theories and indicate their contemporary counterparts in theories of the mind. I hope this will not appear frivolous, though the humour is sometimes hard to resist; there is a serious point to it.

The pre-Socratics were committed naturalists—no appeal to supernatural entities and forces. Not surprisingly, their theories tended to be grossly reductionist. Thales is the paradigm, with his bracingly simple proposal that 'everything is water'. Water comes in several forms—ice, liquid, steam—and is essential to life, so maybe we can reduce everything to water. It *seems* as if there is a greater richness to nature than this—more types of substance— but maybe variations on the water theme can account for everything. Fire? A very agitated form of water (if you pour calm water on it the agitation ceases). Earth? Coagulated water. Air? Exceedingly light thin water. Soul? Well . . . we do need water in order to keep the soul alive. So it's not as if Thales had nothing to say about these natural questions, though indeed the theory looks remarkably far-fetched. It is the same with Anaximines' theory that all is air. The theory certainly has an economical basis—Occam would

---

[4] Democritus' methodology conforms nicely to the Popperian model of science, in that he was not daunted by the ungroundedness of his theory in observation, nor deterred by its lack of confirmation; he freely put forward a bold conjecture, letting his imagination run away with him. He did not, however, seem overly concerned about trying to falsify his theory—though the theory is certainly falsifiable in principle.

have approved—and air is obviously implicated in life through the process of breathing, and maybe air can take solid forms (steam and air are similar, and steam can turn to water), and fire might be very hot air. Like the water theory, the air theory strikes us as too sparing in its allowable theoretical primitives, but it is not as if these theories are just mad ravings or pieces of poetry—they have their rational motivations.

Now what do these two theories remind you of? They remind me of the various brands of materialistic reduction that have gripped more recent thinkers—particularly, behaviourism and 'central state' materialism. Faced with the seeming heterogeneity that separates mind from matter, consciousness from the brain and body, and also with the heterogeneity within the mind, materialists assure us that this is all illusory: really 'all is body'. In the central state version, we are told that neurons and their firings are a sufficient basis for every aspect of consciousness: consciousness itself is 'really' just the firing of neurons, appearances notwith-standing, and the distinctions between conscious states—say, between seeing red and feeling pain—are really nothing but variations on the neural firing theme (faster or slower firings, or where in the brain the firing takes place). There are neural states 'corresponding' to conscious states, so why not invoke Occam's razor and simply identify the two? Granted, it *seems* hard to believe—mental states are not on their face neural states—but then science has often surprised us. Thus the materialist reconciles himself to the less palatable aspects of his view; and he can also ask what *else* you have to offer if you don't like what he is peddling.[5]

Now I am not here attempting to *argue* that materialism is false; I am simply making a tendentious comparison between certain aspects of the debate about materialism and what occurs to anyone

---

[5] Surely the main reason people have for accepting materialism is the avoidance of dualism—that is, the reasons are negative in nature. It is scarcely that materialism is on the face of it an attractive view: it *seems* false—as even its most ardent proponents agree.

thinking about the theories of Thales and Anaximines. And I do think there is a striking similarity here: water and air are taken as given, and then the rest of nature is squeezed into these boxes; similarly, matter is taken as given, and then we have to squeeze the mind into that category in the form of firing neurons—as a minor variation on the basic theme of matter. Might materialism actually be as crude a theory as those old theories? Did the theories of Thales and Anaximines seem crude to *them*? Surely they seemed like the cutting edge of human thought, and anyway no one around at the time had a better theory. Their manifest defects could be put down to their novelty and audacity. Materialism might strike you as counter-intuitive, even absurd, when you first encounter it, but you can school yourself to accept its levelling consequences—and there are always 'moves' that can be made to ward off the doubters.[6]

Or consider Pythagoras: he held, in effect, that 'all is number'. He had the curious view that physical objects were composed of numbers—that they were abstract and mathematical. They don't *look* as if they are composed of numbers, but actually they are; they can be mathematically described, and this is because they are themselves mathematical. Remind you of anything? What about contemporary computational functionalism? Mental processes are computational procedures, abstract properties of brains, which can be modelled by computer programs. Granted they don't *seem* this way to introspection—they seem somehow 'subjective'—but in reality they are abstract functions, mathematically describable

---

[6] Thus contemporary identity theorists will patiently explain to doubters that they are confusing concepts with properties: when it seems to us that pain is not C-fibre firing this is merely a reflection of the distinctness of the two *concepts*, not a matter of there really being two properties here. In the same way, a contemporary Thales who has read his Frege might insist that 'electricity = water' (for example) is true, since the property of being electricity is identical to the property of being water, even though the two *concepts* admittedly differ; and that any opposition to his identification rests upon a lamentable confusion of sense and reference. I will leave it to the reader to play this move out with the Thalean counterpart of black-and-white Mary, etc.

operations. A computer program is an abstract algorithm, which is 'realized' in the hardware of the computer; similarly, a mental state is just a state of such an algorithm, 'realized' in the brain. This is not a materialist view, since mathematical entities are not reducible to physical entities—hence the possibility of 'multiple realization'—but it is reductive nonetheless. In the same way, Pythagoras' theory of physical objects is not 'materialist', since he explains such objects in terms of abstract numbers; and, yes, maybe the same collection of numbers might crop up in (be 'realized by') distinct objects.[7] Pythagoras held that objects are really 'software', just as the contemporary functionalist holds that mental states are just software. After all, we get such a nice *theory* if we adopt these mathematizing reductions: both physics and psychology turn out to be branches of mathematics.

What about contemporary eliminativism—does it have an ancient counterpart? Parmenides was puzzled about change; he couldn't see how it was possible. So he declared it illusory, along with the entire observable world. In his view, 'all is one', and diversity is an illusion too. The world of changing diverse objects is declared unreal, a prejudice of common sense that cannot withstand rational scrutiny. Zeno, influenced by Parmenides, famously declared motion unreal, because of his paradoxes; he 'eliminated' motion from his world-view. These were acknowledged to be extreme moves, radically counter to common sense, but they seemed by their proponents to be backed by solid sceptical arguments. Here I am reminded of the whole eliminativist tradition from Quine and Rorty, to the Churchlands, to Kripke's 'sceptical paradox'. Quine can make no sense of reference (as Parmenides could make no sense of change), so he eliminates it;[8] the Churchlands can't fit folk psychology into their preconceived scientific

[7] Being triangular, say, is a mathematical property of a concrete particular, and it may be exemplified by many such particulars, each having its own varying constitution ('multiple realization').

[8] Hence the indeterminacy of reference: see Quine's *Word and Object* (MIT Press: 1960).

picture of human beings, so it is jettisoned;[9] Kripke's sceptic (just like Zeno) claims to find a real paradox at the heart of the notion of meaning—it just doesn't seem *possible*—and so proposes to abandon the idea that meaning is a *fact*.[10] Each of these thinkers argues himself into the denial that apparently self-evident facts are real— no change, no motion, no beliefs, no meanings, no mind. It turns out there is a lot less to the world than we thought; desert landscapes, etc. The more robustly commonsensical among us shake our heads at such sweepingly eliminative recommendations.

Panpsychism has a beautiful precursor in the shape of Anaxagoras. Anaxagoras was deeply puzzled about how hair grows on the head: hair luxuriantly cascades about the scalp, but where does it come from—after all, there is no hair *inside* the head from which it might proceed?[11] Come to think of it, how does anything turn into anything else? How does bread become flesh and bone? His answer was radical: it's because every substance contains a little bit of every other substance ('all is all', as one might say). Hair grows from the scalp because the scalp itself contains tiny hair-like elements; indeed, hair comes from bread, through digestion, because bread has slivers of hair in it too—though these hairy portions are too small to see. And there must be hairy elements in whatever bread comes from. Pan-hairism! Anaxagoras has a real explanatory problem—how to explain the 'emergence' of hair from heads—and he solves it with a bold stroke—he postulates hair in the head already, but in unobservable form. We might call these theoretical posits 'proto-hairs', since they are not quite full-blown hairs, but they have hair-*ish* properties. Compare: how does consciousness emerge from the brain, given that the brain seems so different from consciousness? Answer: the brain is composed of material elements that themselves have mental properties, and

[9] See Paul Churchland, 'Eliminative Materialism and the Propositional Attitudes', *Journal of Philosophy* 78: 67–90, 1981.

[10] See Saul Kripke, *Wittgenstein on Rules and Private Language* (Harvard University Press: 1982).

[11] On Anaxagoras and the origin of hair see *The Dream of Reason*, ch. 7.

indeed such properties are found in matter generally. Panpsychism![12] These properties might be called 'protomental', since they are not full-blown conscious states, but they do have the seeds of consciousness within them—they are conscious-*ish*. This, too, is a response to a genuine explanatory problem, and the logic of the response seems exactly analogous to Anaxagoras' response to his problem. The resulting doctrines are admittedly startling, perhaps offensive to common sense, but they are the only things that *could* explain what needs to be explained. True, there isn't any direct evidence for hairs in every bit of matter, or for mental states in every molecule, but there *have* to be such things or else the world makes no sense.

What about the more moderate thinkers of antiquity? Empedocles suggested, non-reductively enough, that the natural world is composed of four elements—air, earth, fire, and water. Each is primitive; none can be reduced to the others. For him, Thales was a crude dogmatic reductionist; there was more to heaven and earth than forms of water. Empedocles has his counterpart in the non-reductive theorists of today—everyone from Cartesian dualists to non-reductive materialists like Davidson.[13] Water and fire are distinct, *sui generis* and 'incommensurable'; there are no (strict) water/fire laws; yet there are causal interactions between the two (water puts fires out and fires heat water). Empedocles had four fundamental constituents; nowadays we have two (mind and matter). There is no true completion of 'all is . . .'. Such theorists make no attempt to explain how mind and matter are related—how the former 'emerges' from the latter—just as Empedocles made no attempt to explain how one of his elements might come

---

[12] See Thomas Nagel, 'Panpsychism', in his *Mortal Questions* (Cambridge University Press: 1979), and David Chalmers, *The Conscious Mind* (Oxford University Press: 1996). The doctrine of 'panexperientialism', in its Whiteheadian form, is taken with deadly seriousness by David Ray Griffin in *Unsnarling the World-Knot* (University of California Press: 1998).

[13] See Donald Davidson, 'Mental Events', in his *Essays on Actions and Events* (Oxford University Press: 1980).

from the others or specify what fundamental properties they might share. He was content simply to declare a set of basic divisions within reality. After all, look into what absurdities the reductionist drive had led others!

Then there is good old Socrates, a relative latecomer to these debates. Socrates, it is reported, tired of these ancient debates, after a youthful infatuation with them, viewing them as so much groundless speculation—they were not fit subjects to deliver genuine knowledge.[14] Thereafter, he devoted himself to ethics, which he felt offered a greater chance of knowledge. His position on questions of natural philosophy was one of resolute agnosticism. This, I think, confirms Socrates' reputation for wisdom: he saw that all this speculation was precisely that and didn't want to waste his life in fruitless wrangling over unknowable matters. As it turned out, this wrangling eventually metamorphosed into genuine science, but in the ancient world this was very far from being the case. Socrates was a pessimist about finding out the truths of natural philosophy, so he turned to ethical questions (about which he was also highly pessimistic). His emphasis on human ignorance no doubt reflects his youthful frustrations over the science of nature. His contemporary counterpart is the sceptic who questions all current theories of the nature of consciousness (Nagel would be a good example).[15] I too sense a deep well of ignorance here, with the various theories on offer merely crude attempts to come to grips with the phenomena. But in this paper I am interested in trying out the atomist vision; not because I think we will soon (or ever) be able to convert this vision into an actual theory—rather, as a speculation about what the *form* of a correct theory might be like. And I expect my speculations to be at least as crude and groundless as Democritus' were; that, indeed, is part of my point.

[14] See *The Dream of Reason*, 87.
[15] Thomas Nagel, 'What is it like to be a Bat?' in his *Mortal Questions*, in which agnosticism is the dominant note.

But let me first make a comment about materialistic atomism—the theory that the mind consists of material atoms, the same ones that compose brains. This is the thesis that the varieties of conscious phenomena are simply aspects of the atomic constitution of those phenomena: chemical kinds are aspects of atomic constitution, and so are phenomenal kinds. Properties of consciousness are therefore explicable in terms of the properties of physical atoms, just as properties of chemicals are. This is clearly a highly reductive theory, and the reduction proceeds upon the basis of an atomistic conception of the nature of mental phenomena. The point I want to make about this theory is that it is a responsible and respectable materialistic theory of the mind—though one that we have no good reason to believe and a lot of reason to disbelieve. But it has the *form* of a decent theory, because of the explanatory obligations it acknowledges; it accepts the same obligations as an atomistic theory of chemical phenomena does. It is no mere 'identity theory', according to which it is more or less *stipulated* that mental states are physical states like neural firings. Atomism is a claim of explanatory power, and it earns its right to be taken seriously by making good on its explanatory obligations. The simple identity theory does not do this. Thus the difference between, say, seeing red and feeling pain must be reductively explained in terms of the differences in the properties of the underlying physical atoms, since materialism of this kind must claim that every distinction is a physical distinction, and physical distinctions must always come down to differences in the properties of atoms—in particular, the nature of the particles that make up the atoms (electrons, protons, etc.). I think it is obvious that no such explanation of the phenomenal has ever been given, and indeed it is hard to see how it *could* be given. So there can be no atomistic reduction of the mental in the way there is an atomistic reduction of the chemical. The broader kind of atomistic reduction I am contemplating in this paper will not then take the form of reducing the mind to *physical* atoms (of the kind now known about). Mental kinds are not *this* type of atomic kind. I am envisaging a theory that does for phenomenal kinds what our physical atomic theory does for chemical kinds—and cannot do for phenomenal kinds.

The kind of atomism I have in mind is not committed to any such materialism. It says simply that conscious states and processes consist of underlying states and processes that are not observed but which combine to produce what we do observe. We can assume that these underlying entities are not elsewhere observable; they are not part of what we ordinarily take the world to contain—any more than the atoms of Democritus or modern atoms are. So I am *not* taking them to be *phenomenal* atoms—that is, elements of consciousness derivable by phenomenological analysis. They are nothing like the constituents of sense-data that some philosophers have posited. They are essentially *hidden*, and presumably conceptually alien—just like physical atoms.[16] Of course, I have no idea what they are like intrinsically; all I am suggesting is that they exist and compose the mind according to some principles or laws of combination. When you put the atoms together in certain ways you get a sensation of red, say; and this result is wholly explicable in terms of the properties of the atoms—just as the properties of a chemical are so explicable in terms of physical atoms. The appropriate theory is therefore fully reductive. We can also suppose, following the physical model, that the types of consciousness atoms are relatively few in number, so that we can derive the richness of mental life from a smaller set of primitives; an underlying uniformity is masked by the surface variety of the mind. Physical atoms consist of a nucleus and revolving charged particles; from this we can derive the properties of the composed substances. In the case of the atoms of consciousness we can expect a similar simplicity of underlying reality; so the mind is

[16] See my 'The Hidden Structure of Consciousness' in *The Problem of Consciousness* (Basil Blackwell: 1991). I am here suggesting an atomistic conception of the hidden structure I postulated in that earlier paper.

simpler than it seems—just as the physical world is. Physical atoms also exist in space and enjoy spatial relations to each other. It is doubtful that mental atoms can be conceived in this way, at least as space is now understood, because the mind does not appear to be spatially describable (in current terms);[17] but presumably they too must exist in *some* sort of medium, within which they can separate and combine. Physical atoms can also exist in a detached form, not as part of a macroscopic object; at any rate, they can be conceived apart from other atoms. So we might expect that atoms of the mind can (be conceived to) exist in a detached form, pre- or post-consciousness. Where these atoms might exist, independently of constituting a full-blown mind, we cannot say; but we cannot rule out their existence in other places (or 'places').

Is this panpsychism by another name? Well, it doesn't say that mental atoms are everywhere, nor that physical atoms have conscious (or proto-conscious) properties, nor that we have any idea what the intrinsic nature of the atoms of mind is. It shares with panpsychism only the idea that there is a hidden theoretical level of specifically mind-generating properties—but unlike panpsychism, properly so called, it does not identify these properties *as mental*, in the sense that the concepts that express them are anything like our concepts of the mind.[18] Also, panpsychism isn't generally an explicitly atomistic doctrine, claiming that conscious states have atomic structure in their own right. For all we have said, the atoms of mind might compose a Cartesian immaterial substance; so there is nothing in the theory as such to entail the distinctive doctrines of

[17] See my 'Consciousness and Space', in *Conscious Experience*, ed. Thomas Metzinger (Schoningh: 1995); also my *The Mysterious Flame* (Basic Books: 1999), ch. 4.

[18] It is vital here to distinguish ontological from conceptual questions: of course the putative atoms of mind are ontologically mental, since they constitute consciousness; but it does not follow that the concepts appropriate to their articulation are anything like our current mental concepts. My expectation is that the appropriate concepts will bear little resemblance to our present concepts, though they will be *of* the same thing—that is, they will be concepts that somehow make reference to mental phenomena. Compare the way the concepts of quantum theory refer to what we comonsensically think of as tables and chairs.

panpsychism. Just as Anaxagoras' doctrine includes some atomistic ingredients, because the bits of hair in everything are microscopic, so panpsychism contains a hint of atomism; but Anaxagoras' doctrine is not the same as Democritus'—as panpsychism is not the same as mental atomism. In fact, atomism about the mind is not itself a theory of emergence at all; it is a theory about the intrinsic nature of mental phenomena. It doesn't attempt to explain how consciousness arises from brain cells; it says what kind of *constitution* conscious minds have.[19]

Is there any positive reason to believe the atomistic theory? Very little, so far as I can see—just as there was very little reason to believe the atomic theory at the time it was first enunciated. I am describing the theory, not endorsing it—as anything other than a hunch, a theoretical throb. But there are a couple of points that might seem suggestive. First, it does appear that consciousness is ontologically dependent on the brain (not just causally), and the brain is a physical substance composed of physical atoms—so it would make sense to suppose that consciousness has an atomic structure too. It would be odd if it were a *continuous* thing, given that it arises from a non-continuous substance. And it would be odd if its atomic nature were not hidden, given that the atomic constitution of its basis (the brain) is hidden. How can brain and mind mesh if one is atomic and the other is not?[20] (I mean this to sound like one of those suspicious but ingenious arguments that the ancient Greeks were so fond of.) Secondly, what model of

[19] So mental atomism is *not* being offered as a solution to the mind-body problem, any more than atomism about material objects (such as the brain) is meant as a solution to that problem.

[20] Might there be some sort of detailed *isomorphism* between brain and consciousness, given that the constituents of a complex neural correlate probably play a role in constructing the fine structure of the correlated state of consciousness? That is, it seems likely that the complexity of the neural correlate plays a constructive role in generating the mental state, thus suggesting that the mental state has a corresponding complexity—which may be hidden to introspection (as the complexity of the neural correlate is). This kind of fine-grained dependence suggests atomism about the mind—a hidden articulation to the mental state.

change do we have if we cannot base it on the idea of atomic structure? When physical objects change their atomic parts get rearranged; there is no macro-change without a micro-change. The mind changes too, of course, as mental states come and go; it seems reasonable to suppose that this also is a matter of the rearrangement of its parts.[21] The changes we observe are the reflection of changes at the underlying level, as the atoms come and go and connect to other atoms. Changes in the stream of consciousness are the visible upshot of a vast sea of changes at the atomic level. Of course, none of this is probative, to put it mildly, but at least the idea makes some sort of theoretical sense—it is not just groundless assertion, or fatuous poetry.

Let me emphasize that I don't *want* this theory to be provable, on empirical or a priori grounds. My view is that our ignorance is far too deep to allow any such knowledge. I mean to be occupying a position analogous to that of Democritus so long ago: this is a theory to which I have taken a fancy, that has come to me from thin air, that I really have no right to hold. But, as Democritus' theory was eventually so stunningly vindicated, so this theory might be (or might not); in any case, it has been stated. At least I have the success story of Democritus to encourage me; he had nothing but an obscure intuition with no antecedents. To tell the truth, I have a stubborn conviction that the atomic theory of consciousness *has* to be true—that nothing else is on the cards; but, as I say, I have no right to this view, or to my reader's assent to it. Have I even had anything like Democritus' experience of the dust motes in the light? Not really, except perhaps seeing those little points of iridescence that inhabit the visual field as one tries to go to sleep at night; and maybe an obscure intimation that beneath the surface of my consciousness there throbs a universe of discrete

---

[21] I don't of course mean anything as innocuous as the rearrangement of concepts that occurs when we think different thoughts; I mean something much further removed from the way we now break thoughts into parts. Compare the way an engine has functional parts and the way *those* parts have a hidden atomic structure.

and buzzing nodes of sensitivity—little blobs of mind dust. But here I stray, lamentably, into poetry, worthy perhaps of a bemused and probing ancient Greek. I know not whereof I speak, but the words come to me anyway.

Democritus felt that there had to be more to reality than meets the eye; the observable world cannot explain itself. One part of it cannot supply the true nature of another part—as Thales in effect believed. There has to be an underlying reality, relatively simple, subject to rigid law, highly structured, that accounts for what we observe. The surface needs support from something else. I have the same conviction about the mental: what I introspect of my consciousness cannot be the whole story—there has to be another level of reality that brings it all together. I don't believe the so-called physical world can do this, at least as currently conceived; so I am compelled to posit a hidden world of mental atoms and their interactions, where these atoms may be conceptually distant from anything we now ascribe to consciousness (though of course they constitute it). The atoms of consciousness might have properties that are not at all predictable given the way consciousness naturally appears to us. Will they take the form of a nucleus surrounded by a shell of particles? That sounds like too slavish an adherence to the physical model, but they might have a complex structure, and hence not be strictly *atoms*, i.e. indivisibles. Will these atoms combine to form molecular compounds? That sounds more likely, since there must be a hierarchical process of construction that takes us from the most primitive level to the level of felt experience: atoms, then molecules, then manifest kinds. Physical contiguity is not likely to be the preferred mode of combination—adhesion to neighbouring atoms—but there will have to be something analogous to it—some principle of concatenation. Electromagnetism won't be the force that binds the atoms into bigger wholes, but again something analogous to it needs to be assumed; for something must cause the atoms of mind to come together into stable, if shifting, forms.[22] We know nothing about any of this, except perhaps that something playing these roles must be postulated, given the very structure of an atomic theory. We know what the atoms of mind have to *do*, but we have no idea what they *are*.

An interesting question to consider is whether a distinction between primary and secondary qualities will be a part of the atomic theory of consciousness. Galileo and others distinguished the intrinsic properties of objects from properties that depend upon the observer's response—shape from colour, for instance. The atomic theory was intended to apply only to the former properties; the latter properties were not held to be subject to atomism. This distinction between primary and secondary qualities is essential to the success of physical atomism, given that some of the properties of objects—the mind-dependent ones—are not capable of analysis in terms of physical atoms. Thus atomism cannot account for the colour of objects, according to Galileo and company, but this is no defeat for an atomic theory of the mind-independent *intrinsic* properties of objects. My question is whether such a distinction would arise for the case of the mind itself: do we need to distinguish intrinsic features of consciousness from features it has in virtue of its appearance? The answer, I think, is that we might make such a distinction but that it would not have the result of exempting the secondary qualities of the mind from the reach of atomism. The reason is obvious: those appearance-dependent qualities would themselves be aspects of consciousness, and so a general atomism about the mind has to account for them. Put

---

[22] Will the atoms of mind be subject to gravity? I have no idea, though gravity itself is sufficiently mysterious (and pervasive) that it might play a role here; and certainly the mind is strongly dependent on something that is subject to gravity (the body and brain). It is odd, I think, that, though we constantly experience the force of gravity on our body, we seem not to feel it weighing on our mind ... Descartes, no doubt, would have seized upon this as a further proof of the immateriality of the soul.

differently, atomism about the mind has an obligation to account for the appearance-dependent qualities of the mind as much as for the intrinsic qualities; there can be no shifting of these qualities elsewhere, as with physical atomism.

Suppose that being in pain is a secondary quality of mind, with some primary quality basis—we know not what: we would then need to produce an atomistic account of pain, and not merely of its basis in the primary qualities of consciousness. So the *significance* of any distinction between the primary and secondary qualities of consciousness would be quite different in the environment of an atomic theory of the mind.[23] The atomism needs to go all the way up, so to speak. And, clearly, any attempt to reintroduce a primary/secondary distinction at the level of an appearance-dependent property would run foul of an infinite regress, since there will always be an appearance-dependent residue.

Would the production of such an atomic theory solve the mind-body problem? Not necessarily, though it might contribute to such a solution. For there is no guarantee that the atoms discovered to constitute the mind will relate intelligibly to the atoms that constitute the brain; there might still be an explanatory gap (indeed, as I have noted, this kind of atomism is in itself consistent with dualism). A yet deeper analysis of the world might be necessary to bring the two schemes together—to make the two sorts of atom interlock (which I assume they must eventually do). We already know, I think, that physical atoms cannot do the job of constituting the mind, so there will certainly be no *identity* between the atoms of the mind and the atoms of the brain—the one atomic theory will not *reduce* to the other. On the other hand, surely the atomic theory of mind would provide a deeper understanding of what the

---

[23] The significance would lie in what is explanatorily basic, not in what could be conscientiously ignored. The primary qualities of consciousness would simply be those that explain why the introspective appearances are as they are (these being the secondary qualities)—primary in the sense of theoretical primacy, then.

mind *is*, and hence illuminate how it might fit into the material world. It might, for example, help us to understand psychophysical causation: how the rearrangement of one sort of particle brings about the rearrangement of the other sort.[24] But, again, we are flailing in the dark here, in view of our pre-Socratic predicament. Conceivably, the correct atomic theory of consciousness might make the psychophysical divide look even more unbridgeable, and some quite new conceptual framework be needed in order to get a unified picture—say, something that revealed both sorts of atom as expressions of a deeper reality (Neutral Monist String Theory anyone?).

Finally, I want to say a few (amateur) words about chemistry. Modern chemistry is the area in which the atomic theory of matter receives its fullest confirmation. Bohr's theory of the atom makes sense of the periodic table of elements, in terms of atomic numbers and weights, and predicts the behaviour of chemical substances. It is worth reflecting briefly on the structure of this understanding. Chemists used various techniques, such as spectroscopic analysis and crystallization, in order to arrive at a table of the elements, the basic building blocks of the substances we observe; only later did the atomic theory, involving orbiting electrons, come in to give this mass of observation a solid theoretical foundation. So the order of discovery was, initially, taxonomic and macroscopic, and only subsequently explanatory and microscopic. Question: could there be anything analogous to the periodic table for mental

[24] It seems to me surprising that contemporary philosophers are so ready to believe that once the causal relation has been invoked the naturalizing project has been completed. I don't say this because I think the causal relation is inherently puzzling (like Hume) but because we surely need some idea of how the causation is *working* in a particular case. In the case of mechanical phenomena we have the model of contact causation, but this is hardly the obvious model for the case of psychophysical causation. We need more than the bare assertion of causal related-ness; we need an account of the causal *mechanism*—of what implements the causality. Just consider the causal theory of reference as applied to a Cartesian immaterial spirit!

phenomena? This would not be a purely phenomenological classification, but would have to involve some techniques of experimentation and analysis; it would have to isolate the underlying building blocks—the ingredients of mental compounds and mixtures. What sort of experimentation and analysis? I have no idea—I am but a limping Democritus in all this. Perhaps dissociations caused by brain injury might play a part in this—basic mental modules might approximate to chemical elements. Perhaps these could be ordered in some revealing way.[25] The stage would then be set for a Bohr of the mind to come along and explain how these elements derive from a few basic atomic structures—the analogues of the electrons orbiting the nucleus. In other words, we don't go for the atomic theory straight off; we wait till we develop the mental chemistry far enough. The mental chemistry—exemplified by the periodic table—is the intermediate level of theory, needed to bring together consciousness as it appears and whatever atomic structures might underlie it. We do the chemistry of consciousness before we attempt the physics. Looking at the history of chemistry from the time of Democritus, this sounds like the best strategy for working towards an atomic theory of mind: the chemistry took substantial shape before its atomic rationale ever became apparent. But, as I say, I haven't the slightest idea how we might proceed here; I am merely drawing an analogy that might be worth pondering.

My aim in this paper has not been to defend a theory of consciousness; my aim has been to sketch the form that such a theory *would* have if it were ever discovered. My reasons for putting forward such a sketch are not that I have any real arguments for

[25] If we follow Jerry Fodor's theory of mental modules, then we could order modules along a number of dimensions: speed of operation, narrowness of domain specificity, degree of encapsulation, etc. See his *The Modularity of Mind* (MIT Press: 1983). However, this theory is couched within the framework of the computational theory of mind, and we don't want to confine our mental chemistry to this framework (it works poorly for sensations, to begin with). The chemistry of qualia may not be much like the chemistry of computation.

it, only that it seems like a theory-form that *might* actually be true. It is a pure conjecture on my part, a kind of theoretical hope. Speaking as one of the ancient Americans—seen from a vantage point in the distant intellectual future—I am giving my pre-Socratic self a voice. Democritus had it right, after all, by some combination of chance and strange divination; so maybe an atomic theory of consciousness is also the truth, even though obscurely glimpsed now (even this is putting it too strongly). And who can resist an occasional pre-Socratic spasm when it comes to the topic of consciousness? It is hard to play the wise agnostic Socrates all the time, declining to speculate and devoting oneself to ethics.

7

Consciousness and Cosmology: Hyperdualism Ventilated

Prologue

Something interesting happened to me recently (usually, not much does). Would you like to hear about it? I was dozing in my bed, feverish with 'flu, my mind dwelling obsessively on the topic of consciousness and the brain—how the former springs from the latter and allied conundrums—when I sensed an alien presence in the room, as if a bat had flown in through the window. My consciousness was like something confronted by a consciousness like something other than it.[1] Opening my eyes, I beheld, not a bat, but a numinous volume of light, immaterial-seeming, about the

[1] These higher-order subjective states have received little attention, in contrast to the first-order subjective states discussed (say) in Thomas Nagel's 'What is it Like to be a Bat?', *Philosophical Review* (1974) 83: 435–50. Are there specific qualia whose intentional objects are other qualia? How does externalism about content bear upon that question? Is there really a distinctive subjective state corresponding to the apprehension of subjective states that one cannot grasp: the 'alien subjectivity quale'? And so on. These questions belong to what might be called the phenomenology of other minds.

size of a small man. It floated over to me, hovered for a moment, then enveloped me completely. Being the nervous type, I got a little worried at this point: but nothing untoward happened to me—indeed, it felt as if I had been mentally augmented in some way. I was then levitated from my bed, carried out of the window, and whisked (or was it beamed?) to a tremendously remote galaxy in an obscure corner of the cosmos. Yes, really.

It was a matter of seconds before I was face to face with my kidnappers, who looked almost exactly like ordinary human beings, except for a greater serenity about the countenance—and a larger forehead, of course. One of them, evidently in a position of authority, explained to me why I had been brought there: it was in order to talk philosophy for a while. (Why me?, I wondered.) More specifically, he wanted me to explain, and if possible justify, the world-view accepted by us late twentieth-century earthlings; and he desired to put to me the merits of the world-view routinely believed in his sector of the universe. He knew a little about our cosmological theories, he said, but his intelligence reports had made our views sound so incredible that he wished to verify whether we were really serious in holding them and if necessary to enlighten us as to the correct cosmological position. Would I oblige him by entering into a full and frank dialogue, after which I would be safely returned to earth? He understood that I was fairly representative of the standard earthly position.[2] I replied that I would be glad to dispute with him (my 'flu seemed to have flown), confident that *he* would emerge the enlightened one. What follows is a record of our conversation, still fresh in my mind, so that you, loyal fellow human, can judge for yourself which of us was

[2] Readers can gauge how representative by consulting my *The Problem of Consciousness* (1991). In that book the assumption of material emergence is central to the argument; in the present paper this assumption will be brought into question (though not by me). I am (currently) inclined to think that the view offered by my eccentric host is the strongest alternative to the position I defend in the aforementioned book. It should be clear that I don't *want* this alternative to be viable. But the opposition must be given its day.

philosophically worsted. Remember, it's your cosmology that's on the line, too. I am CM, my alien interrogator is MC (to be read as 'My Captor').[3]

Cosmology

MC: Let's begin with a brief exposition of your theory as to the nature and origins of the universe, specifically as it relates to the existence of consciousness—about the reality of which I gather there is no disagreement between us.

CM: Certainly not: I take consciousness to be as incontrovertibly real as anything else in the universe—I am no eliminativist. So I'm glad we concur on one thing. I'd have been disappointed if you simply sidestepped the mind-body problem by denying the existence of what creates it.

MC: I can assure you now that you will not be disappointed on *that* score. Quite the contrary, I suspect. We are not shy when it comes to matters of ontology.

CM: Well, our story goes roughly as follows. Long ago an event known as the Big Bang brought the material universe into existence—particles, gravity, electrical energy, space maybe. Large lumps of matter quickly formed and began moving around each other, obedient to the laws of physics. There was, of course, no sentience in the world at this early time: nothing was aware of

[3] The most proximate cause of this paper was a remark Peter Unger made to me (quoting Michael Lockwood, I gather): he said that the trouble with the usual theories of the mind-body relation is that they aren't crazy enough. Being sympathetic to this remark, I set myself the task of devising a theory in which craziness was at a premium: a no-holds-barred theory. Intrinsic plausibility (by earthly standards) was to be ruthlessly sacrificed to weird internal coherence. Call this craziness requirement 'Convention C': a materially adequate and formally correct theory of consciousness must be as wild as possible while still observing minimal standards of explanatory power. As will become apparent, My Captor's theory certainly conforms to Convention C. For comments on an earlier draft I thank my Rutgers colleagues Jerry Fodor, Barry Loewer, Brian McLaughlin, and Tim Maudlin, as well as Peter Unger, Consuelo Preti, and Galen Strawson.

anything else, nothing mental glimmered. After a while, in certain privileged pockets of the material world, the evolution of life began: matter started to replicate itself, sometimes changing a bit in the replication process, some chunks of it better at reproducing themselves than others, with competition for the materials needed for replication, until some quite fancy lumps of matter were dotted around the place. Still nothing of a mental nature, though. After another lapse of time, a few of the fancier lumps started to acquire mental states, primitive at first but soon pretty impressive because this made the lumps more adept at producing viable copies of themselves. Thus, just as life emerged from matter by natural selection—some say by way of crystals[4]—so consciousness duly emerged from life; and therefore, by the transitivity of the emergence relation, we have it that consciousness emerged from matter. Matter became organized in certain ways, you see, under the impact of natural selection, and as a result consciousness, well, came out of it—if you see what I mean. Matter generated consciousness, brought it into being. This part of the story, I freely admit, is still something of a mystery to us: we call it the mind-body problem—*how* matter found the resources to produce states of consciousness. We don't really yet understand, scientifically or philosophically, by what means or mechanism bunches of particles contrived to generate something so apparently different from themselves: but we don't seriously doubt that they did—and the optimists among us expect that one day we shall understand what the process consists in.[5] Ontologically, then, consciousness is a derived or secondary existent, arriving quite late in cosmic history. Clear?

MC: Your theory is indeed much as it was reported to me. Remarkable! You are certainly audacious thinkers, I'll grant you that:

[4] See Richard Dawkins's discussion of Graham Cairn-Smith's crystal theory of pre-DNA replicators, in *The Blind Watchmaker* (London: Longmans, 1986), ch. 6. First mud; then crystals; eventually us. (Then probably back to mud again.)

[5] I am not myself one of these cheerful utopians, convinced a priori that human science will inevitably lead to total knowledge of everything. Cognitive pessimism is the prevailing mood of *The Problem of Consciousness* (McGinn, 1991).

paradox inhibits you not a bit. I hope you will excuse my chuckle when you got to that brilliant part about consciousness being conjured from collections of particles. I had to laugh. Let me now offer you a summary of the way we see things here, so that we can then make a fair comparison. Please try to keep an open mind, because there is a radical divergence in our basic cosmologies, and I know that people are very wedded to their cosmologies—it's almost a religion with some folks! To aid your comprehension, I shall, in deference to certain natural frailties, first describe our system in its theistic version; then we can drop God from the picture to derive the hygenic scientific version. Ready?

In the beginning, God couldn't make up his mind which kind of universe he wanted to create—a material universe or a spiritual one. He was undecided, that is, between creating an insentient world of moving matter in space, on the one hand, and an immaterial world of pure consciousness, on the other. Each seemed to have its attractions. Since he didn't really have to decide, being omnipotent, he opted to create both, so that he could enjoy surveying his heterogeneous handiwork on alternating days, down through all eternity. He put this plan into effect, keeping his two universes entirely separate and insulated from each other; they were set up as closed systems—no causal commerce between them. In the material universe, U_1, matter went its mindless way, while in the immaterial universe, U_2, conscious events and processes displayed their characteristic subjectivity and intentionality.[6]

After a few billion years of this segregated parallelism, God became a little bored with his pair of artefacts and hungered for cosmic novelty. Should he, he wondered, scrap the two independent worlds he had created and generate a completely new order, or should he tinker with what he already had and transform it into something fresh and interesting? Reluctant to admit that his ori-

---

[6] Cf. Nagel's 'all-pervading world soul, the mental equivalent of space-time, activated by certain kinds of physical activity' (1986, 30).

ginal works could cease to inspire interest—for he was a proud God—he hit upon a bold plan, with which he was much pleased. He would think of a way to connect U1 and U2! It sounded impossible, he knew, what with U1 and U2 being so different from each other in the kinds of item they contained and in the laws and principles that obtained in them; but he was God, after all, and the impossible had never deterred him in the past (well, there was that unfortunate business with the round squares...). He would take it as a challenge to his creative ingenuity. Anyway, he could always resort to his old standby if the project proved too tricky—divine fiat. But it would be aesthetically preferable to forge the link by coaxing his existing creations into making the connection themselves, so that no far-reaching nomological revisions would be required. This was going to need careful thought, so he went back to his original cosmic blueprints and tried to see whether the solution to the 'connection problem' somehow lay hidden in his initial conceptions. *Only connect*, he exhorted himself.

Imagine his delight (and self-congratulation) when he discovered that by jiggling around with his now-dusty designs for U1 and U2 he could forge a causal link between them. He must have known all along, omniscience being what it is, that he would some day want to marry his separate spheres of reality. What he had to do was form a few pounds of ordinary matter into a particular configuration, admittedly not easily predicted from the manner of matter's original spontaneous clumping, and the result would act like a kind of inter-universe radio receiver tuned in to the conscious events and processes already occupying U2. The required configuration would be pretty fiddly to put together and needed a dozen or so strokes of pure genius to get right, but God was confident that the engineering work could be brought off; unless he was very much mistaken—which he seldom, if ever, was. He couldn't wait to see his new device in operation.

So the next day he woke up good and early, honed his divine cuticle, and by lunchtime he had created—a *brain*. It didn't look like much, but he knew that its advent heralded a new phase in cosmic history. He sheathed this piece of apparatus in a body (it looked unsightly in its naked form), flipped a switch, and waited for his two universes to start flowing into each other for the first time since . . . well, time. And sure enough, it worked! The brain, located there in U_1, began picking up signals from the conscious events occurring in U_2, causing the attached body to twitch in various interesting ways. Moreover—and this also was part of God's clever plan—the form he had given to this brain, which structured matter in a specific and subtle way, a way in which it had not hitherto been structured, *also* worked to give new form to the conscious processes in U_2, conferring upon them a complexity and structure they had not possessed up to this time. The brain thus functioned as both a receiving and a combining device with respect to the contents of U_2. The form of the brain operated dually to give new shape to both sorts of being—matter and consciousness—so producing an unprecedented hybrid entity: a conscious organism, a psychophysical unit. All the other forms in God's two universes were limited to structuring one or the other kind of 'stuff', but the form of the brain was unique in that it could structure *both* realms simultaneously. Brilliant! Thanks to this universe-straddling form, there was now two-way causal interaction between U_1 and U_2, made possible by the porthole punched through by the brain. (Even entropy looked momentarily to have met its match, though this appearance dissolved when you looked more closely.) God was thrilled with what he had achieved. And how was he to know what these conscious organisms would get up to as history began to unfold? He really should have been more careful with the free-will part of the design.

CM: That's a very amusing fairy tale, but before I point out some of the obvious plot weaknesses I'd like to be regaled with that sober scientific version you promised—the one that doesn't bring in God's mysterious powers at all the creaky points. You did tell me that your creation story is supposed to be literally true.

MC: I was just coming to that. All you need to do, actually, is imagine essentially the same story without the idea of divine design behind it. Thus, there were originally two universes, causally isolated one from the other, either brought into being by some initiating event like the Big Bang or existing from eternity in a Steady State. This state of independence ended only when brains came into existence as a result of natural selection. There was a genetic mutation one day and by luck, if you can call it that, a physical object came to exist that was capable, as no physical object before had been, of tapping into the other universe. It was like a radio receiver evolving naturally on some planet and picking up frequencies that had always pervaded the atmosphere but had never before been detected; where these frequencies carried biologically useful information, say weather forecasts emanating from earth, so that having one of these receivers about your person enhanced your reproductive capacity. Brains happen to have the unique capacity to act as an interface or conduit between the two universes, structuring and moulding what lies on either side of the dividing line; and this capacity enabled organisms to exploit the resources of mental causation. If you like, the genes began to take advantage of the contents of U2 as well as U1, using brains as their way in: genes for universe-hopping turned out to have survival value, as genes for continent-hopping in birds do.[7]

CM: But how did the universe of consciousness come to exist in the first place? You have given me no account of that.

MC: We have no real idea, but then neither do we—or you—know how the material universe came to exist: not when you get right down to it. We know there was a Big Bang, true, and we know a good deal about its nature, but what produced that initial explosion of being—what preceded it? *Why* did it happen? No one can

[7] Obviously, this analogy should not be taken literally: birds really do migrate from one place to another, but brains don't actually travel from U1 to U2, they exploit the contents of U2 while staying put in U1. Still, both sorts of relation to a distant zone (careful!) have proved biologically useful.

say. Something has to be taken as given, after all; explanations of origins must come to an end. But we know the material universe came into existence somehow, because here it is; and, similarly, consciousness came into existence somehow, because here *it* is. What we don't know is how or why the conscious universe came to be: what caused it, what its point may be, whether it might one day cease to exist.[8] But, as I say, this is the kind of mystery we have to live with for the material universe too.

CM: But this is just where your story is inferior to ours—not to mention its intrinsic nuttiness, of course. We *can* say where consciousness came from: it emerged from matter, just as living organisms did. *We* don't have to throw up our hands and wallow in mystery.

Emergence

MC: Now here we have the crux of the disagreement, if I'm not mistaken. Earlier you confessed, with commendable humility, that you earthlings have no understanding of *how* consciousness emerged from matter, though you tell me you are confident that it did.[9] So, if we are counting mysteries, that's one mystery each so far, and mine is a mystery of the same kind that we have to live with in respect of matter anyway. But, on closer inspection, your position is really very much worse than ours *because you insist on the reality of something that we know is impossible.* That is, we see no reason to believe that the primitive and underived existence of conscious processes is impossible, but we see every reason to think

---

[8] So consciousness does not exist for the same kind of reason that hearts and brains do, i.e. on account of biological utility. Consciousness is not inherently biological, according to hyperdualism: the genes exploited its prior existence, as they do many other kinds of intrinsically unbiological material. In this respect, consciousness is more like water than blood; less like an organ and more like what composes an organ.

[9] This is my position in *The Problem of Consciousness* (McGinn, 1991): certainty about the fact of emergence coupled with admitted nescience about the mechanism.

that extracting consciousness from matter is a real impossibility. You speak, forgive me, somewhat glibly of this 'emergence' of consciousness from matter—sensations from brain cells, thoughts from chemical neurotransmitters—but surely such a feat is quite inconceivable. It reminds me of the old myth of spontaneous generation, though in that case at least we are dealing with two kinds of physical thing. You might as well assert, without further explanation, that space emerges from time, or numbers from biscuits, or ethics from rhubarb . . . or matter from consciousness. Isn't it perfectly evident to you, as it is to us, that consciousness simply *could* not be produced by mere combinations of particles, no matter how subtle the combination? Matter is just the wrong *kind* of thing to give birth to consciousness. How can physical properties of the brain generate phenomenal features? From what magical crevice in the cortex derives the peculiar subjective homogeneity of an impression of red? How can the enormous variety of sensations be produced by the dull uniformities of neural structure? Where in consciousness do we find the spatial character of the brain's structures, and why isn't this spatiality preserved in the process of emergence? Isn't it as plain as the smell in the nose on your face that we are speaking here of two radically distinct kinds of being? The physical brain just doesn't have the resources to do the kind of generative work you are asking of it: it's not a miracle-box, you know. The great merit of our cosmology, as against yours, is that we are not compelled to make a leap of faith into a palpable absurdity. We grant consciousness the kind of ontological autonomy it so clearly demands.

CM: Hang on a minute: admittedly, we don't know how the emergence is brought about, but neither do you have any account that I have heard of how this 'brain receiver' works—of how the inter-universe link is mediated. Isn't there going to be a mystery about the psychophysical nexus whatever your underlying cosmology? It shouldn't be taken as an excuse to multiply universes.

MC: That is a fair point, but I don't think you have yet grasped quite how fundamentally we disagree with your understanding of the mind-brain relation. It isn't that we think the emergence of consciousness from matter is a numbingly difficult problem, nor even that it is insoluble by thinkers with our, or your, kind of conceptual/cognitive architecture, as we think the problem of interaction may well be. No, what we hold—and are amazed that you cannot see—is that it is clearly and incontrovertibly the case that consciousness *could* not owe its *existence* to the properties of matter. It could not be some kind of byproduct of matter, owing its very nature and being to the operations of the physical world. Our cosmology is expressly designed to avoid commitment to such an impossibility. Why cling stubbornly to the dogma that there is only one universe, the material one, when this means crediting it with magical powers? Why not drop the voodoo science and go with the double universe hypothesis? To us, your emergence thesis seems as crazy as insisting that there is only the conscious universe and somehow it magically gave rise to the material one—as if matter could emerge from consciousness.[10] Both views are mistaken for the same dualistic reason.

Dualism

CM: Your incredulity has a familiar, if antiquated, ring. As you may know, some earthly philosophers, mainly in days gone by, have shared your misgivings over the idea of emergence, not seeing

[10] This is not the same as Berkeley's (far more defensible) thesis that what we *call* 'material objects' are really ideas in our minds or in the mind of God. Rather, it is the thesis that matter *in the sense Berkeley repudiated* is an upshot of mind, i.e. that alleged substance whose nature differs radically from the nature of mind. What MC can't understand is how you can combine irreducibility (a kind of dualism) with emergence—*either* way round. Once reduction has been roundly rejected, he thinks you have to go the full dualist route and not mystify yourself with talk of emergence. In other words, straightforward materialists and idealists are entitled to the notion of emergence, but no one else is.

how things with such apparently different natures or essences could ever stand in a relation as intimate as that—emergence being so close to reduction: dualists, they are called. Not many people hold this kind of view any more, at least within the academy, but even those who do would recoil from the extremes to which you have taken the idea.[11] Their soul-stuff is taken to reside right here in this universe; they don't concoct another universe entirely in which to house it. If you feel the need to be a dualist, why not pare your dualism down a bit—Occam's razor and all that? Even Descartes would have blanched at a whole independent world of consciousness, joined to the material world only after a long stretch of splendid isolation. Why not stick to one individual mental substance for each person, and have these substances come into existence at the same time as the person's brain does—or thereabouts?

MC: I'm not so sure your earthly dualists are as sober (by your standards) as you—or even they—think they are, especially when one examines their view more closely. But yes, I am aware of this tradition among your more rigorous and realistic thinkers, and I wonder why it is so derided nowadays. My own opinion, though I am hardly an expert in the history of human dualistic thought, is that your dualists lacked the courage of their convictions, so they undermined their position precisely by understating it: they hadn't the nerve to go one step further into full cosmological dualism. And, of course, they tended to advance their dualism against a theistic background, which hardly recommends it to a secular age. Without an underlying naturalistic cosmology on which to base their account of the mind-body relation, they left themselves open to objections they could have countered had they gone the whole way with their instincts.

Surely the most troubling aspect of traditional earthly dualism, at least if you're open-minded about it to begin with, is its inability

---

[11] Academic dualists include Karl Popper and John Eccles, *The Self and its Brain* (Berlin, Heidelberg, London, New York: Springer International, 1977).

to answer the question of origins. Where do all the individual minds come from? If cerebral matter does not create them, then what does? They can't just miraculously pop into existence at the precise moment a suitable body looms into view, coincidentally developing as the organism does. It therefore seems, on the standard dualist conception, very hard to avoid postulating God as an *essential* cog in your cosmology: *he* is the one who must do the creating of each individual mind, as well as ensuring the ongoing coupling of mind and body. Ordinary biological reproduction generates your body, but it is given to God alone to be the author of your soul.

You might, of course, try saying that individual minds have always existed and only get coupled to bodies late in their careers; they are uncreated substances. But first, this brings the theory close to our form of cosmological dualism, the sempiternality of consciousness being the cornerstone of our position. And, second, it is surely overdoing a good thing to hold that my mind, in all its specificity, has existed for ever, poised to become linked to my body—which itself might never have existed. Why have I no memories of this previous discarnate existence? Why do I begin life with a baby's mind? Isn't it preferable to assume, as we do, that the brain plays an essential role in moulding the individual minds that are associated with specific organisms? What pre-exists my body is not my mind in full bloom, as it were, but rather the primitive materials my brain forms into my mind. The brain, remember, can work as a combinatorial device without being called upon to act as a generative one. It's rather like a living organism and the physical materials its biological form shapes into that organism. What pre-exists me as a psychophysical unit are, in addition to my physical materials, my mental materials, as yet unformed into the individual mind I shall possess—not me as I shall eventually become. Your dualists simply needed to make the same kinds of cosmological assumptions about their mental realm that they were historically poised to make about the material world. They were benighted creationists about both the biological and the mental realms; a better form of dualism needs to extend to the latter realm the kind of evolutionary naturalism we now take for granted for the former realm.

And, finally, dualists should refrain from trying to slot consciousness—bodily, as it were—into the world of tables and chairs. There is no room (or too much room!) for immaterial substances in physical space; it is hardly plausible to think of my mind as a kind of dimensionless point hovering somewhere in the vicinity of my body. Matter belongs in space, but the immaterial has no place there. Certainly, it should not be conceived as a kind of vaporous presence, putting up no resistance to other potential occupants of space. It needs its own dimension. In effect, the logic of dualism leads one irresistibly to hyperdualism, but your dualists couldn't quite rid themselves of the prejudice that matter in space is somehow cosmologically basic.

CM: But *isn't* it thus basic? I mean, what about questions of individuation with respect to the denizens of U2?[12] Let me put a dilemma to you about the contents of that other alleged place. Either it contains only mental universals (or types) or it contains both mental universals and mental particulars (or tokens). If the former, then hyperdualism is equivalent to mere property-dualism, given realism about mental properties and an irreducibility thesis. But this is relatively trivial ontologically and hardly warrants the inflated terms in which you are apt to characterize U2. On the other hand, if you wish to allow for a type-token distinction for items in U2, so that there can be many mental tokens of the same type, then you owe me an account of what this might consist in: what *makes* one mental token differ from

<hr />

[12] Fodor urged me to consider this kind of objection, which I am glad to do. Such concerns are familiar from Peter Strawson's *Individuals* (1959), in which the primacy of space in individuation is pressed.

another of the same type if it is not something about their spatial location or material incarnation? How, in short, do you get mental particularization in a world without matter and space?

MC: First, let me be clear that we do intend to populate U2 with tokens as well as types; so our view is not just a notational variant of a platonic conception of (irreducible) mental universals or properties. Accordingly, we accept that there is a question to be raised about the individuation of mental tokens. And the more analytically inclined among our philosophers have provided an answer to this question. In the first place, U2 has a temporal dimension, so that the same type can be instantiated at distinct times; and there may also be some analogue of the notion of self in U2, so that tokens could be distinguished by occurring in distinct selves (or proto-selves).[13] But, in the second place, and more important, the question you raise presupposes the very prejudice I mentioned, as I hope the following line of questioning will reveal to you.

How do *you* distinguish physical tokens of the same type—let's say particular events or processes? You may say in terms of their causes and effects; but we can say that of mental events too: and in both cases the individuative circle is extremely tight.[14] To avoid the circle, you might say the events occur in distinct continuant substances. But we can now ask what makes material substances distinct. You might say that they are made of different material constituents, which just raises the question what differentiates these constituents. A natural reply then is that they are at different locations, so that spatial distinctness lies at the bottom of material

[13] This, in effect, is how Berkeley distinguishes tokens of the same mental type: they occur in distinct selves. Of course, you get a circle if you go on to individuate selves in terms of mental events. Whether this is bad depends upon your individuative ambitions.

[14] Donald Davidson proposes a causal criterion of event identity in 'The individuation of events', in *Essays on Actions and Events* (Oxford: Oxford University Press, 1980). The circle here arises through the obvious fact that the causes and effects of token events are also token events.

distinctness. This must already seem suspect, since it isn't that material things *are* regions of space. But now we cannot avoid this final question: what distinguishes one region of space from another? Either we have to circle back to material objects or we have to take spatial individuation as primitive. This is how it goes, right?

The point of rehearsing this familiar story is just to show that in the end you either accept the circularity or take something as individuatively basic, space usually. But if that is so, then what is to stop us from taking the distinctness of mental particulars as basic? Only, it seems, the prejudice that spatial individuation is somehow privileged—that it is self-explanatory, and hence a satisfactory individuative terminus. But *we* fail to see why space should be unique in this respect: we don't see why the distinctness of one mental token from another of the same type shouldn't be taken as primitive, as not admitting of any reduction to some *other* kind of item. So we see no big problem about insisting on a robust type-token distinction for U2, even before the hook-up to the spatial world occurs.

CM: Okay, I can see you have a line to push on the individuation issue. Let me try a blunter kind of objection, though I think I can anticipate your reply from what you've already said. This is just that it's hard to make *sense* of the idea of immaterial things: one can form no clear conception of what is meant, except as the negation of the idea of a material thing. Isn't U2 ontologically weird?[15]

MC: I was wondering when you would get around to rolling out that old chestnut. I am afraid we don't take such worries terribly seriously here, as indeed many of your own pre-modern thinkers did not. We think you are in the grip of an ontological prejudice produced by excessive attention to the deliverances of sense (as

[15] Orthodox opposition, along these lines, to dualistic immaterialism can be found, for example, in my *The Character of Mind* (Oxford: Oxford University Press, 1982), ch. 2.

well as being smitten by physics idolatory, it goes without saying). You think that if you can't perceive it that's in itself a reason to say it isn't there, even that it's not coherent. The senses do indeed detect (directly or indirectly) many of the properties of matter, but there is much else in reality that they are silent about. In particular—and this is a subject we shall need to return to—you also have a similar bias against the abstract world. Indeed, the ontological revulsion you just voiced concerning the contents of U2 can be reproduced in respect of numbers and the like, since they too have non-spatial immaterial existence. Numbers don't emerge from matter either, *pace* some nominalists, though they are as real as material things: here too we hold that ontological duality is unavoidable. So we simply don't share your neurosis about abstract entities, any more than we do your anxieties concerning discarnate consciousness. Just as we are dauntless dualists, so we are proud platonists. And we resist your ontological cavils against hyperdualism in the same kind of way we resist nominalism. We point out the descriptive and explanatory benefits of a broader ontology than the merely material; we invite you to provide us with an untendentious argument against this broader ontology; and we stress its rootedness in common sense, in contrast to the contortions of an overambitious materialism.[16] We have a saying here: never reject a useful entity just because it doesn't mimic the entities you're already comfortable with.

CM: I grant you the issues of dualism and platonism are rather similar, and I suppose there is always refuge in numbers. I don't really feel up to getting into the platonism issue now, but your raising it does prompt the following question: where do numbers and other abstracta belong in your big scheme?

---

[16] I don't know if MC has had access to Hartry Field's *Science without Numbers* (Oxford: Blackwell, 1980), in which the virtues of nominalism are hymned: but if he has, he clearly wasn't persuaded (different form of life, I suppose).

Abstract Emergentism

MC: I'm glad you asked me that, because there is a further component to our position—or at least that of some of our more adventurous thinkers—which brings numbers and other abstract entities into the very centre of the picture. But before going into that, let me first offer a simple answer to your question: the abstracta exist in U2, or in its general vicinity, along with episodes of consciousness. God couldn't very well install them in U1 next to matter, on account of their non-spatial immateriality, so he deposited them in the world already devised for states of consciousness. Numbers lack the mutability of consciousness, of course, but the two are alike in not requiring a spatial receptacle. So we prefer not to add a third universe to the two we have already. Two seems enough, does it not?

Let me note, parenthetically, that once U1 and U2 come to be causally connected by virtue of brain activity, it becomes strained to speak of there any longer being *two* universes, since the criterion of identity for universes plausibly consists in considerations of causal relatedness. This causal leakage from one to the other creates a single inclusive closed system out of two hitherto separate closed systems. But let's not embroil ourselves in pedantic questions about how many universes there strictly are on the hyperdualist view: the theory can be allowed to speak for itself. The important point is that numbers and states of consciousness are alike in their immateriality—and this despite their standing in various interesting kinds of relation to concentrations of matter in space.

CM: By all means let's avoid those questions, of which the well-trained analytical philosopher is so fond. What peaks my interest is how you conceive the relation between the abstract and the conscious in U2. Do they just sit beside each other there, minding their own business? Or is there some more intimate relation between them? How intertwined are the essences of the abstract and the mental, on your view?[17]

MC: I see that you are beginning to develop a feel for the cosmological picture I am urging on you: that is just the kind of question you should be asking. The short answer is that these essences are far more closely related than are the essences of matter and consciousness. There is ontic harmony here, if not ontic penetration. Our thinkers actually divide into two distinct schools on this question. The conservative school, known as the primitivists, holds that the abstract and the conscious merely exist alongside each other, leading quite separate and extrinsic careers—aside, that is, from the odd spot of abstract intentionality. The primitivists thus maintain that consciousness is an underived existent, having no essential nature other than that peculiar to it—as ontologically basic as matter or number. By contrast, the progressive school, known as the abstract emergentists, holds that there is a relation of ontological dependence between the mental and the abstract: the nature of the one involves that of the other. So—

CM: Then you aren't really platonists at all! You are conceptualists or intuitionists or something of the sort, since you think numbers and so on are mental products. In effect, you hold that the abstract emerges from the mental, and so you situate both in the same strip of reality.

MC: You have got hold of the wrong end of the stick. The ontological dependence doesn't run that way; it goes the other way around. It is the mental that depends upon the abstract, while the abstract depends upon nothing but itself. Consciousness, contend some, is an emergent characteristic of abstract entities and their properties and relations; so the abstract lies at the heart of the mental. As you believe that mind emerges from matter, and so has a physical essence, so some of us think that it emerges from the

[17] I was prompted to consider this question by a lecture given by Roger Penrose at Rutgers in 1990. Penrose asked how we might integrate matter, mathematics, and mind into a single coherent world-view.

abstract realm, deriving its essence therefrom. So we are platonists in the full sense. If I were to state this abstract emergentism in Plato's idiom, I should say that it is the thesis that consciousness is a byproduct of the World of Forms. The slogan is: consciousness is the abstract in process.

CM: I thought your hyperdualist cosmology far-out enough, but this abstract emergentism business sounds like the kind of thing people used to think up under LSD. Let me get this clear, because I must have misunderstood you. You go along with Plato and Frege and others in thinking that the abstract is not a creature of the mind, holding instead that the mind is a creature of the abstract. Numbers sort of get together in platonic heaven and somehow emit states of consciousness. You multiply 13 by 27, say, and get pain. Is that it?

MC: Crudely put, that is indeed the theory the progressives think has the most chance of being true—explains the most and has the greatest internal coherence. The only major adjustment I would make to your satiric formulation is that the abstract entities are held to be *dispositionally* the basis of mind—the mental is *latent* in the abstract. There has to be some outside trigger, or occasion, for this disposition or potential to become manifest: something has to engage the abstract entities in a temporal and causal process of the right sort. There has to be, as we say, a 'realization' of the abstract reality before you have mentation. The abstract world supplies, as it were, the original materials from which minds are constructed. God recycled his prior abstract creations as the building blocks of mind, involving them thus in a temporal process. A mental event is basically the temporal tokening of an abstract fact.

CM: You make it sound like some kind of bizarre Pythagoreanism of the mind—as if thoughts and sensations were literally composed out of abstract entities. Pain isn't neural excitation, it's arithmetical multiplication!

MC: I'm surprised you're having so much trouble coming to grips with abstract emergentism. Isn't essentially the same idea familiar on earth under the title 'the computational theory of mind', at least when properly conceived?[18] Don't some of you hold that it is necessary and sufficient for something to have mental processes that it realize a computer program—that mental types are programme types, and that mental tokens are these types incarnated? And what is such a program if it isn't just an algorithm defined over abstract objects—numbers, functions, propositions and so on? A computation, literally, is a kind of calculation, and a calculation is precisely an operation whose objects (directly or indirectly)[19] are abstract entities. A computer program typically consists in a sequence of instructions to perform certain abstract operations, like addition, on certain abstract entities, like numbers. Or again, the rules (NB) are defined over a domain of propositional entities, and the program specifies (say) the numerical probability of one proposition being represented given that certain others are. A platonist will accordingly conceive of realizing a program as a matter of standing in a set of relations to the denizens of the abstract world; and if mentation is computation, then mentality itself consists in standing in just such relations. Of course, the abstract system has to be implemented in some concrete way in order to get an actual computation going, this being a type of action or event rather than a purely mathematical fact; but still, according to computationalism, the essence of the mental process consists (at least partly) in abstract facts. The implementation may be of a physical nature but, as some of the more clear-sighted computationalists have pointed out, this is strictly incidental to the central thesis: *any* implementing process, even an ectoplasmic or divine one, could

[18] That is, functionalism of the computer-model variety: see Hilary Putnam, 'The nature of mental states', in *Mind, Language, and Reality* (Cambridge: Cambridge University Press, 1975) and the mighty throng of his followers.

[19] I mean: even if a computation is conceived as an empirical operation on numerals, construed as particular inscriptions, it is still the case that computation is indirectly number-involving, since numerals denote numbers. In fact, of course, it is far more natural to conceive addition, say, as an operation performed on numbers themselves (no doubt mediated by non-abstract entities like marks on paper).

serve to bring the abstract facts to mental life.[20] The type of hardware (or ectoware) is contingent to the mental state; it is the abstract software that is of the essence. What is this but abstract emergentism?

Note here that what cannot be allowed is that the abstract facts should themselves be construed as products of mind, on pain of circularity in the explanation of the mental in terms of the abstract: you can't be, say, an intuitionist about the abstract and a computationalist about the mental. Note too that it is necessary to distinguish between an object's performing a computation and its having a computation performed on it, on penalty of finding mentality wherever mathematics is applied to objects, as in ordinary physical measurement: here the object doesn't perform the numerical operation—we do.

So, you see, your computationalism is a special case of the kind of view our progressives espouse: the mental is latent in the abstract and needs only an implementing process to become temporally tokened. In U2 there exist such processes, though they are not, of course, of a physical nature: these processes are the trigger that elicits mental events from their dispositional basis in abstract entities, and gives to these events their causal potential.

Some of our theoreticians maintain, additionally, that what mediates between U1 and U2 is precisely the circumstance that the brain performs mathematical operations: its physical processes thus map onto the abstract world and hence (indirectly) bring mental states into alignment with the brain, these states being originally emergent upon the abstract realm, which has already turned mental in virtue of the eliciting processes in U2. The brain, as it were, makes a detour through the abstract, reaching consciousness through its basis in that domain. Psychophysical correlations are thus abstractly mediated. However, this is all pretty speculative stuff and isn't part of our orthodox sober hyperdualism.

[20] Thus Putnam: 'the functional-state hypothesis is *not* incompatible with dualism!' (1975, 436).

CM: I suppose I do now see an affinity between your abstract emergentism and our computationalism, though I doubt that our theorists would care to reveal the metaphysical picture implicit in their supposedly hard-headed approach so explicitly.

MC: People do tend to keep their metaphysical assumptions quiet, don't they?

CM: Like guilty secrets, yes. The main problem I see with abstract emergentism, ours or yours, is explaining clearly just *how* it is that the abstract could be sufficient, in conjunction with a suitable realizing process, to produce states of consciousness. Isn't there a rebarbative bruteness to the postulated dependence, redolent of the kind of magic you excoriate in our idea of material emergence?

MC: I grant you that. But my polemical aim was to get you to compare the two theories of emergence, so as encourage a more impartial view of the options. And you have to admit that the mental and the abstract are closer ontological neighbours than the mental and the material; there is thus less of a gap to be crossed by the emergence relation in the former case. I ask you at least to try to give the view a fair hearing: philosophical progress can sometimes come from the least likely directions.

CM: I promise I'll try. I can see you've got quite a system going here, each part cohering with the rest. I suppose it would be *nice* if it were true. But aren't there just too many unanswered questions?

Methodological Queries

MC: You have to expect unanswered questions in these areas. Wouldn't it be strange if all the ultimate cosmological questions could be answered by tiny bounded mortals like us? Here, any knowledge at all is to be marvelled at. Ignorance comes with the cosmic territory. Quantum theory, for example, would never have gained general acceptance if unanswered questions were sufficient to undermine a theory. You should ask yourself what overall picture of the universe provides the best general account of the phenomena to which we have access, limited as these phenomena are. What makes for the most coherent *fit* between the basic categories of reality? Which theory ascribes the most intelligible pattern to the universe as a whole? As far as I can see, our hyperdualist cosmology—with or without abstract emergentism—is superior on these counts to your matter-obsessed monistic mystery story. Come on, isn't it only ontic prejudice and the dead weight of (recent) tradition that makes you prefer your theory to ours? Show me one non-question begging respect in which your view has the theoretical advantage over ours. And don't just say ours is bizarre!

CM: Let me think—what *are* the problems with your theory? Well, to begin with, isn't it very uneconomical? I mean, two universes instead of one—it's not terribly parsimonious, is it? Our theory is ontologically simpler than yours.

MC: True enough, if the sheer number of basic categories is your measure of theoretical simplicity. But at what cost do you restrict the number of universes to one? Simplicity of this kind is no virtue if the simpler theory fails to explain what the more complex theory does, and a fortiori if the simpler theory contains a screaming absurdity—like the idea of material emergence. Besides, there are members of your intellectual community, quite respectable ones too, who advocate world multiplication, prompted by considerations of explanatory power and theoretical adequacy. There are the possible worlds theorists, who embrace an infinity of existent (though non-actual) worlds in addition to the one we witness with our senses.[21] And there are even some physicists, the thinkers you earthlings seem to revere most in the current epoch, who propose a theory known as the 'many-worlds hypothesis', where these worlds are taken as not only existent but actual.[22] World plurality

---

[21] See, for example, D. Lewis, *On the Plurality of Worlds* (Oxford: Blackwell).
[22] Otherwise known as the Everett–Wheeler–Graham interpretation of quantum mechanics. For a popular account see G. Zukav, *The Dancing Wu Li Masters: an Overview of the New Physics* (London: Bantam Books, 1979).

is practically *de rigueur* in some earthly circles. And ontological economy easily slides into sheer mean-mindedness—it's not as if the worlds are being rationed! Besides, as I remarked earlier, once the brain has punched its way through from U1 to U2, we may as well say that we have only the one universe on our hands, causal closure being the operative criterion of identity here.

CM: All right, but hyperdualism is also highly unempirical: no one has ever had, nor could have, any experience of U2 except as it bears upon his or her own consciousness and that of other conscious organisms situated here in U1. According to the theory, as I understand it, we are all little pockets or packets of consciousness selected from a much more extensive conscious reality, but we have no access to that larger reality. Except for the little specks of consciousness that find their way into us, as it were, the contents of U2 are completely unverifiable.

MC: I'm surprised to find you still so much in the sway of the empiricist outlook. Think of your own theories for a moment: the world-multiplying ones I just mentioned, as well as quantum theory, relativity theory, string theory, evolutionary theory, and so forth. You can't always get direct empirical access to realities that are needed to make the best sense of the world as you find it. Explanatory power is the thing, not sensory convenience. Anti-realism and idealism are especially out of place in cosmological discussions. And, as I have already argued, the individual pockets on their own raise the origin problem in an insoluble form. Good theory construction, here as elsewhere, calls for the postulation of unobservables.

I suspect you are being misled by a feature of your predicament as a sentient organism that you are failing to interpret correctly. Since you are partly a physical entity, existing in U1, your access to what transpires in U2 is restricted to what your brain—a selective receiving instrument—can resonate to: the rest of U2 lies outside its powers of transduction. Your brain cannot tune in to the same constituents of U2 as, say, a bat's brain can—not to mention the constituents of U2 that no extant brain can tune in to. And this makes you conclude, erroneously, that there is nothing more to consciousness. But that is to inflate a merely epistemological point into a metaphysical or cosmological one. It is like thinking the electromagnetic spectrum is no broader than the band of light visible to terrestrial eyes, yours or those of other species. In fact, theory requires that we recognize that brains dipped into consciousness late in the history of things and quite fortuitously, so that there is bound to be much of it that is not connected to any physical organism. Indeed, what is really remarkable, to a larger view, is that *any* of it should be so connected, given the correct cosmological conception. Our brains are, as it were, windows onto the contents of U2, but they are windows that offer only a partial vista of the full terrain. There is thus an illusion of dependence on the material world, prompted by this very partialness, which is perhaps (partly) why you people are prepared to live with the paradox of material emergence. If you could survey U2 from a perspective outside of your own brain and that of other brains, then you would have no tendency to subscribe to the myth of material emergence. You would *see* that brains are just local sumps into which the vast ocean of consciousness only partially drains.

CM: You're beginning to sound mystical in your desire to shun the magical. Your theory reminds me of a theory some of our more extravagant and mystically inclined thinkers have purported to believe: namely, panpsychism.[23] Panpsychism also takes consciousness to extend very much further than we usually suppose, regarding the psychic raw materials from which individual conscious minds are built as pre-existing those minds. Primitive mentality is thus held to pervade the physical universe: rocks instantiate mental properties. But at least this view, unlike yours, confines the proto-conscious basis to this universe, tying conscious states down to ordinary lumps of matter. Why not take a leaf out

[23] See Nagel, 'Panpsychism', in *Mortal Questions* (Cambridge: Cambridge University Press), 181–95.

of the panpsychists' book and insert your wider conscious reality snugly into the material world? Why have your irreducible conscious properties instantiated by immaterial particulars in U2 instead of material ones in U1?

MC: Now you are asking a perfectly reasonable question, one that proceeds from the right first principles. The panpsychists are, of course, absolutely right to despair of the material emergence idea, which is why they take consciousness to have its basis in something of the appropriate kind to produce it, viz. itself. And viewing the structure of the brain as essentially combinatorial with respect to primitive conscious ingredients, instead of as magically productive of consciousness, accords closely with our own conception: no conscious output without conscious input (setting side abstract emergentism for the moment). They are also large-visioned enough to grasp that this requires a novel conception of reality as a whole, not merely of that small part of it wherein brains reside, in which consciousness is not really the late and parasitic arrival it has seemed to some to be. Consciousness must indeed be seen as a more basic or primordial feature of the universe than your modern materialistic thinkers have hypothesized. (These latter thinkers, by the way, are the true mystics: they remind me of nothing so much as fakirs claiming to make carpets levitate by blowing into flutes—where the flute tunes are neural volleys and the floating carpets are the conscious states that correlate with them.)

The panpsychists go wrong principally because they lack the imagination, or the nerve, to locate their conscious materials outside the spatial world of coagulated particles, to be connected up with that world only subsequently. They seem to assume that conscious properties could not be instantiated save by extended physical things; when the truth is that, strictly speaking, physical things never *instantiate* conscious properties—they merely correlate with items that do. Because of this basic mistake, panpsychism runs into problems that cannot be surmounted under its assumed cosmology. In particular, it cannot explain why it is that these alleged properties of non-cerebral matter make no difference to the way this matter behaves—why particle physics, say, can do without attributing psychic properties to atoms in addition to their physical properties. There is simply no description of the behaviour of a hydrogen atom under which its trajectory needs to be explained by the postulation of intrinsic conscious states—in contrast to the movements of cerebrally guided systems such as ourselves. The panpsychist's alleged proto-conscious states of atoms, tables, and black holes have no causal powers in respect of those physical objects that are held to instantiate them. And this is why there is no *evidence* that such objects possess states of consciousness—they behave precisely as if they do *not* possess such states. In addition, of course, this impotency ill suits these properties to yield mental states as we know them, since these states do have causal powers. The problem here stems, clearly, from the panpsychist's insistence on situating his wider conscious reality within the physical universe: the problems go away when you give consciousness its own universe in which to be independently instantiated. So you don't have to spread conscious properties all across a physical world in which they palpably play no role; you can spread them instead across their own universe, making causal connections only where they are there to be seen. If only the panpsychists, with their wider conscious reality and combinatorial picture of the brain, had put their heads together with the Cartesian dualists, with their appreciation of the need for non-physical instantiation, and then had given a little thought to cosmology, *then* they might well have arrived at the correct hyperdualist theory. Hyperdualism, after all, is really just regular earthly dualism combined with panpsychist elements and then taken cosmic— if that makes it seem any more palatable to you. The truth was thus within earthly reach, if only you humans had the courage to *think big*. When it comes to the problem of consciousness, pusillanimity is the chief foe of progress.

Brain Power

CM: You are certainly not afraid to boldly go wherever the problem may lead you: whatever I pose as a difficulty you embrace as a virtue! Let me try to bring a final objection that is far more concessive to your basic cosmological outlook but which it seems to me you haven't yet properly addressed. This is simply that hyperdualism runs the risk of leaving the essential problem where it was to start with, by allowing that the brain plays a major sustaining role in shaping or organizing the conscious stuff onto which it hooks in U2. Isn't this action of constituting conscious stuff into specific minds, either of individuals or species, just the same old problematic emergence you are so anxious to reject? The brain, a material thing, is still doing essential constructive work in bringing con-sciousness into the form in which we experience it; it isn't, on your view, a mere passive receiver. Now, isn't this generativity uncomfortably similar to the kind of material generation we favour?

MC: Again, you are now asking the right questions: that is, indeed, an issue over which we have lost sleep. You are, of course, correct in saying that, on our view, the structure of the brain is capable of producing conscious novelty—in somewhat the way natural selec-tion can produce physical novelty. That is, its combinatorial powers can yield new forms of consciousness. However, the gen-erativity envisaged here is of a different order altogether from that imagined by your kind of material emergence. You think the brain's physical form can act as a kind of (computable?) function from the instantiation of physical properties to the instantiation of conscious properties—that it can span this vast ontological divide. But we maintain only that it can act as a function from one kind of conscious property to another; as I keep saying, its role is purely combinatorial, not foundational or ultimately creative. It is, indeed, a big scientific question how in detail the combinatorial conversion is effected, but this is a question that begins from sound cosmological assumptions: it makes the brain very clever without requiring that it perform magic tricks. The brain receives and organizes prior conscious components, but that is by no means the same as somehow extracting these components from within itself, as if conscious states could be mined from its neural substrata like precious stones from rock. The brain performs a kind of mental chemistry, yes, selecting its raw materials from U2; but it contains no alchemical capacity—no power to get something from nothing.

The question that most exercises our mental scientists nowadays is whether conscious processes as we encounter them can be somehow analytically broken down into simpler components in the way that we know matter can. What is the deep nature of our states of consciousness? Is there perhaps a table of elements for consciousness as there is for chemicals? Are the conscious states we experience ultimately made up of complexes of these fundamental elements? Are there natural laws prevailing in U2 that govern the way conscious primitives can combine and associate with each other to produce the flora and fauna of consciousness that our brains present to us? What, in short, does the natural science of U2 look like? Does it have the kind of depth and difficulty that the natural sciences of U1 display? Is there, say, a mental analogue of the quark? Might there be fundamental indeterminacies in U2? These are the kinds of question we would like to answer.

The trouble we have in answering these questions, of course, is that our concepts of consciousness are geared directly to the way consciousness strikes us introspectively and through its behavioural expression, which might be but the final result of a complex process of natural construction. These concepts don't, as it were, go straight to the cosmic source, bypassing the brain's complex contribution; it is almost as if the brain disguises from us what the contents of U2 are like in their elementary form. Our concepts seem to represent many conscious states—pain, for example—as if they were unanalysable simples, one-dimensional, as it were—but these concepts may not do justice to the underlying natural structure of the phenomena. Our concepts of consciousness might be deeply superficial, if you follow me, limited by the manner in which our brains serve conscious states up to us. On general theoretical grounds, it seems attractive to think of U2 as having the kind of natural nomological depth exhibited by the denizens of U1, but it is surpassingly difficult to develop concepts of consciousness able to depict such depth. Ironically enough, then, our brains may be preventing us from achieving a scientifically powerful theory of the deep workings of U2, and indeed of the manner of its connection with U1. The messages they send to us from U2 are in all likelihood elaborately coded, are perhaps not even decipherable from our restricted standpoint. We can't infer the ground from the upshot.

This is frustrating, though we are not such idealists as to infer from this lack of accessibility that U2 *could* not have the kind of natural depth I have just been speculating about. It might indeed have a rich and surprising nature that is quite far removed from the ways in which we habitually conceptualize our own little strips of consciousness. And this nature, real though it is, might be quite unknowable to the kinds of being who benefit (if that is the word) from its manifestations[24] Who knows what possibilities might be realized out there in the objective world? I mean, the world doesn't care whether we can figure it out or not, does it?

CM: I see that you are not only unapologetic dualists and unblushing platonists but also unabashed realists. In fact, now that I think of it, your entire position depends upon a firm adherence to realist principles, does it not? You put the metaphysics first and let the epistemology take care of itself—if it can.

MC: Absolutely right; and perhaps it is the inveterate tendency of human beings to fight shy of realism that leads to their persistent

[24] The idea that consciousness might have an unknowable hidden nature is defended in my *The Problem of Consciousness* (Oxford: Blackwell, 1991). This conception of consciousness is not, then, the exclusive property of material emergentists: dualists can be noumenalists too. Indeed, they might need to be in order to deal with the problem of interaction, which MC concedes to be daunting.

cosmological blunders—if I may speak candidly. Your species seems determined to believe that objective reality is somehow limited to that small portion of it on which it can train its meagre epistemic faculties. This is not only metaphysically preposterous; it also reveals a degree of egocentricity that comports all too easily with the dearth of virtue so conspicuous on planet earth. Have some humility! Try not to see everything from your own limited viewpoint! Respect the non-human world!

CM: You won't find me dissenting from those worthy precepts, nor from the realism you prize so highly. I've always tried to consider the bat's point of view, in more ways than one. But I can't assent to your cosmology simply because it has the *ethical* advantage over ours. Isn't it also a form of idealism to suppose that the natural is shaped by the moral? Still, you have my promise that I'll think carefully about it. Anything that cuts human beings down to size has got to be worth serious consideration. You have certainly given me much food for thought, so much so that I can feel an attack of intellectual dyspepsia coming on. Hyperdualism is going to take some digesting. Can I go home now?

MC: By all means: we have no wish to hold you against your will. We merely thought that a candid exchange of philosophical opinion might prove beneficial to all concerned. I have to say, though, in that spirit of honesty, that you have said nothing to change my original impression that human thinking on these matters is woefully misguided. I had half-supposed that you might be able to say something to remove the appearance of paradox that so glaringly afflicts earthly orthodoxy, and to put up some kind of cogent case against our hyperdualism. But—no such thing.

CM: You have, I must confess, made me ask myself what *does* justify my firm commitment to the monistic cosmology I have hitherto taken for granted, in the light of the alternative you have pressed upon me. I shall have to decide whether, after mature reflection, there really is any rational foundation for my long-held conviction. Who knows, maybe in twenty years I might be able to see my way clear to joining you in hyperdualist heaven! (Somehow I doubt it, though.)

MC: Then we have achieved our purpose in bringing you here. It has been trying for us to observe a race of otherwise relatively intelligent creatures persisting in such perverse error. I hope that you will endeavour, upon your return to earth, to bring the hyperdualist creed to the attention of your fellows, so that they may assess it for themselves. They may, indeed, find it more eupeptic than you. . . . You may now board the neutron transporter and return to earth. Bon voyage!

Aftermath

And so I was returned safely to my home planet, physically all in one piece, though mentally shaken up (= order in U1, chaos in U2). I still suffer from insomnia worrying about the mind-body problem, but now at least I have another position to occupy my thoughts. It feels strange, though, to lie there in the dark, focusing hard on my consciousness, and to think of it as a kind of fortuitous infusion from another dimension, sucked through by my overactive brain: I am a hybrid being whose nature is to bestride two universes that were never intended to cross paths. While all around me the other material objects are confined to just the one universe. Where exactly am *I*? It gives new meaning to the phrase 'to have your head in the clouds'. My brain is a key for opening the combination lock to a different world. Am I glad that nature invented this key? What if it hadn't? And, what happens to me when I die? But at least I'm not the only one to exist in this divided condition: if hyperdualism is true, then you are all in the same boat as me—we all live on the border of two worlds. Our nature as conscious organisms is to bring two autonomous spheres into unlikely propinquity. That would explain a lot, philosophically and otherwise.

8

The Problem of Philosophy

I

The question of the scope of human knowledge has been a long-standing preoccupation of philosophy. And that question has always had a special intensity where philosophical knowledge itself is concerned. A certain anxiety about the nature and possibility of such knowledge is endemic to the subject. The suspicion is that, in trying to do philosophy, we run up against the limits of our understanding in some deep way. Ignorance seems the natural condition of philosophical endeavour, contributing both to the charm and the frustration of the discipline (if that is the right word). Thus a tenacious tradition, cutting across the usual division between empiricists and rationalists, accepts (i) that there are non-trivial limits to our epistemic capacities and (ii) that these limits stem, at least in part, from the internal organization of the knowing mind—its constitutive structure—as distinct from limits that result from our contingent position in the world. It is not merely that we are a tiny speck in a vast cosmos; that speck also has its own specific cognitive orientation, its own distinctive architecture.

The human mind conforms to certain principles in forming concepts and beliefs and theories, originally given, and these constrain the range of knowledge to which we have access. We cannot get beyond the specific kinds of data and modes of inference that characterize our knowledge-acquiring systems—however paltry these may be. The question has been, not whether this is correct as a general thesis, but rather what the operative principles are, and where their limits fall. *How* limited are we, and what explains the extent and quality of our limits? Can we, indeed, come to understand the workings of our own epistemic capacities? Hence the enquiries of Descartes, Locke, Leibniz, Hume, Kant, Peirce, Russell, and many others.

The most recent major theorist in this tradition, and perhaps the most explicit, is Chomsky.[1] According to him, the mind is a biologically given system, organized into discrete (though interacting) subsystems or modules, which function as special-purpose cognitive devices, variously structured and scheduled, and which confer certain epistemic powers and limits on their possessors. The language faculty is one such module: innately based and specifically structured, it comes into operation early in human life and permits the acquisition, or emergence, of an intricate cognitive system in a spectacularly short time—this being made possible by the antecedent presence of the principles of universal grammar in its initial design. As Chomsky observes, the knowledge so generated is no simpler, by any plausible objective standard, than knowledge of advanced mathematics or physics; but the human mind is so adapted that it yields this knowledge with comparative ease—somewhat as we effortlessly develop a complex physiological structure in a pre-programmed way. (Compare the ease with which our visual system converts two-dimensional arrays into

---

[1] See Noam Chomsky, *Reflections on Language* (London: Pantheon Books, 1975); and *Language and Problems of Knowledge* (Cambridge, Mass.: MIT Press, 1988). See also, Jerry Fodor, *The Modularity of Mind: An Essay on Faculty Psychology* (Cambridge, Mass.: MIT Press, 1983).

three-dimensional percepts, but the difficulty we have in making even simple two-dimensional drawings on the basis of our three-dimensional visual experience.) As a corollary, however, this faculty is poorly adapted to picking up conceivable languages distinct in grammatical structure from that characteristic of human speech. Its strength is thus also its weakness; in fact, it could not be strong in one way without being weak in another.

With language as his model case Chomsky develops a general conception of human intelligence which includes the idea of endogenously fixed cognitive limits even for conscious reason. Here, too, the price of ready success in some domains is fumbling or failure in others. He says:

> The human mind is a biologically given system with certain powers and limits. As Charles Sanders Peirce argued, 'Man's mind has a natural adaptation to imagining correct theories of some kinds. . . . If man had not the gift of a mind adapted to his requirements, he could not have acquired any knowledge.' The fact that 'admissible hypotheses' are available to this specific biological system accounts for its ability to construct rich and complex explanatory theories. But the same properties of mind that provide admissible hypotheses may well exclude other successful theories as unintelligible to humans. Some theories might simply not be among the admissible hypotheses determined by the specific properties of mind that adapt us 'to imagining theories of some kinds,' though these theories might be accessible to a differently organized intelligence. Or these theories might be so remote in an accessibility ordering of admissible hypotheses that they cannot be constructed under actual empirical conditions, though for a differently structured mind they might be easily accessible.[2]

Among the theories that he thinks may *not* be accessible to human intelligence, in virtue of its specific slant, Chomsky includes the correct theory of free creative action, particularly the ordinary use of language. We seem able to develop adequate theories of linguistic competence, i.e. grammars, but when it comes to actual

[2] *Reflections on Language*, 155–6.

performance our theoretical insights are meagre or non-existent. And this is a reflection of the contingencies of our theoretical capacities, rather than an indication of objective intransigence.

Now much could be said in explication and defence of Chomsky's general position, but that is not my purpose here. I wish to start from something like his general perspective and explore some questions seemingly at some distance from Chomskyan concerns: in particular, I want to ask whether the phenomenon of philosophical perplexity might be a consequence of the kind of constitutive cognitive inaccessibility of which he speaks. Is the hardness of philosophy a result of cognitive bias? Might our difficulties here be a side-effect of our adeptness in other areas? Where does the felt profundity of philosophical questions come from? But first I shall have to make some further general remarks about the idea of cognitive limitation; for we will not be in a position to approach my main question unless we have properly taken the idea of cognitive limitation to heart.[3]

First, it is easy to see that comparable limitation theses hold with respect to other aspects of our mental life. We cannot experience every possible type of sensation, nor every emotion; neither can we desire everything that might conceivably be desired. Differently constituted minds from ours might well enjoy a different range of phenomenal, affective, and conative states. There are also sensory thresholds of various kinds which fix the bounds of our perceptual acuities, and which can vary across perceivers, as well as obvious restrictions on our memory capacities and reasoning power. These limits are not in any way dictated by objective phenomena but stem rather from our species-specific endowments. They give us a particular psychological profile, not necessarily shared by other species, actual or possible. Indeed, it is hard

[3] Nor will my project have much appeal for those who detect no particular epistemic oddity in philosophical inquiry—for them I have no real *explanandum*. Scientistically minded philosophers will certainly not sympathize with my motivation. You have to feel that the quintessentially philosophical questions have a special profundity or refractoriness.

to know what it would be like for a psychological being not to have limitations of these kinds, since such limitations are a direct consequence of having any determinate psychology at all.[4]

Second, we should distinguish between two potential sources or loci of cognitive limitation: one relating to the content of our mental representations, the other to the specific character of the operational system within which those contents occur. That is, there is the question of what range of concepts we can in principle deploy in our thought; and there is the separate question of the processing principles and architecture of the system that contains these concepts. Even with unlimited access to concepts, a system might be confined by what it can do with them—say, because of attentional or memory limitations. And a system might be quite impoverished conceptually but be capable of amazing feats of processing and deployment. So when considering whether a certain cognitive system is capable of a given task we need to ask both whether it can acquire mastery of the relevant concepts and whether it has the organizational resources to put these concepts to work in the necessary way. One live possibility is that the mind is not notably lacking at the level of individual concepts but that it lacks the capacity to combine these into systematic explanatory theories of some given class.

Third, if there are the kinds of cognitive predisposition Chomsky suggests, then we should be on the lookout for tendencies to mislocate the source of our epistemic triumphs and failures.

[4] Only the wilder flights of behaviourist psychology could seem to impose no constraints whatever on the kind of mental profile a creature exemplifies. No doubt this idea of indefinite plasticity and unboundedness carried millenarian connotations, which added to its appeal. The irony, of course, is that a purely S-R organism would be incapable of learning anything of interest (as Chomsky has long stressed). What I am assuming is (in effect) that there is something called human nature—as distinct from dog nature and cat nature and bat nature and gnat nature. And I am extending that conviction into our intellectual parts. (I suspect that the tendency to deny this has part of its roots in the metaphysically absurd notion of the 'bare particular'—the featureless underlying reality that carries its properties extrinsically, like a suit of clothes. The *tabula rasa* image is the bare particular in its mental version.)

Since the limits imposed by our mental organization are not guaranteed to present themselves as such, we may find ourselves attributing blame to the wrong thing: we may assume that what comes easy to us *is* (intrinsically) easy, and that what comes hard is somehow objectively recalcitrant. Thus we might be forgiven for supposing, mistakenly, that grammar is objectively simple compared to (say) relativity theory; but, rightly considered, this is a projective fallacy, borne of our peculiar endowments and correctable by an impartial examination of the structure of the systems of knowledge in question. The ease of accessibility of a knowledge system to our cognitive capacities is no measure of its internal complexity or subtlety or profundity—still less of the ontological fibrillations proper to the subject matter of the system. Indeed, it is unclear, ultimately, whether there is any (useful) notion of simplicity or complexity that is quite unrelativized to the specific aptitudes of a selected cognitive faculty. That reason is flummoxed by a certain class of problems is thus no proof that those problems possess any inherent refractoriness, nor that there are no other conceivable epistemic systems that might take these problems in stride.

It may be thought that the existence of non-trivial epistemic limits is a peculiarity of a particular philosophical tradition and that other viewpoints will have less restrictive consequences. Let me then dispel this impression by surveying briefly some standard theories (or theory-sketches) about the nature of thought; we shall see that limits are actually the norm, at any rate by implication. In fact, one of the recurrent faults of the usual theories is that they tend to delimit our conceptual powers *too* narrowly. In any case, it is hard to see how any substantive theory of concepts could avoid imposing *some* limits on concept possession, since certain constitutive conditions will have to be laid down—and hence not necessarily be satisfied. And the more substantive the theory is the clearer the limits are apt to become; only vacuous theories give the impression of boundlessness—as if concepts were entirely weightless and shapeless beings. It might help in counteracting this subliming tendency (as Wittgenstein called it) to consider non-human thinkers, like dogs and dolphins, when reviewing the theories on offer; for deification comes harder in their case than for our own superlative species—at least for us. Here the idea of cognitive limits seems only right and proper.[5]

Three broad types of theory can be distinguished: sensory, behavioural, external. By sensory theories I mean those that base concepts on the contents of perceptual experience—Locke and Hume being the usual suspects. When concepts are construed in this way they are clearly, as those two were keen to stress, constrained by the sensory powers of the creature in question; they are just the traces left by the activity of the sense organs on the memory faculty. Abstraction and association may enlarge the mind's stock of sense-based representations, but concepts of the strictly non-sensory are ruled out. The key tenet of empiricism, indeed, is just that thought cannot transcend the experiential (hence the impossibility of metaphysics, according to the positivism that sprang from these empiricist principles.) It is not, then, just the rationalist tradition, with its emphasis on rich innate structure, that issues in restrictions on thinkability; in fact, in its very cognitive sparingness, empiricism imposes even more pronounced limits than rationalism. The acuity and scope of the senses is the measure of conceptual power, and where creatures differ in their sensory equipment they must also differ in what they can think.

Behaviour-based theories also impose limits, at least under pretty unavoidable assumptions. The central point is simply that behavioural theories tie concepts to the bodily repertoire of the

[5] The tendency to find, or impose, a sharp cut-off point between human and animal minds fuels the idea of boundlessness for the human case. Once a continuity has been admitted the evident limits of animal minds will suggest a comparable position for human minds. (It is quite amazing that philosophers who pride themselves on their biological naturalism should also wish to draw a *cordon sanitaire* around human cognitive capacity.)

thinker and bodies have determinate structure and powers, vary-ing from one kind to the next. Behaving bodies are natural objects in the world, finite and bounded, with limited histories and sets of dispositions. An organism's bodily characteristics fix the nature of the inputs and outputs it can handle, but these are bound to be restricted by the facts of anatomy and physiology. If concepts are to consist in the motion of bodies, then the natural limits on motor capacities become the limits of concept possession. A vivid (if controversial) illustration of the kinds of limits that can result from behavioural theories is provided by Quine's indeterminacy thesis.[6] If concepts come down to dispositions to assent to sen-tences in specific stimulus conditions, then (i) theoretical concepts lapse into radical indeterminacy and (ii) we cannot expect to distinguish concepts that apply under the same conditions of stimulation—as with those rabbits and their undetached parts. Concepts have content, for Quine, only in so far as they are keyed to discrete dispositions to assent, but then any putative concepts not so keyed turn out to be either cognitively inaccessible or plain impossible—despite the reality of the properties they purport to represent. Much the same can be said of Dummett-style 'manifestation' requirements on meaning, which cannot make room for any concepts that call for a 'realist' interpretation.[7] The requirement of an effective mapping from concept to behav-ioural capacity confines concepts to the causal powers of the body in question. Functionalist theories have much the same upshot, since the causal role of an internal state clearly depends upon the contingent make-up of the organism; and if a body fails to provide a basis for some role then the corresponding concept will not be available to the creature whose body it is. Since, presumably, human bodies (say) do not instantiate every logically

---

[6] W. V. Quine, *Word and Object* (Cambridge, Mass.: MIT Press, 1960), ch. 2. (I am not suggesting Quine would see his position in this way.)

[7] Michael Dummett, 'What is a Theory of Meaning? (II)', in *Truth and Meaning*, (eds.) Gareth Evans and John McDowell (Oxford: Clarendon Press, 1976).

possible causal role, there are bound to be concepts that are not open to us (given that every such role corresponds to a potential concept). Just as functionalist theories impose limits on the sensations a creature may possess, so they impose limits on its conceptual powers. And so it is with any theory that equates concepts with dispositions of the body. Even Wittgenstein's much more relaxed emphasis on the connection between meaning and acting has limitative consequences, which he did not forswear.

Third, there are externalist theories that see content as fixed by head/world relations: causal, nomic, teleological, and so forth.[8] Take, as representative, the simple idea that the concepts you have are determined by your history of environmental elicitations. Then your concepts will be limited both by the nature of the impinging environment and by the capacity of your sensory transducers to respond to what is offered up to them (what you can 'interact' with). According to some theories, you simply cannot have concepts for things you have not had causal commerce with—for example, natural kinds whose instances you have not encountered. At the extreme of causal isolation, as with the brain in a vat, you cannot even have concepts of the ordinary perceptible world.[9] Similarly, if we are now not suitably hooked up to some part or aspect of the objective world, then we will not be able to form representations of that part or aspect. The danger in theories of these kinds is actually that they impose unreasonably restrictive conditions on concept possession, underestimating the creative resources of the mind; they certainly do not allow untrammelled conceptual access by sheer effort of will.

It is not that I think any of these theories of concepts is really adequate; my point is just that it is not merely an eccentricity of the

[8] For a tortuous discussion, see Colin McGinn, *Mental Content* (Oxford: Blackwell, 1991).
[9] See Hilary Putnam, *Reason, Truth and History* (Cambridge: Cambridge University Press, 1981), ch. 1.

tradition in which Chomsky locates himself that thought should be subject to significant limits. This is implicit even in theories that are not advanced with this kind of issue in mind; and, as I remarked, it is hard to see how a theory could be both substantive and free of limitative consequences. For what could a concept consist in that was *not* in some way bound by inherently variable and potentially absent facts? Certainly, it is scarcely plausible that every logically possible concept should be necessarily accessible by any mind capable of grasping *some* concept or other. Only a kind of mystical thinking about concepts could occlude recognition of the virtual truism that someone might be able to think some things without being able to think all things. (Compare the question whether humans possess every conceivable motor skill in virtue of possessing some.)

II

I hope now that the sourness of the idea of cognitive limits is recognized, however grudgingly, as simply that of real life. I want to assume, anyway, that it is reasonable to expect, on general grounds, that some areas of human enquiry or interest will be subject to problems of cognitive penetrability, perhaps as a result of our talents in other directions. Then we can ask, with this general expectation in mind, whether we can identify any such areas in particular. Let us thus conduct an impartial survey of human cognitive effort to see whether anything looks like a plausible instance of epistemic boundedness. What actual evidence is there, with respect to particular areas, that the general expectation of selective cognitive failure is being fulfilled? This kind of question could, of course, be asked about many areas of human effort, and its general motivation and evidential status are much the same across the board. For example, we suppose, on general grounds, that humans will exhibit certain areas of strength in motor activity but also certain areas of weakness or total incompetence; and we can enquire into the empirical facts of the case to determine where in particular the capacities and incapacities fall—as we can for any species. Thus we learn to walk quite naturally and everyone is pretty efficient in this department; our swimming abilities, however, are laboriously acquired and show much individual variation; and when it comes to flying, well, it shouldn't even be attempted. This pattern of motor skill is presumably innately based and irremediable (short of fanciful surgical intervention). So, comparably, let us survey our cognitive skills to see where we are strong, weak, and downright inept. And let us not be put off by, or misread, the general difficulty of empirically establishing the absence of a capacity. Admittedly, it can always be maintained that the capacity is possessed but has somehow never quite locked onto its appropriate realizing conditions, but after a point this just looks like special pleading and an unwillingness to take the evidence of incapacity at face-value. There are no doubt those who stubbornly insist that humans have the ability to fly if only they would flap their arms in exactly the right way, in the right wind conditions, and with the right degree of confidence in their hearts; and it is hard to dislodge this fantasy when not every such way has been tried and tested. But we can all see that this is not the rational conclusion to draw from the evidence: it is simply that humans, unlike birds, are not naturally equipped to fly, which is the precise reason we have not yet succeeded in doing it. Similarly, I suggest, we should assess the evidence of intellectual incapacity in the same impartial way, according the relevant indications their due weight.[10] In short: no wishful thinking!

Some of what we know comes very easily. As Chomsky has long emphasized, we develop a complex competence in language with remarkably little effort; and this is best explained by supposing an

[10] I notice that intellectuals will readily concede the point for motor capacity but optimistically hold out for intellectual unboundedness; I wonder whether sports people have the opposite prejudice...

innate and specific preparedness on the part of the human cognitive system. Similar hypotheses are also plausible for visual perception, face recognition, knowledge of common-sense psychology, and no doubt other areas. General evolutionary considerations, as well as ease of acquisition and uniformity across individuals, suggest the idea of unfolding innate endowments, special-purpose modules. But not everything we know comes so readily or shows the same independence of individual intelligence: some human knowledge requires conscious deliberate mental labour. Chomsky cites knowledge of physical science as an obvious example: here it appears plausible to suppose that the knowledge in question is not antecedently targeted or anticipated—rather, it is made possible by the deployment of cognitive capacities that serve some other primary purpose (I shall consider later what this might be).[11] There is no innate structure in humans that already encodes the laws of physics. Such hard-won knowledge is genuinely learned; it is not merely triggered by outside stimuli. It is to our innate cognitive capacities what ballet dancing is to our innate motor capacities: a kind of offshoot or divagation, calling for much stretching and cultivation. The will enters essentially into its generation. While humanly possible it is not (in one good sense) humanly natural.

But are there yet other areas of cognitive effort where we find things tougher going still—in which we seem chronically unable to make significant progress? Are there areas in which we simply lack the capacity to generate the kind of knowledge we desire? Signs of such an underlying incapacity would be: a stubborn lack of progress over time, both individually and across generations, with no obvious explanation in terms of objective complexity or remoteness or other exogenous factor; a subjective sense of intellectual cramp, intersubjectively verified, where the very concepts with which to initiate and prosecute enquiry seem not to be at hand,

---

[11] See Chomsky, *Language and Problems of Knowledge*, ch. 5.

the problems presenting an appearance of internal recalcitrance; the monotonous recurrence of the same unsatisfactory alternatives, with short-lived fashions instead of the steady elimination of unworkable theories and a growing convergence of opinion; a temptation to put all this down to the malign effects of disguised pseudo-problems. None of this would, of course, *entail* that the domain in question is one to which the human cognitive apparatus is constitutionally unsuited, but to an impartial observer it would provide prima facie evidence of a mismatch between the kind of theory needed and the cognitive tools being brought to the search. It would suggest the hypothesis that we are beyond the rim of human intellectual competence.

And now my point is just this: large parts of what is called 'philosophy' exemplify the above general description, so that the hypothesis of cognitive transcendence is at least a reasonable conjecture.[12] If this hypothesis were right, then the search for philosophical knowledge would be an attempt to do with our epistemic capacities what cannot be done with them. Our minds would be to philosophical truth what our bodies are to flying: wrongly designed and structured for the task in question. Let me emphasize that this is a *hypothesis*: it is to be viewed as the most plausible explanation of the data, compared to other proposed explanations, and it fits our best picture of the kind of thing the knowing organism is. Like any hypothesis of comparable scope and generality it might, of course, be mistaken; but I suggest that it is worth taking seriously and examining on its merits. After all, it simply applies to the so-called 'higher cognitive functions' what is acknowledged to be the general condition of our various faculties, bodily and psychological. It competes, say, with the hypothesis (never to my knowledge advanced) that in fact humans do have a natural adaptation towards philosophical understanding,

---

[12] I shall henceforth simply say 'philosophy' to cover the subset of problems I am interested in; my position is not, of course, that whatever people discuss in *departments* of philosophy is subject to cognitive closure.

comparable to their innate expertise in language, but that this adaptiveness operates only during a 'sensitive period', say from five to eight years old, in which great strides would be made in philosophical inquiry if only we exposed our children to an intensive course in philosophical training during that period. We just don't get them early enough! Presumably this hypothesis, though implausible in the extreme (but why exactly is that?), is not *logically* excluded, and has never been empirically tested in any systematic way. It is at least among the range of hypotheses about human knowledge that we have learned to take seriously, at least as to its form. Well, my competing hypothesis asserts, not that we are missing a sensitive period for solving philosophical problems, but rather that the human cognitive system is just not set up for dealing with problems of this general type. This does not exclude the possibility that a differently organized intelligence might relate to philosophy as we do to physics, or indeed to language or common-sense psychology. For all I know, there are forms of intelligence out there that *do* go through a sensitive period for solving the problems of philosophy: if you miss it, you never pick up what your conspecifics take for granted—a thorough understanding of the phenomena that so perplex our earthly philosophers. According to my hypothesis, however, humans are constitutionally *in*sensitive where philosophical problems (of a certain kind) are concerned. In the rest of this paper I shall consider the prospects for this hypothesis.

III

Let us call the hypothesis 'transcendental naturalism', TN for short, because it combines deep epistemic transcendence with the denial that what thus transcends is thereby non-natural. How well does TN account for the oddities of philosophical inquiry? I have considered this question, and allied issues, at some length in a book, and I cannot here repeat everything I say there.[13] Instead I shall try to summarize the main points, providing what I hope will be a synoptic overview of the position. To this end, I begin with a sketch of the typical geography of philosophical debate; the suggestion will be that TN both predicts this geography and is itself superior to the sorts of position routinely adopted within it. After that I shall offer a conjecture about what it is that distinguishes (certain) philosophical problems from other problems we find cognitively amenable. All this will be highly speculative, naturally, and excessively compressed, and no doubt grievously flawed: but speculation can be audacious and risky without being irresponsible—and what else is philosophy for anyway?

When human minds interact with philosophical problems, especially those of the form 'How is X possible?', they are apt to go into one of four possible states. Either (i) they try to *domesticate* the object of puzzlement by providing a reductive or explanatory theory of it; or (ii) they declare it *irreducible* and hence not open to any levelling account; or (iii) they succumb to a *magical* story or image of what seems so puzzling; or (iv) they simply *eliminate* the source of trouble for fear of ontological embarrassment. For ease of reference, I call this pattern of responses the DIME shape. The topics on which it imprints itself, and which I have discussed in some diagnostic detail in the aforementioned book, include: consciousness and the mind-body problem, the nature and identity of the self, the foundations of meaning, the possibility of free will, the availability of a priori and empirical knowledge. In each of these areas, I claim, we can discern the same fundamental pattern of debate as the object of perplexity taxes our intellectual resources, pushing us in one direction or the other. For example, consciousness familiarly provokes the following set of philosophical

[13] Colin McGinn, *Problems in Philosophy: The Limits of Enquiry* (Oxford: Blackwell, 1993). The present paper is best taken as an abbreviated version of that book, designed to focus on the larger forestry; arboreal detail, at least down to trunk morphology, can be found in the longer version. I do not regard this paper as self-sufficient.

reactions: attempts to explain it in naturalistic, usually physicalistic, terms; declarations that is brutely irreducible and *sui generis*; invocations of non-natural forces and relations; denials that there is really any such thing as consciousness to begin with. And much the same can be said for the other topics mentioned, despite some variation in the details. (I must here leave it to the reader to impose the DIME shape on debate about those other topics; or she can always have a look at my book.) Basically what we find, quite generally, is the threat of magic or elimination in the face of the theoretical obduracy of the phenomenon that invites philosophical attention. The phenomenon presents initial problems of possibility, which we try to dissolve with a domesticating theory, but there is always the danger that the failure of this undertaking will leave us facing magic or elimination or unwanted inexplicabilities. Free will, for instance, looks upon early inspection to be impossible, so we try to find some conception of it that permits its existence, but this conception always turns out to be dubiously reductive and distorting, leaving us with the unpalatable options of magic, elimination, or quietism.[14] And so we hop unhappily from one unsatisfactory option to the next; or dig our heels (squintingly) into a position that seems the least intellectually unconscionable of the bunch.

Now TN has a view about this familiar fix: it is because the correct theory is inaccessible to the human intellect that we inflict the DIME torment on ourselves. Since we cannot get our minds around the portion of intellectual space where the correct theory lies, we are prone to dart off in inappropriate directions. Suppose

[14] As I use the term, a *domesticating* theory is always to some degree distorting or deflationary—an attempt to trim the phenomenon of what is essential to it and what makes it so puzzling to us. But it is part of the TN doctrine to insist that any real phenomenon is subject to some true theory or other: this theory, though, which may be beyond our capacities, is such that *were* one to grasp it one would not have any sense of distortion or deflation—for it would be fully adequate to the phenomenon. Such adequate theories, when they can be grasped, are the bread and butter of successful science. A domesticating theory-attempt, by contrast, always carries a powerful odour of revisionism.

that M is the right theory of the mind-body link but that we cannot, constitutionally, reach M: then we are apt to settle for some deforming domestication programme, or to say that there is just no theory to be had, or to conjure up a pseudo-explanatory magical story, or to get rid of the thing that leads to the problem. If we *could* reach M, then we would be able to accept consciousness in its undistorted form, and dismiss the usual DIME options: for we would have a proper theory of precisely the kind of thing that consciousness is. What TN counsels is that we be guided by the truth of that counterfactual, accepting the undiluted existence of something we cannot comprehend. TN says that it is because we cannot gain access to the concepts and principles required to make sense of consciousness (say) that we allow ourselves to be taken in by the DIME shape. But it is better to accept that the world contains things whose ultimate nature we cannot penetrate.

In such a case, according to the TN hypothesis, there comes to be a subject called 'philosophy', with its peculiar addiction to insoluble mysteries. Minds that were better tuned to the requisite theories would have no use for the category of the philosophical, or might perhaps include a quite different set of problems within it. Science, then, might be aptly characterized as that set of questions that does not attract the DIME options—where our cognitive faculties allow us to form the necessary concepts and theories. The distinction between science and philosophy is, on this view, at root a reflection of the cognitive powers we happen to possess or lack, and is therefore creature-relative: it does not correspond to any interesting real division within objective reality. Conceivable creatures might invert the classification we make with these concepts, finding consciousness and free will easy to penetrate and explain scientifically, while being quite mystified by the movement of the planets or the nature of digestion. For it is not, for TN, *intrinsic* to consciousness and free will that they should occasion the kind of perplexity they do in minds like ours; such perplexity results, rather, from the *interaction* between a certain natural phenomenon and a certain type of cognitive set-up. It is not beyond the bounds of possibility that our brains would have to be made of something other than neurons in order for us to have the kinds of cognitive powers needed to solve the problems philosophy poses; at any rate, this is the *sort* of diagnosis TN offers for our philosophical retardation. Evolution selected neural tissue, suitably arranged, as the machinery for making intelligence, but that decision is surely substantive; perhaps other materials are used elsewhere in the universe, producing different sorts of intelligence from the earthly kind. The hardness of philosophy is thus an upshot of the particular way that natural selection has built our thinking organ, not an objective trait of the subject matter of philosophical questions.[15]

IV

So far we have seen some general motivation for TN, deriving from a certain conception of cognitive capacity, and we have considered some evidence that can be interpreted as favouring the hypothesis, though not of course conclusively. Crudely put, the idea has been this: philosophical problems are uniquely recalcitrant, chronically so, though nothing about their subject matter entails this; but it is actually quite predictable that there should exist problems with this degree of intractability, given the most plausible view of the kind of system the human mind is; hence philosophy is a good candidate for being an instance of what is bound to be so on general grounds. But it would obviously be desirable for TN to have some positive theory about the inner

[15] This remains the case even if, for some deep nomological reason, the only naturally possible way to make intelligence is by using neurons; for that is still a point about mental architecture, not about the objective world one is trying to penetrate. Indeed, strictly speaking, the point holds even if philosophy is uniquely hard for *any* logically possible mind: nothing follows from that fact alone about the queerness of the philosophical subject matter itself. (It is instructive to consider this question with respect to the infinite.)

structure of our theoretical capacities from which the claimed partition among problems would follow. In the case of language, universal grammar is what plays this role: the language faculty is internally structured according to that specific set of principles, and any possible language that fails to conform to these principles will not be accessible to a faculty so structured. Linguists have theories about the form of universal grammar, so in effect they have theories about the limits of the human language faculty. Can we come up with anything comparable with respect to the human theoretical capacity? What specific characteristics of conscious reason put philosophy beyond its scope? What kinds of theories are accessible to our belief-forming mechanisms? What does it take for something to be intelligible to us?

Let me begin by rehearsing a suggestion of Chomsky's about our grasp of number theory.[16] He observes that natural human languages possess the property of 'discrete infinity'—roughly, they comprise a system of distinct basic elements that can combine to produce infinitely many complex wholes. Bee languages, by contrast, lack discreteness, being analogue systems, while other animal signal systems fail of infinitude. Presumably the property of discrete infinity arose from some specific biological adaptation, which was then exploited to generate languages as we know them. Chomsky speculates that this feature of our linguistic competence may be the basis of our ability with numbers, since the number series also exhibits discrete infinity, albeit over a distinct domain. If so, then our arithmetic faculty is a by-product of our linguistic faculty, got by abstracting from one domain to another. Pursuing Chomsky's speculation, we might go on to see the cognitive structure thus made available by this extension from language as a central element in our general ability to formulate intelligible theories of the world. That structure enables us to conceive of arbitrary domains in terms of combinatorial rules that generate a

---

[16] See Chomsky, *Language and Problems of Knowledge*, 167 ff.

potential infinity of derived entities from a fixed set of individual elements. Thus it is that the crucial notion of *compositionality* enters our thinking, cropping up in many unrelated areas, and allowing us to generate theories in which it essentially features.

Suppose now that a representation of this abstract property were to join with the kind of spatial representation employed by our senses, notably vision, so that a kind of cooperation of faculties was initiated.[17] Then we might expect a mode of cognition that deals in discrete elements embedded within a continuous medium and capable of rule-governed processes of agglomeration. This would be suitable as a basis for representing the world of material objects in space, these being systems of combined elements, variously located, and capable of assuming indefinitely many different forms. So we can understand, at least in broad outline, how our grasp of physics might arise from grammar plus spatial representation—as arithmetic arises, according to Chomsky's speculation, from the iterative character of language. Here then we can tell the beginnings of a by-product story about our knowledge of physical science, and incidentally explain why such knowledge does not arise with the kind of spontaneity we observe elsewhere.

But if any area of human enquiry required us to go radically beyond the kinds of cognitive principles thus made available, we would find ourselves bereft of the intellectual resources with which to handle that area: our cognitive equipment would not be adequate to the objective properties of what confronts us. (Compare the blankness exhibited by most animals with respect to any representational medium: they lack the idea of *reference*.) That we can understand a given domain depends, according to this story, on a more or less fortuitous match between that domain and the domains targeted by the faculties from which the relevant

[17] Chomsky comes very close to suggesting this in *Language and Problems of Knowledge*, esp. pp. 183–5. (I am grateful to Carol Rovane for reminding me of this passage.)

modes of representation were derived. In other words, cognitive accessibility is a function of similarity to the concerns of our linguistic and perceptual faculties; crucially, it turns upon the applicability of the combinatorial paradigm supplied by language.[18]

This line of thought then suggests the following conjecture: what distinguishes the two kinds of questions is the applicability or otherwise of the 'discrete infinity' mode of understanding, supplemented by the sorts of representation with which our senses operate. That is the demarcation line that separates what we can make theoretically intelligible to ourselves and what we cannot. I refer to this as the CALM conjecture: Combinatorial Atomism with Lawlike Mappings.[19] It says, roughly speaking, that we can understand what conforms to CALM principles, and we cannot understand what does not. According to the Chomskyan speculation, as I interpret it, the CALM schema has its roots ultimately in the structure of language itself, where words combine by rules into phrases and sentences—the abstract character of this property then being detached from the particular atoms to which it originally applies. I think this explains pretty well (though rudimentarily) how we come to have geometry and arithmetic and linguistic theory and physics and even biology—the domains that are tolerably transparent to us. The question now is whether it also hints at why we do *not* have philosophy. Do our difficulties here arise from the circumstance that the phenomena of interest to us cannot be made to conform to the paradigm of a collection of elements that combine lawfully into complex wholes which

[18] General remark: by-product accounts of some particular cognitive attainment are empty unless backed by some specific derivational story. You have to be able to indicate *how* the basic faculty gave rise to the secondary one. It is mere irresponsible hand-waving to suggest, for example, that philosophical knowledge is possible because it is (somehow!) a by-product of 'human intelligence'.

[19] There is much more on this in McGinn, *Problems in Philosophy*, where the CALM conjecture is tested in application to the issues of consciousness, the self, meaning, free will, the a priori, and empirical knowledge.

depend for their properties upon those of their constituent parts? Is it a basic lack of CALM that generates philosophical perplexity?

To answer this question fully we would need to conduct a careful survey of the standard and central problems of philosophy, trying to determine whether it is a systematic breakdown of CALM that produces these problems. I have attempted this in the aforementioned book; let me here cite just one area in which the conjecture seems to carry considerable plausibility—namely, the mind-body problem. Consider how consciousness relates to its neural substrate: then the problem is simply that no intelligible generative relation can be identified. In particular, we cannot regard conscious states as complexes made up of neural elements. So one good way to formulate the mind-body problem is precisely to say that conscious states cannot be regarded as compound structures derived from the neural units that correlate with them. Sensations do not stand to neurons as sentences stand to words or as macroscopic bodies stand to molecules. Hence the usual (and reasonable) talk of radically emergent properties, of explanatory gaps, of peculiar kinds of novelty in the world. In some of its aspects the brain no doubt conforms to CALM principles, as cellular structures do generally; but there must be other aspects of it too, if it is to be capable of generating conscious states, since such states are not, evidently, merely CALM products of neural units and their relations. The principles governing the brain's operation cannot be purely combinatorial, or else it *could* not be the basis of consciousness. Thus the correct theory of the psychophysical link must deal in properties that are not subsumable under the CALM schema. Some kind of projection from the neural basis is apparently what we must assume, but this type of projection cannot be reconstructed from within the CALM framework that controls our thinking. Ultimately, if the Chomskyan speculation is on the right lines, the problem is that in some deep way the brain is not organized after the pattern of language—its properties are not merely those of a system exhibiting combinatorial principles.

Because of the basis of our theory-forming capacities we are prone to conceive of the brain on the model set by language (and perception), but this does not suffice to disclose the properties in virtue of which the brain contrives to produce conscious states. Thus theoretical reason is targeted away from what it seeks to understand.

I think what I am suggesting should become clearer if I enter another speculation, geared to a rather different conception of the psychophysical link. To many theorists a double aspect view of the mind-body relation has seemed attractive, where each aspect is not supposed to be a *product* of the other.[20] The difficulty with such a view is that the aspects seem merely juxtaposed; no intelligible relation binds them together. Now suppose we take seriously the idea that our sense of intelligibility derives from language, specifically from its combinatorial features. Then we might hypothesize that the notion of a semantic whole governs the way we conceive of joinings of other kinds—at least by analogy and extension. For instance, the subject–predicate relation is the kind of joining of elements that we find maximally transparent; so we yearn for joinings that approximate to this. The hooking together of pieces of matter is not so far off, so we do not fret unduly about that. But the concatenation of the mental and the physical looks far too much like a mere ungrammatical string, exhibiting no inner co-herence: we cannot make it fit, even by analogical extension, the paradigm of a well-formed unitary sentence. Thus we are per-plexed that such a juxtaposition should obtain at all, especially when we have good indirect reason to believe that it cannot be merely accidental. Our sense of intelligible linkage is set by the linguistic basis of our theory-forming capacities—that is, by the principles of syntactic and semantic combination—but the kind of linkage that connects mental and physical states cannot be subsumed under this paradigm. It is as if we cannot locate the

[20] See Thomas Nagel, *The View from Nowhere* (Oxford: Oxford University Press, 1986), ch. 3.

argument-places of the function that would connect the mental to the physical. We cannot grasp what kind of unitary whole the mental and the physical combine to generate. Thus our language-based sense of intelligibility lets us down in the present case.

I might summarize our cognitive predicament by distinguishing two types of novelty that the world may contain. Type 1 novelty is the kind subsumable under the CALM schema: it applies to linguistic novelty and to the sort of novelty that results when material particles are arranged in various ways. It is fundamentally combinatorial, iterative, and transparent. Type 2 novelty is the kind that cannot be regarded in this way, and which therefore invites the epithet 'genuine': the emergence of consciousness from the brain is a case in point. It is just when we find ourselves reaching for ideas of type 2 novelty—with the attendant notions of radical emergence, underdetermination, and irreducible duality—that we are entering philosophical territory. And a characteristic response to the consequent bafflement is an attempt (always doomed) to construe a type 2 case as really a type 1 case, as with typical domesticating projects. We have a natural drive towards the combinatorial, so we try to assimilate everything to that, frequently distorting reality in the process. We yearn for CALM, even when this is not the appropriate attitude to adopt in the circumstances. When that happens we become fixated on the DIME shape, and philosophy is the outcome.

Simply put: philosophy exists because not everything you are interested in resembles what you say and see.[21]

V

Up to this point I have been discussing the limits of conscious reason, claiming that this particular human faculty is a poor

[21] Of course, I am keenly aware that I have not established such a sweeping claim in this paper. A fuller attempt is made in my *Problems in Philosophy*. There is, as we

instrument for the discovery of philosophical truth. But it does not follow from any of this that *any* epistemic system must be so bounded; it does not follow that *no* form of cognition could solve philosophical problems. This is a point that has already been made with respect to imaginary creatures, but I want now to consider some actual forms of representation that might plausibly be said to deal with the problems that elude reason. In effect, I have been saying that our reflective belief-forming system cannot solve philosophical problems, but it is left open that we might possess some other faculty that is better equipped for the task. Some other human faculty, that is, might not be subject to the constraints that follow from the fact that conscious reason is structured by the prior faculties from which it derives. Such a faculty might, indeed, have been specifically selected to contain the kind of information relevant to answering philosophical questions, so that it is not mere luck if there is a convergence between the output of the faculty and the subject matter of the relevant questions. So: do we contain anything that has been *built* to encode the kind of information we seek when trying to answer philosophical questions?

I want to suggest, perhaps surprisingly, that there are at least two plausible candidates for human epistemic systems that already contain the data conscious reason cannot reach. Neither is plausibly regarded as a by-product of some other faculty, with the limits attendant upon that; rather, both are expressly designed to represent what reason is not designed to represent. These are: the subconscious self-monitoring representations employed by the brain as it goes about its business; and the information contained in the genetic code. Since the latter is easier to expound in a brief space I shall focus on it. And the basic point is straightforward enough: since, as is commonly supposed, the genes work

know, a well-established tradition of making large meta-philosophical announcements without doing all the necessary spade-work; and such exuberance can serve a useful purpose, if taken in the spirit intended.

symbolically, by specifying programmes for generating organisms from the available raw materials, they must contain whatever information is necessary and sufficient for this feat of engineering. So, for example, they must somehow specify the structure and functioning of the heart, and they must supply rules for generating this organ from primitive biological components. The genes are, as it were, unconscious anatomists and physiologists, equipped with the lore pertaining thereto. But what goes for the body also goes for the mind: the genes must also contain the blueprint for constructing organisms with the (biologically based) mental properties those organisms instantiate. They must, then, represent the principles by which mental properties supervene on physical properties. They must, that is, specify instructions adequate for creating conscious states out of matter. And the same holds for other mental attributes: the genes 'know' how to construct organisms with intentionality, with personhood, with the capacity to make free choices, with rich systems of knowledge—just as they contain instructions for making organisms that embody innate universal grammar.[22] This requires a grip on the natural principles that constitute these attributes, as well as mastery of the trick of engineering them from living tissue. The genes represent unconsciously what creationists ascribe to the mind of God. And since God has to know the answer to the philosophical problems surrounding these attributes, so too do the genes. In fact, they have known the answers for a very long time, well before we ever formulated the questions.

---

[22] We need not take the word 'know' literally here; Chomsky's technical term 'cognize' will serve equally well: see Chomsky, *Rules and Representations* (New York: Columbia University Press, 1980), 70. It is hard to see how the thesis of genetic cognizing could provoke dismay in anyone who was already comfortable with unconscious cognizing of other sorts. And, for what is it worth, the current stabs at explaining reference causally or teleologically can be pretty obviously applied to putative terms of the genetic code. The genetic instructions have compliance-conditions which are fulfilled if and only if the embryological process produces an organism of the kind the genes specify.

Clearly this claim depends upon a robust acceptance of the idea that the genetic code constitutes a genuine semantic system, just as our belief system does. The epistemic pluralism thus presupposed comes naturally once modularity and subconscious representation have been admitted—but of course I am well aware that not everyone goes along with this. My point here is just that *if* the representationality of the genes is admitted, *then* we can see that the limits of reason need not be the limits of all human epistemic systems. The genes really need to contain the information required to generate psychological organisms, this being their task in life, but conscious reason is under no particular obligation to recapitulate that achievement. So the genes have philosophical insight built into their very job description. Hence each cell in the human body 'knows' more philosophy than shall ever be accessible to the frontal lobes.[23]

What is galling about this is that conscious knowledge is associated with intellectual pleasure, with the satisfactions of understanding. But the information contained in our genes is not hooked up to our pleasure centres in this way, so we gain no enjoyment from their relative omniscience. Consciousness is what makes knowledge pleasurable, and without it even the most profound insight has no power to scintillate. Still, we can console ourselves with the thought that we can, after all, solve philosophical problems—though with a part of ourselves we cannot reach.[24]

[23] From a larger perspective, the frontal lobes are mere epistemic parvenus, recently installed to give us the benefits of planning and flexibility; they are not the very origin of all that is representational (though they are wont to arrogate this privilege to themselves). For a discussion of the peculiarities of frontal-lobe representation, see my *Problems in Philosophy*, ch. 8.

[24] I am grateful to Carol Rovane for her comments on an earlier version of this paper, and to Galen Strawson for suggesting the title.

9

Inverted First-Person Authority

Generally speaking, we can distinguish facts from our ways of knowing about them. On the one hand, there is a property instantiated by an object; on the other, there is our knowledge of this instantiation. The instantiation of the property is one thing; the faculty by means of which we detect it is another. This distinction simply reflects the familiar realist separation between ontology and epistemology: the object of knowledge is not to be conflated with the knowledge itself. Knowledge is a relational matter, an interaction between an object and a knowing subject; so the idea of a conceptual inseparability between a fact and a given way of knowing about it sounds wrong as a matter of deep principle. The *objectivity* of a fact seems to imply that it can always be conceptually distinguished from our means of gaining epistemic access to it.

Given this fundamental distinction, we can expect various contingency theses to present themselves—to the effect that a given range of facts is only *contingently* known about in a certain way. For example, we know about light by means of the sense of sight and sound by means of the sense of hearing: but can't we conceive of an *inversion* of these faculties with respect to those properties? Thus light waves might have interacted with our (or some other creature's) senses in such a way as to produce sensations of hearing, and similarly for sound and sensations of seeing: we just need to rig the sensory receptors up so that light stimuli are processed in the auditory cortex and sound waves are processed in the visual cortex.[1] The objective property is one thing, and our perceptual reactions to it another. Accordingly, the connection between them is metaphysically contingent.

Then there is spectrum inversion: here the same subjective sensation might lie behind different discriminatory behaviour, and different sensations might lie behind the same such behaviour. The behavioural evidence is thus inverted with respect to what it is evidence for—the two are only contingently connected. The behavioural evidence for the sensation is not the same as the sensation, so we can conceive of inversions in how the two line up with each other (this possibility is partly what generates the problem of other minds). In a similar way we can keep sensory impressions constant while varying the facts about the external world, as with brain in a vat scenarios and so forth; again, fact and evidence can be pulled apart.[2]

Or consider our knowledge of the near and the distant, and the micro and the macro. We generally have better epistemic access to near objects than far ones, but this seems like a mere contingency: we can easily imagine that our senses were sensitive

[1] Of course, I mean 'sensations of seeing/hearing' phenomenally: the inversion involves a phenomenal similarity combined with a divergence in external causation. I don't, however, mean this to imply some sort of non-intentional conception of phenomenal character; in my view, the inversion case involves a mismatch between the intentional content of the experience and its actual causal source—say, an experience as of certain *sounds* produced by what is in fact *light*. But I won't get into a defence of this way of conceiving phenomenal character (viz. 'representation-alism').

[2] Verificationists and extreme externalists will disagree that this is the right way to describe the brain in a vat, but I am an unreconstructed Cartesian about this, for reasons it would be out of place to pursue here.

in the opposite direction, so that we are better tuned to the properties of far objects than near ones (in fact, of course, in the case of sight there is such a thing as *too* near). If objects were more damaging to a creature's senses the nearer they were, or caused sensory overload, then further objects would be better detected and categorized. Likewise, it does not seem inconceivable that our differential sensitivity to the micro and macro might be inverted: a creature might be sensitive to the molecular structure of objects but overwhelmed by their larger-scale features; and a creature might respond to the properties of whole galaxies as we respond to medium-size objects but not be able to make out tables and chairs at all. This seems no more difficult in principle than the possibility that hearing might be a more discriminating sense than sight (as it is for bats). There seems to be no *necessity* that these types of fact should have the epistemic privileges they actually do have. It is not *intrinsic* to the fact that it is known about in a certain way or with a certain authority. The power of a given faculty seems to be a function of that faculty itself, not the type of fact it can take in.

But there is one area in which it has been assumed that there is no such contingency—namely, our perceptual knowledge of the external world of material objects and our introspective knowledge of our own mental states. External objects *must* be known perceptually, with the accompanying sources of error for such knowledge; and one's mental states *must* be known introspectively, with all the authority that springs from this mode of knowing. I want to explore and question this venerable assumption. Can there be inversions of first-person authority, whereby external objects can be known about with all the authority accorded to introspection, and mental states become subject to all the frailties and fallibility of perceptual knowledge? The question, then, to be a bit more precise, is whether the physical properties of external objects might be known about using a faculty analogous to introspection, while mental properties of the subject are known about by means of faculties analogous to perception. Of course, if we simply *define* the mental and physical in such a way that they are known about by introspection and perception, then the answer will obviously be negative; but I take it that the assumption at issue contains a substantive claim—namely, that fact and faculty necessarily march together. Presumably, there is no *analytic* necessity that they should. It is not that we are stipulatively defining a mental state to be precisely one that is known about introspectively, and a physical state to be one known about perceptually—that would be a gross conflation of the ontological and the epistemological— rather, it is held that as a matter of metaphysical necessity you cannot detach the faculty from the fact. In other words, it is not that it is part of the *concept* of shape, for example, that it be known perceptually, and part of the *concept* of pain that it be known introspectively; yet nevertheless it is necessarily the case that perception and introspection line up with the physical and mental facts this way. We don't want to say that, in a putative possible world in which square things are known about introspectively and pain is known (in the first-person) perceptually, the former is automatically mental and the latter automatically physical! So my question does not have a trivial answer. What is at issue is whether the connection between introspection and the mental— or perception and the physical—is *metaphysically* necessary.[3] I shall be arguing that any such claim of necessary connection is questionable.

---

[3] I am not taking any stand on the nature of such necessity; I am simply observing that it is highly implausible to suppose that 'mental' *means* 'known infallibly' and 'physical' *means* 'known fallibly' (or some such). For if these pairs were synonyms, then an evidently meaningful question would be meaningless. How, positively, to define 'mental' and 'physical' is not an easy question, and depends on the purposes for which such a definition is sought. For my purposes here we can sidestep these difficulties by considering sensation properties and shape properties as representative; then the question is whether we can invert knowledge of these specific properties in the way I am interested in. From now on, then, my talk of 'mental' and 'physical' should be interpreted in this unambitious way.

I now need to distinguish two different questions. First, is it possible for creatures to introspect physical facts and perceive mental facts? Second, is it possible for the *reliability* of knowledge of physical and mental facts to be inverted? The latter question takes no stand on whether it is really introspection or perception that mediates the knowledge; it is concerned solely with whether the customary epistemic privileges of introspection can be inverted—infallibility, self-intimation, incorrigibility. Maybe such inversion is possible even while the faculties deployed are not themselves inverted, so that perception of the physical comes to have the infallibility that introspection of the mental has, and introspection of the mental comes to have the fallibility of ordinary perception of the physical. I am more concerned with this question, but I am also interested in whether faculty inversion is possible; in any case, the questions need to be distinguished, so that a negative answer to the first is not construed as automatically leading to a negative answer to the second.

Of course, not everyone agrees about the nature and extent of first-person authority, but for the purposes of this paper we can take it in the strongest way—this will give the question more bite. That is, I shall assume a strong contrast between the two types of knowledge—taking first-person introspective knowledge to be non-criterial, non-inferential, direct, infallible, incorrigible, and certain; while perceptual knowledge will lack all of these features.[4] This will make the question of inversion as hard for me as possible.

[4] To fix ideas, it helps to focus on the question of whether there is an 'experiential intermediary' involved in the generation of the appropriate belief. When I perceive an object and judge that it is a certain way, my judgement is mediated by an experience that is identical neither to the object nor to the judgement; but when I introspect a sensation there is no such experiential intermediary standing between the sensation and my judgement. The question, then, is whether we can construct a case in which the former type of judgement lacks such an intermediary while the latter rests upon one; and I shall argue that we can. (Of course, talk of an 'experiential intermediary' carries no commitment to a sense-datum theory of perception or the like; nothing I am supposing goes against a 'naïve realist' view of perception.)

How might we argue for the possibility of inversion? First, I want to make two assumptions, which I think are not terribly tendentious: (a) that the property in question and the state of knowing about it are distinct existences; (b) that the two are causally related.[5] Thus, the sensation of pain is not the same as knowing you are in pain, and the former causes the latter; and, similarly, an object's being square is not the same as someone seeing and knowing it is square, though the former causes the latter. These assumptions at least raise the prima facie possibility that the fact and our awareness of it might come apart.

Now let us first consider states of the brain: these states may cause beliefs in us, either as part of the mechanism of introspection or by means of perception (as when I look into my brain with a mirror). Thus some brain states cause others, and these others may realize knowledge of their causes (though not necessarily under brain descriptions). The causal process will involve suitable brain hardware that mediates the causal connection—neural pathways and so on. Call the brain states that prompt introspective knowledge I-states (strictly, it is their mental correspondents that are known), and call those that are known about perceptually P-states; then the question is whether I-states *could* be known perceptually and P-states *could* be known introspectively. That is, could the causal pathways leading from the underlying brain states be inverted in such a way that the corresponding mental state is known perceptually and the (merely) neural state is known introspectively? Might we be able to know our sensations by means of perception and our (non-mental) brain states by means of introspection?

---

[5] (b) entails (a), given plausible assumptions about causation, but it is useful to separate the two features, because of the key role of distinctness in what follows. The causal theory of introspection might be defended in the way a causal theory of perception is typically defended, namely by pointing out that unless there is a causal connection between object and judgement it is hard to see how the judgement can be *of* the object. It is not sufficient for introspecting a given sensation that you have the sensation *and* the judgement; you have to have the judgement *because* of the sensation—*mutatis mutandis* for perception.

Take the second part first. As far as I can see, there is no deep conceptual obstacle to simply rigging up the brain in such a way that the presence of a P-state simply registers with the subject: he spontaneously finds himself believing that the neurons in such-and-such an area are firing at so-and-so rate. He does not see the neurons firing, and he makes no inference from anything else; he simply finds himself with this belief. The neural state in question has caused him to have a belief in its presence—directly, non-criterially, etc. Moreover, he never has such a belief unless the causal relation in question obtains, so there is no possibility of hallucinating or some such. The causal route simply doesn't go through a perceptual channel; there is no perceptual experience *of* the neural state—just an immediate intimation that it is there. It is experienced as a sort of 'intuition', a powerful conviction that something is so in his brain. I don't see why this should be impossible—it seems like a simple rewiring job. We might compare it to a kind of blindsight, in which beliefs are formed without the basis of visual experience; or, less dramatically, forming beliefs on the basis of subliminal 'perception'—that is, the belief comes to you without the mediation of a sensory state *as of* the object of belief. You are struck with the conviction that your brain is thus and so, and this is because it is thus and so and is causing you to believe it.[6]

But if this can work for brain states, there is no reason of principle why it shouldn't work for physical states outside the head. Couldn't we in principle rig the world up in such a way that facts about physical objects are immediately fed into a person's brain and trigger beliefs in their existence, without any perceptual mediation? This may be difficult, scientifically, to be sure; but is it logically impossible? We just need a totally reliable causal pathway

[6] There is no reason why this belief cannot be *conscious*; it is merely that it has no experiential cause. It is as conscious as any belief, such as our logical and mathematical beliefs, which are not caused by sensory experiences either. The beliefs of the blindsighted are also clearly conscious, though not backed by any conscious visual experience.

between fact and belief, which passes through no perceptual stage. Couldn't God have made a world like this? People are blind and deaf (etc.) in this world, but they can form beliefs about the external world with remarkable reliability: they know what is going on out there, and they never make mistakes.[7] Then we could describe this as a case in which either the subjects are 'introspecting' external facts or have a mode of access to them that mirrors introspection in central respects; in any case, we have a kind of 'direct knowledge' of the external world—not perceptually mediated. The causal connection is totally reliable and the perceptual state has been eliminated from the process of belief formation: isn't that the essence of our knowledge of our own mental states? Beliefs about external objects just pop into your head and they are (almost?) never wrong (certainly, we could *increase* the reliability of such beliefs dramatically). So the perceptual and error-prone character of our beliefs about the external world is really a contingent fact about them, not a metaphysical necessity.[8]

The first part of my question is harder: could mental states be known by means of something analogous to perception? Of course, they often are so known—in the third-person case—and this opens the possibility that they might be similarly ascribed even to oneself. What I want to suggest is that the following is a conceivable creature (call him *C*): *C* has mental states, the ability to ascribe them to others on behavioural evidence, but no

[7] Couldn't this just be a basic law of nature in that world, as exceptionless as the gravitational law in our world? There is a nomologically necessary biconditional linking fact with belief, so that believers *must* get it right, and must always get it. In other words, our propensity to error and ignorance is contingent.

[8] Think how different the discipline of epistemology will look for people in that world: with no experiential intermediary to contend with sense-datum theories will not even suggest themselves; there will be no argument from illusion to worry about; there will be no notion of the perceptual given to ground a hoped-for foundationalist epistemology. Being an epistemologist in that world will be a breeze, relatively speaking; it is our specifically experiential access to the world that is responsible for vast tracts of human epistemology, good and bad.

introspective faculty. Thus *C* has pains, can ascribe pain to others, but has no faculty for introspecting his own pains—no first-person ascriptions of the usual type. *C* is the mirror image of a creature that can introspectively self-ascribe mental concepts but has no ability to other-ascribe them (perhaps this creature has no perceptual faculties at all). All that is needed for my introspectively bereft creature *C* is brain damage to the region of the brain that subserves introspection, and presumably there is such a region. I take it that animals and infants can have mental states that they cannot self-ascribe; well, my creature *C* is like them, except that he can ascribe such states to others—that is just the way his brain is configured. But if so, there is no problem about his ascribing mental states to himself on the *same* basis he uses for others—that is, his observable behaviour. Thus he might (a) be in pain, (b) judge that he is in pain, but (c) do so purely on the basis of behavioural criteria. He never ascribes the concept *pain* on any other basis than behaviour. This, I say, is logically possible. In such a case his knowledge that he is in pain is perceptually based and subject to the usual sources of error. We are familiar with the idea that an unconscious mental state might be self-ascribed on behavioural grounds; I am suggesting that the same might be true for a conscious mental state—though one that does not involve introspective awareness *of* it (i.e. introspectively based judgements about it). I am firmly distinguishing the conscious state itself from introspective knowledge of it—for these are distinct existences—and then claiming that we can have the former without the latter, *even when* the subject has the ability to self-ascribe in the third-person mode.[9] This is no doubt a mind-bending idea for creatures like us, who are so used to introspective knowledge, but I don't see any incoherence in it. We could also tell the same kind of story by envisaging a creature that knows his own mental states by means of direct perception of the brain, inferring from the latter to the former. Instead of inferring he is in

[9] Clearly, then, I reject 'higher-order thought' theories of what makes a mental state conscious, for reasons I won't go into here.

pain from perception of his own pain behaviour, he makes this inference from the observation that his C-fibres are firing. In us it is pain itself that triggers first-person introspective ascription of the concept *pain*; in my creature *C* it is perceptually accessed evidence for possession of that sensation, i.e. observable behaviour or correlated brain states.

The fully inverted subject thus combines non-inferential access to external facts with inferential knowledge of his own mental states. Such a putative subject raises a number of very tricky questions, which I will articulate if not resolve. First, what is the nature of the concepts that are applied in the judgements made—are they our usual concepts differently deployed or are they radically new concepts? The subject non-inferentially judges himself to be in a certain neural state, I suggested: but is this really the content of what he judges? The property ascribed is physical, but is the concept used to express this property the same as *our* concept *neural state N*? It might be thought that it cannot be, because concepts are individuated by their conceptual role and the inverted subject invests his concepts with a very different conceptual role from ours: he applies his concept non-inferentially, we do not. Maybe, then, his concept is a *mental* concept—for a physical property? The description 'the cause of the sensation of heat' can denote a physical property while being itself a mental concept—is this what is going on with the inverted subject's concept of his neural state? (Of course, the same question could be raised with respect to his judgements about the shape properties of external objects.) Actually, I doubt this way of looking at the matter: I think that his concept is individuated more by the reference it has, and this is the same as the reference of our concept. The epistemic characteristics of the faculty of ascription do not enter into the identity of the concepts ascribed; indeed, I think the thought-experiment of the inverted subject is a good way to see that it is wrong to tie concepts and epistemic faculties too closely together (see below). I also think the inverted subject has the same mental concepts as us, since his concepts refer to what ours refer to (but see the Postscript). Concepts are individuated by reference; the use of a different evidential basis for applying these concepts does not create a new concept. It is no more true that *C* has a different concept of pain from me than it is that I use different concepts in first- and third-person ascriptions; concepts are not evidentially individuated, in my view (of course, I am not purporting to establish this view here). Those, however, who favour such evidential views may prefer to ascribe different concepts to the inverted subject; my points will still go through under this different mode of characterization.

We can also ask what becomes of phenomenology under inversion: does the physical gain it and the mental lose it? Is phenomenology a function of the mode of epistemic access—so that qualia now attach to the physical, while the mental is robbed of them? I think not. The sensation of pain is still phenomenally individuated, even though it is not ascribed on the *basis* of its phenomenology— just as with third-person ascriptions. And the physical properties of external objects, like shape, do not miraculously grow a phenomenology just by being known about non-perceptually; they are still ordinary physical properties—albeit ones that signal their presence without the benefit of inference. Being non-inferentially and infallibly known is not sufficient to confer a phenomenology on the subject matter of what is known. In short, phenomenology does not have an epistemic ground or analysis. It is not that conscious states *acquire* their phenomenal character from being introspectively known; it is intrinsic to them.

How does the appearance/reality distinction fare under inversion? Is it that the physical loses this distinction while the mental gains it? It is true that my creature *C* perceives the evidence that leads him to ascribe mental states to himself (his observable behaviour or brain), and this evidence is not identical to the mental state it is evidence for; and it is also true that his counterpart does not perceive anything in connection with his knowledge of the external world, so there is no perceptual appearance to contrast with the reality of the thing perceived. But I don't think these truths should make us relocate the appearance / reality distinction in the way suggested. For, first, it is still the case that the feeling of pain cannot be pulled apart from pain itself (though introspective *knowledge* of pain can be pulled apart from pain); and, second, the physical fact is still the kind of thing that *could* appear differently from the way it does—since it *could* be perceived, and perceived differently by different senses. This physical fact doesn't appear perceptually to our inverted subject, but it could appear thus to others (as it does to us)—and these appearances can be pulled apart from the reality of the fact (it could exist and not appear at all). This is really another way of saying what I just said: that the phenomenal appearance of pain is intrinsic to it, while properties like being square can be conceived apart from any particular appearance they may have. The mode of *knowing* is indeed extrinsic to the facts in these cases—that is what the possibility of inverted first-person authority tells us—but that is not the same as the question of how reality and appearance relate in the two cases. So, again, I think there is a constancy in the facts that holds even as we vary the mode of knowing. Concepts and phenomenology (or the lack of it) stay fixed under variations in mode of epistemic access. Ontology is independent of epistemology—yet again.[10]

Another way to see that epistemic privilege is a separate matter from phenomenology is to consider a priori knowledge. We also have certainty in respect of much of our logical and mathematical knowledge, but this obviously has no tendency to show that numbers have phenomenal character. Authoritative, even infallible, knowledge has nothing intrinsically to do with subjectivity,

---

[10] Generally speaking, verificationism is vulnerable to inverted evidence arguments, since they pull facts and verification procedures apart. The same concepts, representing the same states of affairs, are applied in different evidential conditions.

or else numbers would have subjectivity. I emphasize this because so many people seem to think that phenomenology is somehow a function of the special access we have to our own mental states—as if it is somehow projected from the unmediated way that mental concepts are applied in first-person judgements.[11]

Inverted first-person authority has an obvious bearing upon scepticism. The standard Cartesian position is that scepticism applies to the external world but not to knowledge of one's own mental states. I have no desire to contest that position, but I do want to contest the correlative modal claim that *necessarily* scepticism applies in this differential way: I suggest that it is only contingent that there is this difference of application of scepticism. In other words, physical facts are not intrinsically vulnerable to scepticism and mental states intrinsically invulnerable. If the inverted subject knows about his mental states by perception-based inference from his behaviour, then clearly scepticism will gain purchase—just as it does for other minds, and for the same reason. It will make sense for the inverted subject to wonder whether he really is in pain, since his behaviour is neither necessary nor sufficient for this to be so. The evidence for his self ascriptions is indirect and fallible.[12] On the other hand, since his knowledge of the external world is not mediated by perception, and depends upon an absolutely reliable hook-up between fact and belief, he will not be able to entertain the hypothesis that things

[11] I take Brian Loar to be a clear representative of this point of view: see his 'Phenomenal States' in *The Nature of Consciousness*, (eds.) Ned Block, Owen Flanagan, and Guven Guzeldere (MIT Press: 1997); but I think the general view is quite widespread.

[12] It might be thought that he can know if he is *pretending* to be in pain, so the case is different from our knowledge (or ignorance) of other minds. But this is not to take the thought-experiment far enough: he must *also* conjecture that he is pretending on the basis of his own behavioural evidence (maybe he is not putting on a very convincing display of being in pain). Indeed, his only access to his *intentions* is through the behavioural manifestations of these intentions: he knows that he intends to take a beer from the fridge, say, because he *sees* himself taking a beer from there and makes a defeasible inference.

may perceptually seem just this way without there being any corresponding external state of affairs. He makes no inference from his perceptual state, so his knowledge cannot be threatened by the possibility that this inference may lead to a false conclusion; he is simply visited with the primitive conviction that things are externally thus and so, and this conviction is reliably connected to things being that way. There is no perceptual interface, nothing that could stay mentally fixed while the external facts vary. There can be no such thing as hallucination or illusion (and hence no such thing as sceptical arguments from these possibilities). There is no perceptual appearance from which external reality might diverge.[13]

It may be said that it is at least *logically* possible that the inverted subject is a brain in a vat, in which case he will have the same conviction about the external world that we have, but this conviction will be false—thus allowing scepticism to gain a foothold. This is notoriously tricky territory, but let me make the following brief remarks. First, it is quite unclear what this notion of logical possibility is and why it is relevant. There is no *logical* impossibility in the idea of your having a mental state and forming a false introspective belief about it—logic alone does not ensure infallibility here. We are not here in the realm of analytic truths. So the impossibility of scepticism with respect to knowledge of one's own mind is not ensured by any kind of simple conceptual necessity;[14] it must arise from some sort of strict causal reliability. In other words, it must come from the truth of some suitably strong

[13] Thus the super-blindsighted (and super-deafhearing, etc.) cannot be made subject to classic Cartesian scepticism: they cannot be troubled by the thought that all their experiences could be as they are and yet the world not be as it is experientially represented (though they may be troubled by other sceptical thoughts).

[14] Such as an a priori *identity* between the sensation and the judgement that you have it: this would clearly preclude the possibility of having one item in this pair without the other, and thus secure self-intimation and infallibility. However, such an identity thesis is grossly implausible, since (among other things) it rules out the possibility of creatures with pains that lack the *concept* of pain.

counterfactuals—to the effect that if one were to believe one was in pain then one would be in pain, where the reliability is extremely well entrenched. But the same could be true of the inverted subject with respect to the external world: God has arranged it so that similar counterfactuals relating fact and belief hold—the subject thus never gets it wrong. I think this is enough to give him knowledge, indeed certainty.[15] His knowledge would resemble our knowledge of elementary logic or arithmetic.

What is clear is that the inverted subject cannot perform the standard sceptical thought experiment of detaching his sense experience from its usual external cause, thus creating a sceptical set-up in which appearance is pulled apart from reality, since his knowledge of the external world is not perceptual to begin with. He cannot entertain the thought: 'Everything might perceptually seem this way, but it does not follow that reality is as it appears.' Thus he cannot contemplate *our* sort of scepticism. Perhaps we (and he) can make sense of the metaphysical possibility that the cause of his convictions is just some internal brain state, with no external object to correspond to the belief; but we equally seem to be able to formulate a comparable alleged possibility with respect to our introspective beliefs—namely, that they are not caused by mental states but by some other purely physical cause in the brain.[16] No asymmetry can be constructed here, precisely because of the absence of a perceptual intermediary between fact and belief. The essential point is that the standard way of creating a

[15] I am here assuming the correctness of some sort of reliability account of knowledge and justification, the details of which need not be spelled out here.

[16] I can certainly *say* this and not contradict myself, given the causal and distinctness assumptions we have been working with. And, after all, won't there be some most proximate physical cause of my introspective belief that could in principle operate without the prior mental state that the belief purports to be about? It can hardly be that introspective certainty depends on the empirical fact that the mental state causes the belief in its presence without the mediation of any physical mechanism. There must surely be neural pathways in the brain that link the sensation to a belief in its presence; so why can't we have a set-up in which only the final portion of the pathway is kept intact, with the initiating mental cause deleted? This certainly *seems* like a describable situation.

sceptical possibility about the external world is inapplicable, namely keeping the perceptual data constant and varying the external facts. So, even if there is a type of scepticism that can be generated for the inverted subject, it will not be *that* kind of scepticism—the kind that seems so natural and inevitable in the light of the way we *actually* form our beliefs about the external world.[17]

If there can be an inverted subject, therefore, then there can be an inverted scepticism. The inverted subject will be troubled by scepticism about his own mind, but not about the external world. Not that this *answers* scepticism, of course—for him or us; it simply notes that the way scepticism falls out is a contingent feature of the way we happen to form our knowledge of reality. It is not *inherent* in mind and matter that the former should be invulnerable to (traditional) scepticism while the latter is prey to it. Scepticism arises from the *relation* between fact and faculty, not from the nature of the fact alone.

It may be heuristically helpful here to think about God's knowledge. Presumably, God does not *perceive* the world of physical objects, in the sense that he directs his senses towards it and receives experiences from which he makes inferences; his knowledge must

[17] It might be illuminating to distinguish two types of scepticism: the natural from the contrived, the pressing from the pedantic. The traditional problems of other minds and the external world are of the former type, proceeding from the ease with which we can intellectually separate the basis of judgement from what the judgement aims to get right (behaviour and mental states, experiences and external objects). The idea of an impenetrable interface certainly gains a ready hold on the philosophical imagination in both cases. On the other hand, types of scepticism that trade simply on the possibility of error seems far less gripping—as when we are told that our mathematical and logical beliefs might all be wrong because we have made mathematical and logical mistakes in the past. Then we might say that my inverted subject can be exposed to the uninteresting scepticism that insists that his holding the beliefs he does fails to logically entail their truth, while not being susceptible to the more visceral kind of scepticism that so grips us—the possibility of a vast mismatch between the perceptual appearances and outer reality. The feeling that one really has access only to one's own experiences can only arise if one *has* experiences (and there is, I think, no comparable feeling with respect to one's beliefs—for reasons it would be interesting to investigate).

be more 'direct' than that, more intimate. Equally, it is not to be supposed that he introspects our mental states (they aren't his!), and obviously he doesn't infer them from our behaviour. Omniscience doesn't work like that (or so we naturally suppose). God must enjoy some other mode of epistemic access to his creation, some sort of infallible intuition about how things are. He is not troubled by Cartesian worries about widespread illusion and the like—so he has no need of a further God to guarantee the correctness of *his* beliefs, with the threat of infinite regress that ensues. In any case, his knowledge of the material world cannot be modelled upon our perceptual knowledge of it. And why *should* it be so modelled? When the material universe has been created it has yet to be settled how it might come to be known; installing senses like ours in creatures like us is just one way—faculties that generate experiences from stimuli upon which beliefs are based. We can surely envisage other methods by which material facts come to be registered in knowing creatures. What about that idea of universal super-blindsight—reliable knowledge of the world without any experiential intermediary?

If we imagine a community of inverted subjects, with philosophers among them, we can suppose that they have no particular problem about knowledge of the external world, but they do fret over something called the 'own mind problem'. How, they wonder, can they really know whether they even have mental states? Some have noticed that they must have *some* mental states or else they couldn't be wondering (just like Descartes), but they still worry that their usual attributions might be wrong: they *think* they are in pain when they groan and grimace, but this is a fallible inference—maybe they have never felt pain at all! Some are convinced sceptics about self-ascriptions of mental states, while entertaining no anxieties about their knowledge of the external world— this not being based on inference (where there is no criterion, there is no possibility of it being misapplied). Maybe one eccentric among the philosophers starts to wonder whether their epistemic predicament is necessary or contingent, and formulates the idea of an inversion of modes of knowing—in which the external world is known by fallible perceptual inference and mental states by some strange sort of infallible direct intuition. Her colleagues may suspect that she has a screw loose in conjuring up such an odd idea, but she persists nonetheless.

It is sometimes supposed that the special character of first-person knowledge of mental states is what gives rise to the impression that they are irreducible to physical states of the brain. We misinterpret merely epistemic features of our concepts of the mental for deep truths about the very nature of mental states.[18] We know about brain states in one way—by perception—and about mental states in another way—by introspection—and we suppose that this merely epistemic difference reflects an onto-logical distinction. Is this a plausible diagnosis of the root of the mind-body problem? The inverted subject thought-experiment gives us a way to think about this question. If the mind-body problem arose from different modes of epistemic access, as a kind of misplaced projection, then we can make certain predictions about inversion cases: that the properties that are known with first-person authority should strike the subject as the problematic member of the pair, and that sameness of access should eliminate the felt problem. Consider, then, our inverted subject's conception of material objects—the conception he has as one who knows about them 'directly': does he believe that such objects are spooky relative to mental states? Is it that, in reflecting on his concepts, he comes to the view that physical properties are problematic in comparison with mental properties, perhaps inviting reduction or even elimination? And does he, correspondingly, take mental

---

[18] See n. 11. The idea is that we mistake conceptual differences for ontological ones, projecting the former onto the latter—rather as it is sometimes supposed that we mistake the distinctive characteristics of moral concepts for a special category of moral properties. I myself don't find this kind of 'error theory' plausible in either case, and I am suggesting that the inversion cases are a good way to see that this diagnosis is on the wrong track in the case of the mind-body problem.

properties to be unproblematic, in view of his indirect perceptual access to them?

These strike me as odd and implausible conjectures: I don't think his sense of the conceptually problematic would be inverted in this way. I suggest that he would have essentially the same physical concepts that we have, and not regard the denoted properties as peculiar; his mode of epistemic access would not colour his sense of the ontological peculiarities. For how can the physical become problematic just by being known about differently? Surely there would be no temptation to conflate ontology and epistemology here—so why make that diagnosis for our current conception of the mental? Furthermore, let us suppose that we are dealing with another type of case—that in which the subject has the *same* mode of access to both sorts of fact: either he knows about both physical and mental directly or he knows both indirectly. In the former case, he has *no* perceptual knowledge; all his knowledge is 'intuitive' knowledge—knowledge not based on inference, with no experiential intermediary. Are we to suppose that this would dissolve the mind-body problem for him? The claim might be that, since he knows about both mental and physical properties in the direct way, he enjoys the theoretical comforts of conceptual homogeneity, and hence has no sense of a gap between mental and physical. Again, I find this highly doubtful: the identity of the modes of epistemic access wouldn't cause him to assimilate the denoted properties—he would still sense the difference between these properties. All he needs to appreciate the mind-body problem is knowledge of *which* properties he is referring to, and this he could have despite the differences in the authority with which he applies the corresponding concepts. (So if you are thinking of having inversion surgery in order to cure yourself of the mind-body problem, don't do it.) Making his ascriptions non-inferential (and so on) doesn't imply that he loses his grip on the nature of what he is referring to. And making both sorts of ascription inferential and perception-based likewise does not obliterate the felt problem. So, in our case, why assume that we are somehow bamboozled by our modes of access into conjuring an ontological divide that isn't really there? The inverted subject thought-experiment is thus a good way to evaluate this sort of diagnosis of the source of the mind-body problem.

What this suggests, more generally, is that an epistemic treatment of concepts is on the wrong track. I think we can detach mental and physical concepts from the epistemic faculties within which they are actually applied: thus the same concepts can be applied either inferentially or non-inferentially, with a perceptual basis or without (though I don't expect that what I have said here will persuade proponents of epistemic theories). Therefore, we need a three-way distinction—between properties, concepts, and modes of access. We have (say) the property of neurons firing, the concept *neurons firing*, and then the particular epistemic faculty that is employed when that concept is applied—either perceptual or non-perceptual. Whether a concept is applied on the basis of a perceptual criterion or not is strictly irrelevant to its identity.[19] As I said earlier, I prefer to individuate concepts in terms of their reference, not the epistemic characteristics that happen to govern their application.[20] No doubt there is something stipulative about how we are to use the word 'concept', but the important point is that *something* cognitive is kept constant as we vary the epistemic faculties—it is not merely an identity of reference, but of sense. As an analogy: the very same concept *square* can be applied within

[19] So it would be wrong to suggest that having the concept *square*, say, consists in having a propensity to judge that things are square just when one has an experience as of a square thing. That is not a necessary condition for having the concept *square*, given that my inverted subject is possible; there is thus no essential connection between possessing the concept and undergoing the corresponding experience.

[20] A referential theory of concepts faces questions of individuation: how can concepts differ if their reference is the same? I am not trying to solve this familiar problem, though I think that one can go a long way here without invoking anything but properties. My present point is that invoking epistemic faculties is not the way to handle such questions: it is never a good move to say that concept C_1 is different from concept C_2 because C_1 is applied infallibly (etc.) and C_2 is not.

different sense-modalities, say touch and sight; it is not that the difference of faculty generates a new concept with no cognitive overlap. In a slogan: concepts transcend epistemic faculties. I suppose this is really just to say that verificationism is false—which, of course, it is.

Putting together scepticism and the mind-body problem, then, we can say that the latter problem does not arise because of the differential applicability of scepticism to the physical world and the mental world. It is not that our sense of the mind-body problem is a result of the fact that we can doubt the external world but not the internal world—since if we invert these we don't make the problem go away. The indubitability of the mind is not what underlies our sense of the distinction between mind and body.[21] It is true that, as things are, scepticism applies to the physical world but not the mental world, but this is independent of our inclination to insist on an ontological distinction between them. So Descartes' two big problems turn out not to be interconnected. It is *not* that we think the mind cannot be the body because we can see that the mind cannot be doubted but the body can; this epistemic difference is orthogonal to the mind-body problem.

What I have basically argued is that mind and matter cannot be epistemologically defined: that is, we cannot define matter as what is known about by perception and mind as what is known about by introspection. The possibility of epistemic inversion shows that ontology and epistemology are not this tightly linked. The idea that matter can be defined as what is imperfectly known and mind

[21] This goes against the spirit of one of Descartes' arguments for dualism, namely that the mind must be distinct from the body because the existence of the former is indubitable while the existence of the latter is not. If this epistemic difference is contingent, it is hard to see how it could be *essential* to the distinction between mind and body, *constitutive* of it; and of course Descartes' argument is notoriously suspicious for conflating ontology and epistemology (i.e. trading on an opaque context). The distinction between mind and body cannot *consist* in a difference in how well they are known; this epistemic difference must spring from something about their nature, antecedently established.

as what is perfectly known is wrong. This should not seem terribly surprising once one has made a sharp distinction between facts and our knowledge of them. How else mind and matter may be defined is a separate question, and one that may not have a good answer.[22]

Postscript to 'Inverted First-Person Authority'

I should address myself to a rather glaring tension between this paper and what I say in 'What Constitutes the Mind-Body Problem?' and elsewhere. In 'Inverted' I suggest that my inverted subject has the concept of pain even though he has no first-person access to pain, i.e. no introspective acquaintance with it. In 'What Constitutes' I say that one cannot have the concept of pain without being acquainted with pain. Something has to give. On the one hand, I am motivated by the well-known point that concepts of experience require for their possession that one has self-awareness of instances of their extension; on the other hand, I am influenced by the plausibility of 'referentialist' accounts of concepts and by the implausibility of 'conceptual role' accounts of concepts. Both forces seem to me strong and not easily brushed off—yet they conflict with each other. What to say?

One option would be to restate the thesis that concepts of experience require acquaintance with the relevant experiences; say instead that one cannot have such a concept without *having* the experience—but that one need not be *acquainted* with it. Then my inverted subject *can* have the concept of pain, despite his lack of introspective awareness of it, since he does *have* pains. This dissolves the tension, but I think it understates the way concepts of

[22] I am thinking here of trying to define that difference in such a way as to make the definition useful to formulating a substantive doctrine of physicalism. I argue in 'What Constitutes the Mind-Body Problem?' (Chapter 1 of this book) that this is a hopeless task, following others. However, for my purposes in the present paper, we don't need to answer the broad question of how to define 'mental' and 'physical' in order to see that epistemic definitions won't work (see also n. 3).

experience depend upon experiences: one really does need to be directly acquainted with pain in order to have the concept—at least the concept *we* have.

A second option is to say that the inverted subject lacks *our* concept of pain, on account of his lack of acquaintance with pains, but that he has *a* concept of pain—one that resembles ours in certain important respects. Compare the blind man and colour concepts: true, he lacks our concepts of colour, but he has *some* sort of concept of colour—he is not like someone who has never heard of colour and knows nothing about it. The blind man has a kind of *schematic* concept of colour, based on all the things he knows about it—rather as we can arrive at a schematic concept of a bat's echolocatory experience. What he lacks, we are inclined to say, is the *full* concept of colour; his grasp is *partial*. Similarly, we might say that the inverted subject does not have our concept of pain but still has some sort of concept: he can apply the word in its third-person uses perfectly well, and he may know other things about pain, e.g. that it contrasts with pleasure and betokens injury. He might have a *functional* concept of pain, which coincides with our concept at certain points. Then we can say that the inverted subject has and applies this schematic concept of pain, despite his lack of first-person acquaintance. Certainly, as I say in the paper, pain is what in fact lies at the other end of the relevant causal chains that prompt his use of 'pain': he is *referring* to pain, even if he doesn't conceptualize pain as we do.

A third option would be to say that he is acquainted with pain after all—it is just that he has no ability introspectively to ascribe the concept to himself. He can engage in acts of acquaintance with his pains but he cannot judge *that* he is in pain on the basis of these acts; his acquaintance never functions as the ground of his self-ascriptions. This is logically consistent, just about, but it is surely deeply unattractive, since it dissociates self-awareness by means of acquaintance from the capacity to make introspective judgements. It is as if the subject can directly tell that he has a pain but he cannot judge that he does, even though he has the concept of pain and the capacity to make judgements involving that concept (only not on the basis of introspection). This is hard to make sense of.

Of these three options I find the second the least unpalatable, because it grants cogency to both of the conflict-generating forces. If we take this line, then the correct description of my inverted subject is that he can self- and other-ascribe the concept *pain**, where this concept shares its extension and some of its intension with our concept *pain*. What is perhaps less clear is that he could fully appreciate the mind-body problem with respect to pain by possessing only *pain**. He certainly lacks the most basic way that we grasp that problem, as I articulate it in 'What Constitutes', since he has no direct acquaintance with his sensations. Of course, all of this is very difficult to judge, because we are dealing with a far-out thought-experiment that does not reveal every aspect of itself, and the question of concept possession is vexed in any case.

What is important is that the inverted subject can ascribe what is in fact pain to himself (without perhaps having the full concept *pain*), and do so with the same kind of fallibility that afflicts our third-person uses of the concept. That is sufficient for the kind of inversion I am envisaging. (Note that no comparable issue arises with respect to the other wing of the inversion, since the possession of physical concepts is not plausibly tied to their perceptual use: one can employ the concept *square* in judgements applied 'directly'.)

10

The Objects of Intentionality

1. The word 'object' has a number of different meanings in philosophy, marking several kinds of distinction. When used in the phrase 'intentional object' it expresses the idea of what a mental state is 'directed towards': the intentional object of my belief that London is large is London, since that is what my belief is about (plus being large). In this sense, everything and anything can be an object—properties, events, processes, Fregean functions, universals, numbers, gods, and ghosts—since all these things can be what a belief is 'directed towards'. Objects, in this sense, are simply correlative with the idea of content. They are not the same as 'intensional entities'—such items as Fregean senses or intensions in the technical model-theoretic sense. They are not 'abstract', since London is an intentional object—what someone is thinking about. Nor do they necessarily exist, since I can be thinking about Zeus or Pegasus. And it would be equally wrong to suppose that they necessarily *don't* exist, since London exists. The *merely* intentional object doesn't exist, as that phrase is typically used—it is thought about but has no reality. Pegasus is *only* an object of thought. It is futile to ask after the 'ontological status' of

intentional objects: some of them are things like London and Bill Clinton—things that exist—while some are things like Zeus and Pegasus—things that don't exist.[1] The phrase 'intentional object' does not single out some special type of object (in another sense of that word), but simply gives expression to the idea of what a mental state may be about. If you ask me what the object of my search is, I may say 'the fountain of youth'—this is simply what I am searching *for*—and you can agree that this is what I am searching for even if you doubt the existence of such a thing. This sense of 'object' could just as well be expressed by the words 'target' or 'focus' or some neologism like 'intentionalandum'; there is certainly no valid move from describing something as an intentional object to describing it as an object in some of the other philosophical senses—as existent, or complete, or concrete, or whatever. This notion is customary in the philosophical tradition, being roughly equivalent to Husserl's *noema*, and it has an established use in analytical philosophy. I am labouring it here because I am going to make heavy use of the notion in what follows, and I don't want to be misunderstood; specifically, I am not going to be arguing for the utility of 'non-extensional entities' like Fregean senses. If anything, intentional objects belong at the level of reference (though, of course, senses can also be intentional objects if they are thought *about*, as opposed to being the means whereby other things are thought about).[2]

---

[1] See Elizabeth Anscombe, 'The Intentionality of Sensation', in *Analytical Philosophy*, edited by R. J. Butler (Blackwell, 1968). I am generally indebted to this still important but nowadays neglected paper.

[2] Two views can be held about the relation between senses and intentionality: that senses are themselves intentional objects, or that they are merely the means by which references become intentional objects. I favour the latter view: we don't think *about* senses when we have a thought with a certain reference; senses are what *enable* us to think about references (so they don't 'get between' us and the world). If we were to construe senses as themselves intentional objects, we would have the question of what makes them so, and this would threaten an infinite regress of senses. Senses, then, are not to be construed as a type of intentional object—except of course when they feature as the explicit reference of a thought.

The notion of an intentional object can be introduced in a slightly more formal way, as follows. Suppose a sentence of the form 'aRb' is true, where 'a' is the name of a person, 'R' is a psychological verb, and 'b' is a singular term: for instance 'the Greeks worshipped Zeus' or 'Bill is thinking about Susan'. Then we can say that the 'b' part gives the intentional object of the person's attitude. To speak of an intentional object is *just* to speak of the truth of such a sentence, so that if such a sentence is true then it *follows* that the person's attitude has a certain intentional object; in other words, the notion captures certain grammatical facts. If I say that 'b' specifies an intentional object, I am simply saying that there is a true sentence of the form just outlined. I don't myself think it is particularly useful or illuminating to formulate the notion in this formal way, but it serves to pin it down for those who suspect the notion of harbouring some ominous ontological agenda (say, to resurrect Meinong, as they understand him—or misunderstand him).[3]

I need to make another distinction, between *de re* and *de dicto* intentional objects. Again, this is not a distinction between classes of object, since the *same* objects (in the other sense) can be now *de re* and now *de dicto* intentional objects; the distinction has to do with the nature of the intentional relation—or the truth conditions of intentional sentences, if you prefer. Suppose I am aiming my bow and arrow in the direction of a field, and in fact my father is standing in my line of fire—but I don't know it is my father: then my father can be said to be the *de re* intentional object of my aiming—he is the object that my aim is directed (literally) towards. Why would I be aiming at my father in this way? Because my

---

[3] For a scholarly treatment of Meinong see Janet Farrell Smith, 'The Russell-Meinong Debate', in *Philosophy and Phenomenological Research*, 45: 3, March 1985. This article makes it clear that the popular idea that Russell decisively refuted Meinong (so that we no longer have to take him seriously) is wide of the mark; Meinong's views are far more defensible than we have been schooled to think. I also recommend Terence Parsons', *Nonexistent Objects* (Yale University Press, 1980), a rigorous and sensible defence of Meinongian metaphysics.

father looks to me like a tree stump and I am doing some harmless target practice. If you ask me what I am aiming at I will say 'that tree stump', pointing my finger in the direction of my father—this is the *de dicto* intentional object of my aiming. The *de dicto* object obviously corresponds to the content of my intention—how I am representing the world. And of course this object does not exist, since there *is* no tree stump in my line of fire; I have simply mistaken my father for a tree stump. My father exists and is the *de re* object of my mental state; the tree stump does not exist and is the *de dicto* object of my mental state. If we ask what I am aiming at in this situation, we get two answers—a man and a stump—only one of which is a real object. In one sense I am aiming at something that does not exist; in another at something that does. This point will be important later, when I argue that this kind of case is a lot more common than people have thought.

2. I now want to become a little more controversial. I am going to sketch a portrait of non-existent objects—which many philosophers find repugnant. I am not going to defend this notion here, though that has been done elsewhere.[4] I don't actually think the sketch ought to be very controversial, once it is clearly understood; but experience has shown me that many people find the idea of non-existent objects intensely distressing. My purpose here will be to put this idea to use in unexpected ways, not to provide a full justification for it; so the paper will have only a conditional interest for those subject to the distress just mentioned.

By a non-existent object I mean such things as Zeus or Pegasus or Vulcan or Allen Smithee[5]—things that are thought about, maybe even believed in, but which don't exist. These are objects of thought, but not existent objects of thought; and perhaps it

---

[4] See ch. 2 of my book *Logical Properties* (Oxford University Press, 2000). Unfortunately, I had not read Parsons' *Nonexistent Objects* at the time of writing my book, but I would now want to cite it enthusiastically.

[5] Allen Smithee is the non-existent movie director that real directors attribute their movies to when they don't like the way they turn out.

will ease some of that distress if I observe that 'non-existent object' is simply short for 'non-existent *intentional* object'. Some philosophers think to make some argumentative headway here by asking, in a sneering tone of voice, 'How can there be non-existent *objects*?'—clearly intending some other notion of object. But this rhetorical question loses all force if we ask instead 'How can there be non-existent *intentional objects*?'—since that cancels the other sense of 'object', in which existence is already presupposed. There is obviously no strain whatsoever in saying 'The object of Jones's search is entirely non-existent'—that is, the intentional object of his search does not exist. In any case, I intend to be speaking of intentional objects that don't exist—corresponding to sentences of the 'aRb' form in which 'b' is an 'empty' singular term. These are simply cases in which 'aRb' is true but 'b exists' is false (obviously, then, I reject the idea that a sentence of the former form can be true *only* if a sentence of the latter form is). Of course, there are a great many cases like this, whenever so-called 'empty terms' occur in the language. And the source of these cases are such familiar phenomena as misperceptions, hallucinations, dreams, mental images, deceptive verbal testimony, novels, theoretical error, and so on. Many of our intentional objects fail to exist, and life goes on regardless.[6]

Let me then simply state what I take to be the chief characteristics of non-existent objects. First, they are not mental—except, of course, when they are (for example, that non-existent pain I deceived you into believing I had yesterday). Zeus is not a mental object, but a divine object—which fails to exist. No doubt Zeus's properties are conferred by human acts of mind, like the characters in a novel; they certainly don't come from his mind-independent reality. The properties of fictional characters are the upshot of creative mental acts, but it would be wrong to assimilate such

---

[6] I think we tend to assume that non-existent objects are relatively rare and parasitic on existent objects; and we also assume that they invariably arise from some sort of cognitive malfunction. Not so, as I shall be arguing later.

characters to mental entities like beliefs and intentions—Zeus is not himself a belief (otherwise he *would* exist). Second, non-existent objects are not senses, even if these are taken to be non-mental: I am not speaking of the *sense* of 'Zeus' when I speak of him—and if I were, again he would exist. Such objects belong in the realm of reference. In fact, I think there is no problem in saying that 'Zeus' *refers* to Zeus: this is perfectly correct and natural English.[7] And it surely follows from the fact that the Greeks worshipped Zeus that they referred to him—for how could they worship him (have that mental attitude) unless they could make him the object of their thoughts, and hence refer to him?

It is possible to make true statements about non-existent objects: that they don't exist, that they are sometimes believed to exist, that they have such properties as being divine, irascible, and powerful. Indeed, I think *anything* can be truly predicated of them *except* existence: Sherlock Holmes is a detective, a man, a concrete entity (not an abstract one), has causal powers (he is a noted pugilist), lives in London, and so on. He has the properties he is represented as having, though only by virtue of being represented as having them. He is a perfectly ordinary individual—except for the small matter of not existing. In other words, there are true subject–predicate statements with 'Sherlock Holmes' as their subject term.[8]

Non-existent objects are no more 'bundles of qualities' than existent objects. It is not that they somehow reduce to their properties, while existent objects do not: they *instantiate*

[7] A prejudice against admitting this has grown up in analytical philosophy, but it is really nothing more than the plain truth that we can use the words 'about' and 'of' in connection with non-existent objects: for how could our discourse be *about* something to which we could not *refer*? Stipulatively restricting the use of 'refers' to the case of existent objects results from a kind of metaphysical hypochondria—as if using it also for non-existent objects might lead one to come down with a bad case of Meinong's syndrome (symptom: a bloated ontology).

[8] Parsons' *Nonexistent Objects* is particularly good on this.

properties, they don't collapse into them. It is often argued, correctly, that objects cannot be sets of properties because that would make them abstract entities, and they are not; but this point applies equally to non-existent objects. Also, of course, if they were such sets or bundles, they would have to exist, since the sets or bundles do—but *they* (the objects) don't. The non-existence of these objects amply distinguishes them from their existent fellows; it is a symptom of confusion to try to find some other way to distinguish them—and these ways always end up negating the very non-existence they are trying to capture (that they are mental or are senses or reduce to sets of properties).

Non-existent objects exhibit a marked degree of indeterminacy: not every predicate either applies to them or its negation does. This is a very familiar point: it cannot be said either that Hamlet has a mole on his left shoulder or that he does not; the number of lines under his eyes is utterly indeterminate; the colour of his underwear is not just vague but radically unsettled. This is really a result of the conferred status of the properties of such objects: when an object is merely intentional there is nothing to confer properties on it *but* the mental acts of its entertainers. Non-existence and indeterminacy go together.

There is also a clear sense in which there is no appearance/reality distinction for merely intentional objects: they have no properties beyond, or other than, those bestowed upon them. As a result, we cannot make sense of widespread error about their properties—it cannot be that we have got it all wrong about Zeus. This is because what Zeus *is* consists in what we take him to be, so he has no nature that might diverge from the one we attribute to him. Of course, there is room for local errors, based on false testimony, mistranslations, and so on; but there is no room for the idea that everyone had it wrong all the time—any more than Conan Doyle might be fundamentally mistaken about his own fictional creation.[9] There is thus no 'reality' apart from the appearance—truth and believed truth cannot be pulled apart. Non-existent objects are individuated by the way they are represented, while existent objects can generally be quite other than the way they appear and are described.

I have said that non-existent objects can be referred to; so semantic predicates apply to them. There are truths of the form 'x refers to y' even when y does not exist. Presumably, it is obvious that this precludes a perfectly general causal theory of reference—if this means that the object of reference has to play a causal role in producing instances of the name (or some such). A causal theorist of this (simple) kind will have to contest my claim about reference and non-existence. I do not intend here to contest his contestation; I am going to assume that reference to the non-existent is possible, and that as a consequence a (simple) causal theory of reference is wrong for such reference.[10] My claim will be that such reference is extremely widespread, and is in fact the primary case.

What we need to take from this brief discussion of non-existence is that some intentional objects don't exist but that otherwise they are just like existent objects. It is not that I accept an 'ontology' of non-existent objects—if that means that I believe that they enjoy *some* sort of existence. I accept no such thing: merely intentional objects do not exist in *any* sense—that is their whole point. What we have is terms in our language that refer to such non-existent objects of thought: that is all. I am separating reference from existence, not claiming that we have reference to some special exotic brand of quasi-existing entities. Nor am I introducing some such notion as *subsistence*: I am using the single notion of

---

[9] The reason for this, of course, is that the properties of a fictional character are stipulated not discovered: Conan Doyle knows a priori that Sherlock Holmes is a brilliant detective—just as I can know a priori that this stick is a metre long.

[10] A causal theory of reference for property reference would not be compromised by the case of reference to non-existent objects. It is entirely consistent to hold that predicates get their reference by virtue of a causal link to properties, while singular terms refer purely by means of associated descriptions.

existence and saying outright that some intentional objects lack this property—*tout court*. It is not that there are two types of 'being', one stronger than the other; there is just being and non-being.[11]

3. With these preliminary matters clarified, I shall argue now that reference to the non-existent is central, ubiquitous, harmless, and theoretically illuminating. Non-existent objects are not things to be afraid of—to quarantine and banish—but things to welcome and put to work; they are our friends not our enemies. They are not merely peripheral anomalies, to be disposed of and disrespected; they are the foundation of all intentionality—the basic case. I expect this to sound shocking now, but by the end of the paper I hope to have rendered the claim banal and innocuous (or at least tolerable). The claim to be established, then, is that whenever there is intentionality directed towards an existent object there is intentionality concurrently directed towards a non-existent object, so that reference to the non-existent is always embedded within

---

[11] I want to make it clear that I am not adopting a 'deflationary' view of reference to the non-existent, along these lines: for a term to refer to a non-existent object is simply for it *not* to refer to an existent object—that is, there is no existent object to which it refers. On the contrary, I maintain that for a term to refer to a non-existent object is for there to be an object such that it is referred to by the term and that object has the property of non-existence. So reference to the non-existent is not the mere *lack* of reference to the existent; it is a kind of reference in its own right. To hold the 'deflationary' view would be flatly inconsistent with my later claim that a term can have both an existent and a non-existent referent, since that latter possibility isn't one if reference to the non-existent just *is* the absence of reference to something existent. The 'deflationary' view, as stated, has the consequence that anything that inherently lacks reference—a table, a mountain, a piece of verbal nonsense—refers to something non-existent, since it fails to refer to something existent; which is plainly false. Reference to the non-existent is a positive intentional act; it is not merely the absence of any intentional act. I think, in fact, that the 'deflationary' view is shown to be erroneous by the non-contradictory status of the claim that a term can have both an existent and a non-existent referent (as with a classic Donnellan case in which the description 'the man drinking a martini' can refer to a real man drinking water as well as to a non-existent martini drinker). Non-existence is indeed lack of existence, but *reference* to the non-existent is not lack of reference to the existent—it is reference to something that lacks existence. (This footnote was prompted by a question of David Chalmers.)

reference to the existent; but the converse does not hold. Moreover, there is a sense in which reference to the existent is *dependent* on reference to the non-existent.

There are two ways to argue for this claim: the argument from error, and the argument from individuation. The former way is less interesting, so I shall spend less time on it. In the case of my father and the tree stump the non-existence of my *de dicto* intentional object results from the perceptual error that characterizes the case: there is simply nothing there that is a tree stump, though it seems to me that there is—so 'that tree stump' does not refer to an existent thing (though it does, according to me, refer to a non-existent thing). I have made a mistake of existence, supposing that something exists that does not; this arises simply because I take a predicate to be satisfied in my environment that is not so satisfied, namely 'tree stump'. In effect, my perceptual state affirms the proposition that there exists a tree stump in my visual field, but there is nothing of that kind there, so my perceptual state is incorrect; hence if I were to give a name to what I seem to see, that name would fail to refer to an existent thing. This is to say that in a case of error my intentional object (or one of them) fails to exist—I have a non-existent intentional object. Now suppose that such perceptual error were widespread, even universal; then it would follow that the majority, or even all, perceptual states introduced non-existent intentional objects—in addition to the real ones that constitute the *de re* objects of perception. Some predicate would be affirmed to be instantiated in the sensory field, and this affirmation would be false. But is there such general error in perception?

Well, a case can be made that there is; but I am less interested in this than in what follows from it—for it would entail my main claim. Three potential sources of error are worth considering, all familiar: solidity, colour, and constancy. Suppose that objects are not solid, but that they look solid; they have gaps between the atoms, but they look to be continuous substances—a respectable, if highly debatable, view. Then all perceptions would affirm that there is a solid object out there, but that would be false, since solid objects do not exist. Thus existential error would infect every perception, and any singular terms employed to denote these ostensible solid objects would be existentially empty—'that solid object' would never have an existent referent. Therefore the *de dicto* intentional object of these perceptions would never exist—just like the case of my father and the tree stump. Or consider colour: if you hold any view according to which the perception of colour is in error, because the way colour looks does not match the way it is, then the same result will ensue. Thus, if colour looks non-dispositional and non-relative, yet is really dispositional and relative, then all colour perception is of non-existent objects (as well as existent ones—the *de re* objects). Colour perception affirms that there is a non-dispositional and non-relative colour quality instantiated there, but there is not—there are no such objects in the world. You do see existent objects, but you see them *as* having qualities that they don't have; hence you also 'see' an intentional object that fails to exist. There is a true existential proposition here and a false one, and the false one generates non-existent intentional objects. Putting it in the formal mode: for any sentence of the form 'aRb', in which 'b' refers to an existent object, there is a sentence of the form 'aRb*', in which 'b*' refers to a non-existent object (or fails to refer to an existent object, if you prefer)—where 'R' is some perceptual verb like 'see' or 'seems to see' or 'visually represents'.

The same point can be made with respect to perceptual constancy—of distance, shape, colour, or whatever. If things in the distance look smaller than they are, then perception contains an error as to size; and this will give rise to false existential propositions—such as that there exists something in the visual field that is both a person and smaller than the coffee cup on my desk. Now I know that many people will resist this description of the case, holding that people in the distance do *not* look smaller than nearby cups—after all, I have no tendency to *judge* that they are thus smaller. But I believe this is wrong: I think distant things do *look* smaller (in one good sense of 'look')—it is just that we automatically correct for this on the basis of background knowledge. Distant objects indisputably take up less of the visual field, and I think this translates into a difference in how they *look*; it is just that we don't take how they look all that seriously, since we *know* that distant objects tend to look smaller than they really are. Anyway, my point here is that *if* you agree with this account of constancy, then you should agree, too, that perception introduces non-existent intentional objects all the time, since it is riddled with illusion—in this case, that things get smaller the further away they are. A nearby gunshot sounds much louder than a distant one, though we don't judge the sounds to be objectively different in volume; but it is nevertheless true that there is an error built into these auditory perceptions—since the sounds are not in fact different in loudness, though they appear to be.

So these relatively humdrum examples of perceptual error actually entail my main claim; that claim ought not then to seem as dramatic as it might have appeared on first statement. But it would be far more interesting if we could establish the claim without assuming these controversial theses of perceptual error, and this is what I propose to do next. I shall do this by considering *temporal* and *counterfactual* cases in which plausible individuation conditions for intentional objects force us to introduce non-existent objects in addition to existent ones. First, then, consider the case of Fido and Rex, a real dog and an unreal one. At time *t* our subject *S* is seeing Fido in a perfectly normal way: Fido exists and is causing *S*'s experience as of a dog meeting Fido's description. Now suppose that we remove Fido from the scene, but that we preserve *S*'s (qualitatively defined) experience—we use some deftly placed electrodes in his cortex or whatever. Let us suppose that *S* has been referring to Fido and carries on using the name introduced when Fido is removed. Now we, knowing what is going on, will not use S's doggy name as he does, because we know he is no longer in the presence of Fido; we know that S is now speaking of a non-existent dog when he says 'that dog'. Suppose we call this non-existent dog 'Rex', being well aware that Rex is not identical to Fido (S keeps using 'Fido'). Then we can say that 'Fido' and 'Rex' have different references, one existing and one not. S's intentional object is Fido at time *t* and Rex at the later time. The question I am interested in is whether 'Rex' has reference *before* the removal of Fido. Suppose that we reintroduce Fido after an interval: does 'Rex' still refer *after* this moment? In other words, does S's experience have *two* intentional objects during the Fido periods, both Fido and Rex? One description of the case says that when Fido is removed a *new* intentional object enters into S's experience, namely Rex, and that when Fido comes back that new object *ceases* to figure in S's experience, being replaced by Fido. Another description—the one I favour—says that no new object enters S's class of intentional objects when Fido is removed, and there is no subtraction of any object when Fido comes back: Rex is S's intentional object all along (as well as Fido when he is around). Restoring Fido as S's *de re* intentional object does not make Rex cease to be an intentional object of S's—Fido adds, he does not subtract. I think this sounds intuitively right, but why is that? Because there is a *qualitative continuity* in S's experience: it seems to him just as if there is a single dog throughout the period. If the whole period had con-sisted of hallucination, then we would have said that Rex was there throughout; but making both ends of the period veridical doesn't abrogate the continuity that encourages this description of the case. And isn't it extremely odd to suppose that adding Fido could eliminate an intentional object? How could Fido *supplant* Rex? But if Rex is S's intentional object *after* the period of hallucination, is he not also S's intentional object *before* it—since there is an experien-tial continuity throughout? Didn't S have an experience as of a *single* dog the whole time—though, of course, no such single dog exists? But if so, his intentional state took a *non*-existent dog as its intentional object.

Here is another case: You see what you take to be a man crossing the street, but in fact this is a rapid succession of distinct men cunningly arranged by God to look like a single man. God splices all these distinct men seamlessly together so that there is an appearance of manly unity. You call the man you seem to see 'Bill'. The *de re* object of your seeing is a succession of (say) ten men, but there seems to be a unity to the object of sight, which is why you introduce the one name. I suggest that in this case there is a single (*de dicto*) intentional object, *as well as* ten (*de* re) intentional objects; and this single object does not exist—there *is* no unique man who performed the sequence of movements you observed. Your perceptual experience affirms that there exists a unique man who crossed the road, but no *one* did—Bill does not exist. So the identity conditions for your *de dicto* intentional object are not the same as for the *de re* object(s): it persists over the time in question, while they do not. If this were happening to us all the time, then we would constantly be presented with non-existent intentional objects of perceptual experience.[12]

The logic of these arguments resembles the well-known case of the statue and the piece of clay that composes it. The clay is made into a statue and then reduced to a mere lump again. Does the lump persist throughout these changes? It would be extremely odd to say that the creation of the statue put the piece of clay out of existence, and there are good reasons to distinguish statue from lump. In the

[12] The same is true of the content of perceptual judgements (as distinct from the experiences that prompt them): you would certainly *judge* that you saw one man over the interval in question, whose name is 'Bill'. The assumption of object continuity is what generates the non-existent object, since there is no such continuity in this case. I don't doubt that this assumption is generally justified: our experience presents a world of continuous objects, and this is generally the way the world is. If, however, you became convinced that there is no such object continuity in objective reality—perhaps for metaphysical reasons—then our experience would have to be deemed misleading, and a host of non-existent objects would thereby be generated.

same way, if we start with Rex, then add Fido, and finally remove Fido again, leaving Rex to bark once more, it seems odd to suppose that Rex disappears during the middle phase; rather, we have Rex *and* Fido in the middle phase. *Both* of these objects are present in S's total intentional state: if the non-existent object is an intentional object in the phase when the experience is non-veridical, then this object is not eliminated when the experience turns veridical and a new intentional object is added. And these two objects cannot be identified, since one exists and the other does not. Imagine that all your experiences up to now were hallucinatory—hitherto you have been a brain in a vat—but now you are suddenly hooked up to the world normally and actually see real things. Can we plausibly maintain that your erstwhile non-existent intentional objects are now no longer objects of thought for you, having been replaced by existent objects? How can *adding* existent intentional objects *subtract* from your stock of intentional objects?[13] What happens, rather, is that hooking you up to real things creates a condition of *double* reference in you.

[13] It might be objected that this principle, though generally correct, fails for the specific case of non-existent objects, because adding existent objects removes the very ground for saying that non-existent objects are being entertained. That is: it is a necessary and sufficient condition for there being a non-existent intentional object that no existent object fits the conditions that are laid down in the content of the intentional state in question. So in the move from the hallucinatory case to the veridical case the very conditions that generate the non-existent object are abrogated, since now there is an existent object that satisfies the content of the experience. In other words, it is error that produces non-existence, and when there is no error the constitutive conditions for the non-existent intentional object are lacking. To add an existent object *is* therefore to subtract a non-existent one, given the nature of non-existent objects.

This seems to me a difficult question, and I am not sure I have a full answer to it. The question rests on whether error is the sole and sufficient basis for an attribution of non-existence. I certainly don't think that a statement of non-existence *means* that an error has been committed, so there is nothing analytic about the conditions of non-existence the objector is invoking. My intuition is that there is a kind of *independence* to the act of taking a non-existent intentional object, so that adding an existent object that satisfies the conditions laid down does not eliminate the former intentional act's object. Thus, if I invent a fictional character, and then it turns out that a real person satisfies all the conditions I have specified in describing my character, it is not that I thereby fail to refer to a non-existent object, referring

Now for the crucial counterfactual case: the argumentative structure is basically the same as the temporal case. Suppose you are a normal perceiver in the actual world—you perceive what you seem to perceive. Now consider the counterfactual world in which you are a brain in a vat but have the same experiences as in the actual world. In that possible world you have a range of intentional objects that do not exist but for which you may have names. So in the actual world you have names for existent objects, but in the counterfactual world you have names (that sound just the same) for non-existent objects. Question: do you *also* have those non-existent intentional objects in the actual world? In other words, does removing the existent objects create *new* intentional objects in the counterfactual world? My suggestion is that those non-existent intentional objects were already present in the actual world, alongside the existent intentional objects. Intuitively, if I think away the existent object of my mental state, I simply reveal an intentional object that was there all along; I don't create a fresh intentional object just by subtracting the existent object. And this is basically because the merely intentional object is qualitatively individuated (perhaps relative to a person), and these qualitative conditions obtain even in the veridical situation.[14] We can put the

instead (willy-nilly, as it were) to an existent object. Similarly, if I am a brain in a vat entertaining a range of non-existent objects, these objects don't cease to be available to me just by making me hooked up to real objects. Couldn't I, knowing that I have made the transition to the real world, just *decide* to keep referring to my old non-existent objects, as well as to the new existent ones? The fact that now my experience is veridical and my beliefs true doesn't seem to rob me of what I used to think about; it just adds new objects of intentionality to my stock. So there must be more to reference to a non-existent object than merely the absence of an existent object that satisfies the conditions associated with such reference: non-existent objects are not obliterated simply by ensuring that their associated descriptions are satisfied. (Again, this footnote was prompted by a conversation with David Chalmers, though I'm not sure the objection I am discussing is the one he intended; in any case, his actual objection, cited in n. 11, made me think of it. The present objection seems to me much harder to deal with than the previous one.)

[14] By 'qualitative' I don't mean 'non-intentional'; I am not assuming some sort of non-representational qualia conception of experience. I mean instead to be speaking of content that is general in nature, i.e. involves reference to properties of objects. So

same point in terms of reference: I refer to non-existent objects in the counterfactual world, existent ones in the actual world—but do I *also* refer to the same non-existent ones in the actual world? I think I do—and if so there has to be a kind of double reference in the actual world: my names have to refer to both existent and non-existent objects concurrently.[15]

The argument I am giving can be compared to a similar view of senses and experiences themselves. If we subtract reference from sense we don't eliminate sense: it would be very odd to say that senses are *created* in the counterfactual situation in which references are removed; better to suppose that there is *both* sense and reference in the actual situation. It is not that we invoke sense *only* when reference fails: it is common to both referential success and the lack of it. Similarly, we don't suppose that experiences exist only when they are non-veridical: removing the object doesn't *create* an experience; it simply leaves as a residue what was there already when there was a perceptual object.[16] I am saying the same about non-existent intentional objects: they are not created by the removal of existent ones; rather, they were there all along,

I am supposing that in the actual and counterfactual situations the same range of properties is predicated by the subject's experience and thought.

[15] We don't have to put the point quite so provocatively: we can say that a name refers only to one object but that there is an *associated* reference (perhaps only in thought) to another object—I *refer* only to the real Kripke when I say 'Kripke' but I *think* of his non-existent counterpart too. Or we could do it the other way around. Truth conditions will then be specified accordingly. There don't seem to be any very powerful constraints forcing one way of proceeding over the others (is it 'indeterminate' whether a name refers to one of these objects instead of the other?). Of course, we don't want to say that a single *proposition* contains both of these objects, or else we will be faced with propositions that are both true and false (consider existential propositions); rather, a given sentence is 'ambiguous' between two propositions, one about real Kripke and the other about his non-existent counterpart. (This is not perhaps a case of straight ambiguity, since it is hard to see how to recover a reading of 'Kripke exists' that makes it false. It might be better to say instead that there is a systematic mapping between the sentence and a proposition that contains a suitable non-existent counterpart.)

[16] I suppose that 'disjunctivists' will want to disagree with this, holding that there is no common factor uniting the veridical and hallucinatory cases. I am an unregenerate 'conjunctivist' obviously, but I won't argue the point here.

capable of being referred to. So, right now, I have a range of non-existent intentional objects in my mental sights—those that I *would* have if all my experiences were non-veridical. Indeed, for all existent intentional objects I now have, there is the non-existent object I would have if the existent object were not there—and I have this non-existent intentional object as things actually are. Put brutally, I am now experiencing an existent coffee cup *and* a non-existent one—the one I *would* be experiencing if there were no existent cup to be seen. And whenever I use a name to refer to a real person I am also referring to an unreal person—the one I *would* be referring to if the real person did not exist. This follows from the simple principle that removing intentional objects from a person's mental landscape does not create new ones; it simply exposes to view what was there already.

I hope it is clear that my ubiquitous non-existent intentional objects are nothing like sense-data. Sense-data are mental entities that exist, but objects like Pegasus or an hallucinated tree stump are not mental and do not exist. Nor are they senses or concepts or modes of presentation or ideas; they are what such items are *about*—they belong to the level of reference (albeit non-existent reference). Merely intentional objects are just like ordinary objects, except for the small matter of their existence (as I observed earlier). I am emphatically not making the platitudinous point that in any intentional act there is both the object of the act and the act itself. My claim is that there is always a *duet* of intentional acts, each taking different objects (one of them non-existent). And my general thesis is that reference to such non-existent entities is actually the normal case, not a symptom of malfunction or abnormal circumstances: we are intentionally directed to non-existent objects all the time—without making any *mistakes* of existence.

4. What are the consequences of this view for the nature of perception and reference? As I have said, we now have a kind of double intentionality as a regular occurrence. But it would be

wrong to suppose that these distinct objects are independently represented by the mind; the two references are clearly connected. Compare this with the token-reflexive account of indexicality, according to which an indexical term refers to itself in the course of referring to an extra-linguistic object. For example, 'now' means 'the time of this utterance of "now"' and 'I' means 'the speaker of this token of "I"'. The indexical term refers to an object *by* referring to itself; it asserts a relation between the object and itself as an utterance. There is a kind of concealed double reference here, but the two referents are related. Or compare seeing an object: we can be said to see the surface of the object as well as the object as a whole; so there are two objects of sight. But they are not independent objects, since we see the whole object *by* seeing the surface of it. I think that in the case of reference to non-existent objects there is a similar dependency, or better interdependency. An existent object causes me to see it; as a result I have a specific type of experience, which takes a non-existent object as its intentional object, in addition to the real object that I see. So it is in virtue of seeing the real object that the unreal one becomes an object of intentionality for me. But, on the other hand, I could not see the real object without also seeing the non-existent object; after all, that object can be present to me even when I am hallucinating. It is this act of intentionality, combined with a suitable causal relationship, which delivers the perception of the existent object; the latter piggybacks on the prior intentional relation to a non-existent object. We could define the real object of perception simply as that object which (suitably) causes in the subject an intentional state directed toward a corresponding non-existent object. In the veridical case these two objects will closely resemble each other—they will share many properties. The non-existent object that corresponds to the real cup I am seeing will also be white, shiny, cylindrical, etc. So the two are not unrelated objects, picked out by separate acts of intentionality; they are intelligibly connected. We might, indeed, speak of them as *counterparts* of each other—closely similar objects that differ in that one exists and the other does not.[17] They certainly have an identical *appearance*, since non-existent objects can easily be mistaken for existent ones—that, after all, is what hallucination is all about.

This way of looking at perception provides an answer to the question of what is in common between qualitatively identical experiences one of which is veridical and the other is not. The experiences are the same, to be sure, as is their representational content; but that isn't all—they are also directed to the same non-existent intentional object. I myself have no problem with saying that this object is *seen* in both cases, so that non-existent objects can be seen (I don't think sense-data can be seen, however, because they are mental items); and therefore I am happy to say that in both the veridical and the illusory cases the *same* object is seen.[18] It is just that in the veridical case *another* object is also seen, and in just as full-blooded a sense—namely, the existent causally operative object. So my view is that two objects are seen in the veridical case and only one in the illusory case; but there is a highly significant 'common factor' here because an identical object is seen in both cases. Sense-datum theorists made the mistake of saying that a common *mental* item is seen in both cases: that is wrong, but their instincts weren't so far off, since there is something that is a common object of seeing in the two cases—a non-mental, non-existent (material) object. This view gives no support to the idea that the objects of perception are mental entities, nor does it claim that existent material objects are somehow not really seen. There is no forced choice here: we can be said to see both—just as we can

[17] This notion of counterpart is obviously reminiscent of David Lewis's notion: see his *On the Plurality of Worlds* (Blackwell, 1986). However, Lewis takes all counterparts to an existent object to exist themselves, while not being actual; I take them not to exist *simpliciter*.

[18] Anscombe's 'The Intentionality of Sensation' persuaded me of this, after years of believing that non-existent objects could only *seem* to be seen. She gives a number of examples in which perceptual verbs are rightly used in relation to non-existent objects, the simplest of which is 'I hear a ringing in my ears': pp. 169–71.

be said to see both the surface of an object and the whole object. It is, of course, true that on this view we can be said to be perpetually hallucinating, even in the most veridical of cases, since there is always a non-existent object of sight in the offing; but once it is appreciated that this is not incompatible with the idea that we are *also* seeing an existent object the sense of outrage ought to dissipate.

Theories of reference will look rather different in the light of this conception. What theory of reference works best for reference to non-existent objects? Not a causal theory, as I noted earlier. In fact, since such objects are individuated in terms of our beliefs, some sort of description theory seems natural. Of course, a social dimension will need to be included, which leaves room for error about the object, but at bottom the community will refer by means of suitable descriptions. Zeus *has* to fit the descriptions that initially introduce his name, even if later speakers are misinformed about his properties (they come to think he is vindictive when he is benign, say). So Russell and Frege were basically right about names, *if* we construe them as talking about non-existent objects of reference (not that they were).[19] The causal theory will figure in roughly as follows: the existent reference of a name is defined as that object that causes reference to a non-existent object, which is itself a matter of description-fitting. Thus, if I use the name 'Saul Kripke' I refer to the real Kripke in virtue of the fact that he is the cause of my using the name to refer in addition to Kripke's non-existent counterpart—which latter reference is descriptively mediated.[20] If there is no real Kripke (he is the result of an elaborate

---

[19] Kripke and others were notably not discussing reference to non-existent objects in their critiques of description theories of reference; I am suggesting that this is no accident.

[20] Maybe Kripke has no unique non-existent counterpart; maybe he has (or could have) many, depending upon the number of illusory 'Kripkes' that might be around. Obviously, this depends upon how liberally non-existent objects are individuated (do the many monotheistic world religions worship the same non-existent god or many such gods?).

hoax), then I refer *only* to this non-existent object; but if there is, then he is the cause of that other act of reference. Looked at this way, the causal theory is hardly fundamental: I can refer to things without the aid of a causal relation to them (if they are non-existent), and when causality does come in it piggybacks on description-based reference. Not that the causal theory of names is wrong; it is just not as central as might have appeared. It seemed central because we didn't think much about reference to the non-existent, and we didn't recognize the ubiquity of such reference.

5. Is reference environmentally determined? Straightforward reference to the non-existent can hardly be, since the environment cannot contain non-existent objects that interact with thinkers and speakers. We can perhaps construct a twin earth case for a term like 'Pegasus', by stipulating the same social history of the term and so on; but if the uses of the name in the two communities refer to different non-existent objects that will not be because of any impact of the non-linguistic environment on speakers (it may simply be a function of the difference of speech communities). The reference of the term can exert no causal control over tokens of the term, so this kind of causal relation cannot tie the name down to two distinct environmental referents. We normally allow that different tokens of 'Zeus', uttered by different people at different times, can have the *same* reference, but it is less clear what to say about different (causally isolated) communities on earth and twin earth—perhaps this is enough to make us say that *distinct* non-existent objects are referred to, perhaps not. In any case, this will not be a classic twin earth case.[21]

---

[21] If the mere difference of communities makes earth and twin earth speakers refer to different (though qualitatively identical) non-existent objects, then this is a still a fact about the communities themselves and not their environment—so it still counts as 'internal' to the speakers. The numerical distinctness of the two communities is what brings about a difference in what they refer to, instead of their internal states—but this is still not a matter of their contextual embedding in the world.

What about terms that do refer? Does 'water', which has distinct existent references on earth and twin earth, also have distinct non-existent references? According to me, 'water' on earth refers to water (an existent substance) *and* to a suitable counterpart non-existent object (not identical to water, obviously): but is this the *same* non-existent object that my twin on twin earth refers to? Questions about the identity conditions of non-existent objects can be tricky, but I think a case can be made that they are the same. Let us suppose, plausibly, that 'water' is associated with the description 'the (unique) watery stuff', on both earth and twin earth (where 'watery' here just expresses the common appearance of the two liquids on earth and twin earth). Then the qualitative facts about the terms are identical—the speakers are in the same qualitative state when they use their term. But since non-existent objects are qualitatively individuated, the two sets of speakers will be referring to the same non-existent object. Think of it this way: Consider what the two sets of speakers *would* be referring to if H_2O and XYZ did not in fact exist on their planets (it is all a huge illusion). These non-existent intentional objects would be associated with exactly the same qualitative states, and so would naturally be identified. Even if we let the identity of the communities figure in the individuation of these objects, it is still clear that the actual existent substances don't play a constraining role in tying down the reference of 'water' to these non-existent objects. In short, the non-existent reference of 'water' is not environmentally sensitive—unlike the existent reference. So there is no twin earth case for such reference, and hence externalism is not true of it. (The identity conditions of the non-existent referents mirror those of what some people call 'narrow content'.)

This limits the scope of externalism. If we think of reference in terms of an inner and an outer shell, then the inner shell is not subject to externalism, while the outer shell still is. Externalism is never true for the inner shell, no matter what kind of term we choose, since this kind of reference is environmentally insensitive—it coincides pretty much with the speakers' qualitative states.[22] There is broad reference and narrow reference—the kind that varies from earth to twin earth, and the kind that does not—and the narrow kind is to the non-existent. This kind of reference *is* 'in the head'—that is, supervenient on brain states and so on. The other kind of reference is not, being dictated by the existent environment. I take it that this corresponds to the intuitions that most people have had about twin earth cases; I have merely recast those intuitions in terms of a covert reference to the non-existent on earth and twin earth. That is what the semantic overlap consists in.

6. It might be wondered whether the apparatus of non-existent objects of reference could replace the notion of sense. Can we say that a pair of co-referring names also refer to two distinct non-existent objects, and that these objects account for the semantic difference between the names? That might seem tempting once we decide that non-existent objects are individuated qualitatively, since different descriptions will give different such references. Consider what we *would* refer to with 'Hesperus' if Hesperus did not exist, and similarly for 'Phosphorus': it is doubtful that these would be the same thing, since the two appearances will generate distinct non-existent objects. So might not these references do the job customarily assigned to sense? This might seem like an attractive theoretical simplification, but I don't think it will really work. The problem is that there can be informative identity statements between terms for non-existent objects, so that we will still need a layer of sense, over and above reference, to capture these cases. Clearly, we can assert things like 'Clark Kent is identical to Superman', and these can be both informative and true; so

---

[22] Note again that qualitative states, as I intend them, are intentionally loaded—they are a matter of what properties are attributed to the world, not something inherently non-representational.

we need two senses to account for such cases, and there is only one reference to work with here. Distinct descriptions don't *always* generate distinct references to the non-existent. So senses can be sliced more finely than non-existent objects, and hence cannot be replaced by such objects. Accordingly, the semantics I favour includes two levels of reference *and* a level of sense (which may itself have more than one level): a name will refer to an existent object and to a non-existent one, as well as expressing a sense.

How do truth conditions work out under this kind of semantics? Less simply than we usually suppose, and contextual rules will need to be invoked to capture the way we normally evaluate sentences for truth. Take 'Kripke exists': is that true? Well, it is if we take the name to refer to existent Kripke; but not if we take it to refer to Kripke's non-existent counterpart—the object we would be (solely) referring to if Kripke didn't exist. Generally, we ignore this latter truth condition, and indeed there seems to be a fixed rule that excludes these non-existent counterparts from figuring in truth conditions. It might even be best to restrict the ordinary notion of reference to the former relation, holding only that there is always another intentional object accompanying the existent one—but this object is not strictly *referred* to (where reference and truth are taken as correlative). From my point of view this is a minor issue: what matters is that there is always a non-existent intentional object for any existent one, whether or not this is what our ordinary terms are taken to *refer* to. Theoretically, we could stipulate that all our terms primarily refer to the non-existent objects, so that existential statements all turn out false; and then recover the usual assignments of truth-value by means of a rule linking the non-existent to the existent object—i.e. take the existent object that is the counterpart to the non-existent one and compute truth conditions accordingly. We simply need to coordinate the two possible truth conditions in the right way. This is more complicated than we are used to, but semantics has a tendency to get more complicated than we thought—does it not? Certainly, the role of context in determining the intended truth conditions is well established; the sentence by itself is apt to underdetermine its own truth conditions in use.

7. So far I have focused on reference to ordinary physical objects, and my claim has been that such reference is always accompanied by a non-existent intentional object. But is this true for *all* types of reference? Interestingly enough, it is not. In particular, it is not true for reference to *mental* entities—and also, I think, not for reference to selves or abstract entities. Suppose I say 'that pain', referring to a sensation of pain in my leg: do I also refer to some non-existent counterpart to this existent pain? The problem with saying this is that we cannot make sense of the idea of what I *would* be referring to if the pain did not exist, since I cannot make that kind of error about my pains. If we take all my actual references to my experiences and consider what to say about what I would be referring to were I a brain in a vat, then we find that these references are preserved in that counterfactual situation, since by hypothesis the brain in a vat has all the experiences that I do. Appearance and reality cannot come apart in this case, so we cannot generate a non-existent object by keeping the appearance constant and removing the reality. Accordingly, when a mental entity is the intentional object there is no argument to the effect that there is a counterpart non-existent object in the counterfactual case that must be admitted even in the actual veridical case. There really is only one intentional object here. And that is because mistakes about existence are not possible for such cases.

Much the same should be said about selves and numbers: whenever mistakes about existence are impossible we cannot produce a scenario in which we have the appearance without the reality, and so we cannot establish that another non-existent object is needed.[23] There is nothing *in* the idea of what I *would* be referring to with 'I' if I did not exist![24] So the type of argument I gave for postulating extra non-existent intentional objects has no purchase here. Putting it in the formal mode again: if our sentence form 'aRb' contains a psychological relation and a reference to a mental entity (etc.), then such a sentence cannot be true unless 'b' refers to an existent object. Thus, I cannot be said to feel a pain unless the pain exists—though, of course, I can be said to worship a god who lacks all existence. So these are very different cases, and my claim applies only to the latter kind of case. We are always hallucinating non-existent material objects, I suggested (putting it provocatively), but we never conjure up non-existent mental states (in our own case). But I take it that this difference in the applicability of my claim should come as no surprise, in view of the antecedently recognized difference between intentionality directed to the mind and intentionality directed elsewhere—specifically, to the external world. Real existence is never entailed by the appearances in the case of the external world, but it is in the 'mental world'. And this is why my argument has no application to the latter type of intentionality. It is the *possibility* of error that produces the non-existent counterpart intentional object.

If all this is right, then there are two main types of intentionality: the kind that builds in reference to the non-existent and the kind that does not. When we have intentionality directed towards material objects we have the former type of case; when we have

[23] We need some qualifications here about mode of epistemic access. Clearly we can make mistakes of existence about selves and numbers when our mode of access is third-personal and inferential, respectively; but we cannot when the access is first-personal and 'direct' (as when I think of the number two: here I cannot be mistaken about that number's existence). I won't go into this fully now.

[24] This is just another way of stating Descartes' *Cogito*.

intentionality directed towards our own mental states (and selves and numbers) we have the latter type of case. So the latter type of case fits pretty well the conventional view of how reference works and what the objects of reference are (though, ironically, this has been the area in which some philosophers have wanted to deny that genuine reference takes place). But in the former type of case we seem to have a radical departure from received views, in that non-existence turns out to be central and universal. There are a lot more intentional objects than we thought, and they show a disturbing tendency not to exist. Disturbing, that is, until you have grown accustomed to their company; I now find them nothing to be alarmed about, even to be quite friendly. Brentano said that all consciousness is consciousness *of*; I agree, but would rephrase: all (or nearly all) consciousness is consciousness of *nothing*—that is, of the non-existent (though also of *something*—the existent).[25] I hope this sounds less outrageous now than it did when I started. It is really just a consequence of the fact that consciousness presents its (existent) objects in such a way that were they not to exist consciousness itself would not change its intrinsic character. It is as if the existent object fills a slot already prepared for it by consciousness, and this slot consists in reference to a non-existent

[25] Some readers may be reminded of Jean-Paul Sartre's *Being and Nothingness* (Methuen, 1969). Sartre held that the essence of consciousness is nothingness, and I might sound as if I am saying something similar. Actually, our views are exact opposites: Sartre took the *objects* of consciousness to be defined by Being, with Nothingness entering via the intentional relation; I am attributing Non-being to the objects of consciousness (though not of course to all of them). I sense a kind of convergence, however, in Sartre's stress on the idea of *absence* (the eagerly expected Pierre is *not* there in the café), in which consciousness is haunted by the specter of Non-being. On my view, too, Non-being is with us always, asserting its claims (I won't try to speculate, Heidegger-like, on the relation between this and the prospect of death). What does seem right is that, in my view, it is of the essence of consciousness to perpetually present us with the realm of Non-being; and maybe this does something funny to a person. It is as if behind every direct encounter with the real world there lurks the prospect of being a brain in a vat. In a way, we are both in contact with the real world *and* brains in a vat (since we also contemplate all those non-existent intentional objects)!

object. When it comes to the essence of consciousness, then, non-existence is dominant over existence. In its intrinsic nature consciousness is primarily directed to what is not.[26]

[26] This is not to reject externalism: real objects in the environment do enter the individuation of many mental states. But this kind of externalism is not as universal or basic as has been supposed. See my *Mental Content* (Blackwell, 1989) for a discussion of the scope and limits of externalism. In the terms of that book, concepts for non-existent objects are 'weakly external': the non-existent object itself is what individuates the corresponding mental state (remember that this object is not itself mental), though it does not do so by means of environmental impingement. In effect, I am adopting a 'direct reference' theory of terms for non-existent objects: these objects enter the very proposition itself—which is to say that not all propositional constituents have to exist.

INDEX